The Worlds of Political Economy

THE WORLDS OF POLITICAL ECONOMY

Edited by
R.J. Barry Jones

Pinter Publishers, London and New York

First published in Great Britain in 1988 by
Pinter Publishers Limited
25 Floral Street, London WC2E 9DS

British Library Cataloguing in Publication Data

A CIP catalogue record for this book is available from the British Library.

ISBN 0 86187-946-5

Library of Congress Cataloguing-in-Publication Data

The Worlds of political economy.
Includes index.
1. Comparative economics. I. Jones, R.J. Barry.
HB90.W67 1988 338.9 88-17934
ISBN 0-86187-946-5

Typeset by Arjan Limited
Printed by Biddles of Guildford

Contents

PREFACE

The Worlds of Political Economy is the second volume in a series of general surveys of political economy. The first volume, *Perspectives on Political Economy* was published in 1983 and drew upon the fruits of a series of seminars held in the Politics Department of the University of Reading, England. The present volume seeks to build upon the foundations established by the earlier publication. It offers a wide-ranging survey of the current study of political economy, from various perspectives, and highlights some of the more interesting recent developments within the subject and its constituent approaches.

Considerable appreciation must be extended to those who have ungrudgingly contributed chapters of such interest and undeniable quality. Thanks, too, must be expressed to those who have assisted in, or borne with, the final preparation of this volume.

R.J. Barry Jones

Reading

PART I INTRODUCTION

Chapter 1

1. Political economy: contending perspectives on a changing world

R.J. Barry Jones

The term 'political economy' has featured frequently in the titles of many recent studies of various aspects of contemporary politics, economics and international relations. With the proliferation of such studies, seasoned observers have begun to wonder whether they are witnessing yet another terminological 'fad'; a linguistic talisman to command the attention of the more fashion conscious among academics.[1] The term 'political economy' has also made a gratuitous appearance in the titles of some studies that are not substantively different from many earlier works. There are, however, a number of significant empirical developments, and shifts of intellectual focus, that have encouraged the crystallization of a new (or renewed) area of interdisciplinary activity and warranted the notion that a real 'political economy' has now emerged.

Political economy is now considerably more than the policy-focused aspects of conventional economic analysis. Many examples of modern political economy transcend the arbitrary distinction between the political and the economic. Moreover, the currents of intellectual debate that heralded, and have continued to accompany, the development of many of these approaches are such as to suggest the crystallization of a genuinely *political* economy.

Empirical and intellectual currents

The later 1960s, and 1980s witnessed a number of developments that challenged practical policy-makers, confronted analysts with new issues and raised serious doubts about the efficacy of accepted theories of, and approaches to, many aspects of contemporary political and economic systems. At the 'domestic' level, many advanced industrial countries were experiencing a pernicious combination of inflationary pressure and declining industrial competitiveness—a mixture that threatened to confront these societies with a range of serious difficulties and challenges. Many of the less developed countries (LDCs) were also experiencing the disappointment of their early post-colonial hopes of rapid economic development and enhanced well-being. Declarations of a new, or second, 'crisis' in economic theory soon followed upon the widespread acknowledgement of these developments and difficulties.[2]

Developments within the international political economy also weakened confidence in the post-war order. Much of the harmony of the post-war, free-market, international economic system rested upon the strong position of the United States of America and the relatively small number of significant competitors within the world's markets for industrial goods and advanced services. By the 1970s, however, the recovery of the industrial economies which had been most damaged by the Second World War was complete. Many international markets thus became increasingly competitive and uncomfortable for many of the industries based in those advanced industrial countries that had enjoyed considerable prosperity during the period of post-war recovery. Additional competitive pressures in a number of significant industrial sectors were also being felt from the emergent newly industrialized countries (NICs). The 1970s also saw the traumatic oil embargo and price rise of 1973-4 and the second, and equally serious, round of oil price rises in 1979. Finally, the very principles of the 'liberal' international economic order were themselves challenged by the LDCs' strident demand for a New International Economic Order (NIEO). The emergence of a new 'international political economy' reflected and accompanied these dramatic developments.[3]

Intellectually, there were a number of sources of dissatisfaction with established approaches to the analysis of politics and economics. There was a particularly strong rejection of the separation of politics and economics, conventionally made within many orthodox analytical approaches. Marxists, of one type or another, had long rejected this artificial separation but had been inclined to subordinate politics to economics, analytically.[4] Indeed, conflicts with international politics were commonly attributed to underlying economic causes. In sharp contrast, many, including 'realist' theorists of international politics[5] and modern successors to the mercantilist tradition of political economy, asserted the dominance of politics over economics. Theories that maintain the political domination of economics, or the economic determination of politics, constituted forms of political economy in their clear rejection of the separability of the two areas of activity.

Recent attempts to apply the techniques of economic analysis to the study of political activity constitute a particular variant of the traditional tendency to assert the priority of one or other side in the relationship between economics and politics. This analytical departure does not assert the economic determination of politics but, rather, depicts political, and governmental, behaviour as if it were a form of economic activity. In this vision, the world of politics is an arena of entrepreneurs, value maximizers, resource managers and generally self-interested, economic 'rational actors'.[6] As a metaphor, the perspective provided by this form of political economy is interesting and, at times, illuminating. It does, however, encounter a number of difficulties of empirical veracity, analytical ethnocentricity and implicit political value judgement.

While inclinations to emphasize the primacy of either politics or economics persist, many contemporary political economists are disposed to treat the relations between the economic and the political as intimate, critical, but essentially problematical. Arguments for a new, synthetic political economy reflect this reluctance to prejudge the political-economic balance or to accept simple notions of causal determination. However, there is an even more fundamental sense in which some developments within the field of study constitute a *political* economy.

The philosophical and methodological problems faced in many areas of the study of human affairs are shared by political economy. A fundamental problem, here, concerns the nature of the analytical enterprise, the status of the theories that are adduced and the character of the language with which study is undertaken. A simple empiricist epistemology, and associated methodology, is now rejected by many students of human affairs. The relationship between analyst and referent is seen to be an inherently complex and problematical matter.[7] Indeed, there are many who argue that all analysis is necessarily conducted on the basis of prior theory and that much of that theory is constructed from terms that are often, if not always, inherently *political*.

A number of propositions underlie the view that the study of human activity is an inherently complex and problematical matter. The world of human and social activity is seen to be both extremely complex and constantly dynamic. The complexity of human affairs is, in large part, a result of the 'social construction' of human reality, wherein the ideas that human beings hold about human activity are the primary basis of their own subsequent behaviour. However, the manner in which complex patterns of human action, and interaction, often have unintended and unexpected consequences renders the issue even more complex. An arena of activity in which the actors' belief influence, if not wholly determine, their behaviour, but in which the whole may often be greater than the sum of the parts is, indeed, a challenge to analysis.

The methodological problems with which a complex and dynamic world confronts political economy are compounded by the role of unintended, and unexpected, consequences and outcomes. Where phenomena are extremely complex and dynamic, any empirical order may reflect the existence and operation of factors and forces that are not immediately apparent to the observer. In such circumstances, analysis must incorporate reference to such non-observables if it is not to neglect a vital, and often fundamental, element. Devotees of a number of approaches to political economy, including structural analysts and some neo-Marxists, do indeed assert the central role of such non-observables in theory and analysis.[8]

Value preferences determine much of the subject matter that analysts choose to investigate and the kinds of interpretation towards which they will be drawn. Moreover, ideas about complex and dynamic aspects of reality constitute simplifying intellectual devices. The simplifications that are found to be acceptable will be those that reflect the analyst's established preferences. Moreover, if causal significance is attributed to non-observable factors and forces, then it is likely that the non-observables selected for analytical inclusion will reflect prior views about, and judgements upon, the subject matter of study. Such dispositions and judgements are, in large part, a 'political' matter.

Within political economy there is a further sense in which the enterprise may, indeed must, be an essentially political matter. The term 'political' is being used here to denote fundamental and unavoidable arguments about the way in which the relationship between the individual and the collective should be determined and ideas about the actual and desirable range and nature of intentional collective activity. Activity in the political economy is largely governed by such ideas. Moreover, such ideas occupy a central place in any true form of theoretical political economy, however contentious the political principles upon which that form of political economy is based.[9]

Fred Hirsch's *Social Limits to Growth*[10] provides a perfect example of political economy, in the essentially political sense being considered here. Hirsch seeks to identify many of the damaging implications of the dynamics of the modern, capitalist economy. The analysis is conducted on the basis of a number of critical ideas: the destruction of 'conviviality' by the promotion of self-interest; the proliferation of intermediate goods that provide little or no primary satisfaction; and the prevalence of positional goods, which can be enjoyed only at the expense of the frustration of others. In developing his arguments, Hirsch implicitly challenges many of the basic terms within which conventional economic analysis is undertaken, including spontaneous harmony, efficiency, growth and prosperity. In *Social Limits to Growth*, the subject matter is essentially economic, but the analysis and message is overwhelmingly 'political'.

Identifying approaches to political economy

The many contending approaches to political economy are inherently 'political' to a greater or lesser extent. Those that are directly addressed to fundamental arguments about the relationships between government and individual, and the limits of collective activity, in the 'economic' realm necessarily incorporate interpretative and prescriptive arguments. However, the presentation together in one volume of alternative approaches to political economy provides, in itself, a form of argument, for each approach rests upon distinctive views of basic political issues. To undertake the direct comparison of contending perspectives is thus to undertake political economy in the political sense of that term.

There is a widespread recognition of the plurality of basic approaches to the analysis of the political economy, but rather less agreement about the number, nature and appropriate names of those approaches. Three issues have arisen in the development of a widely acceptable taxonomy of political economies. The first is a difficulty created by political economists themselves. Tactical requirements and emotional commitments have encouraged analysts to obscure the existence and boundaries of discrete approaches. Labels that are convenient at one time may be repudiated when they are found to have pejorative connotations, as with the oft-heard claim that there really is no such thing as 'neo-classical' economics. However, others find that their attachment to one or other analytical school is so great that they cannot abandon the label, however far from orthodox principles they subsequently stray. The legitimate boundaries of contending approaches dissolve in the face of such developments and it becomes unclear where one perspective ends and another begins.

The second issue raised by the categorization of approaches to political economy follows from the first. If the boundaries of 'schools' are seriously blurred, and if some analysts actually dispute the very existence of certain approaches, on what basis may classification proceed? Here the choice is between ideal type and minimalist criteria of classification. Ideal typologies[11] involve identifying the basic and typical features of approaches at a high level of abstraction and generalization. Concrete examples of theory and analysis may then be classified as members of one or other of a strictly limited range of such 'ideal types'. The distinctive features of any concrete example of theory or analysis may, moreover, be highlighted by comparison with the definitive characteristics of an 'ideal type'. Significantly for the classification of a diverse, and often diffuse, realm such as political economy, the ideal types that are developed will, inevitably, be highly stylized versions of each 'approach' and may correspond, precisely, with no one actual example of the approach.

A minimalist typology will, in contrast, seek to identify a wide range of features, all of which are shared by two or more examples of analytical political economy. A classificatory description of each individual analytical approach, or group of approaches, can then be constructed in terms of such 'common' features—for example 'neo-Ricardian, evolutionary institutionalism. The range of classificatory 'types' that might emerge from such a procedure may, however, be so wide as to be of little assistance in bringing the wide variety of actual examples of political economy under intellectual control.

The third issue confronted when classifying approaches to political economy is closely related to the second and concerns the basic purpose of the classificatory endeavour. There is a widespread tendency within the 'social sciences' to undertake endless classificatory undertakings in the belief that classification is an intrinsically meaningful achievement in itself, of real value outside introductory textbooks. Unfortunately, classification for its own sake is far from significant and may, indeed, encourage the illusion that the ability to name 'approaches' is, in some way, the same thing as saying something of importance about that real world: mere scholasticism becoming a substitute for significant study and analysis!

Classificatory schemata, if they are to have any real significance for the analysis of the real world, must be based upon substantive notions about the real world, particularly notions concerning the nature and possibility of knowledge about the world, and ideas about the nature of the world, its essential characteristics and dynamic principles. Significant classification of various approaches to political economy must, therefore, be based upon ideas about the generation of knowledge within a world of the type that we encounter. The position adopted here is that human knowledge and understanding of a complex, dynamic and largely socially constructed world is inevitably partial, but driven by the search for internal order. Moreover, ideas about a realm of human activity which is, in a basic sense, political, will also be essentially political ideas. Discernible approaches to political economy will therefore be partial but, as a result of the quest for internal coherence and consistency, often more partial than might otherwise be the case. The kinds of partial approach that develop are also seen to be primarily a product of the current functioning of the political economy: its essential features, dynamic characteristics, and the problems that it has generated in the recent past.

The bias inherent in each perspective will also be political, in embracing one of a number of possible positions on basic political issues. Overall, then, classification will be based upon the construction of ideal types defined in terms of their distinctive, partial views of 'reality' and the positions adopted, implicitly or explicitly, on the fundamental political issues of government-individual relations and the limits of collective activity.

If, as has been argued, reality is so complex and, in many ways, indeterminate, that all interpretations are necessarily partial, then 'truth' will not be a function of any one theory or perspective. 'Truth' is not therefore to be found in the over-confident, or even slavish, acceptance of any one approach but will be approximated through the manipulation of, if not clash among, contrasting views of reality. As the proponents of contending approaches refine their interpretations and arguments, often in the face of external criticism, more insights are generated and further developments of the opposing views stimulated. 'Truth' does not emerge from the linear evolution of any one theory or approach, therefore, but is the product of the dialectical, or more properly polylectical, process of argument and counter-argument, contention and refutation, challenge and innovative respose. The elaboration of ideal types of political economy contributes to this process by clarifying and enhancing the contending arguments and thereby stimulating the polylectic.

Political economy: Liberal, Marxist and economic realist

The survey of contemporary political economy in this volume is organized within three broad approaches: liberal, Marxist and economic realist. The terms liberal and Marxist are widely accepted, even if their content and limits remain contentious. Economic realism has been adopted as a title for a loose, but identifiable, disposition within analytical and practical political economy. Economic realism, however, remains a contentious label, but has been selected for two reasons: first, for the sense that it conveys of an approach that is flexible, responsive, and even pragmatic, towards the variety of conditions and requirements prevailing within real-world political economies; and, second, for its association with 'realist' self-help responses of societies and states to a world of pervasive uncertainty and insecurity.

The idea that there is a distinctly 'liberal' approach to economics and politics is widely accepted. Moreover, it is relatively easy to identify a core of basic values, beliefs and attitudes that are central to any meaningful liberal position: a belief in the moral and practical priority of the individual; a faith in the efficiency of free economic markets; and, finally but by no means least, a belief that the role of government should be as limited as is practically possible.[12]

If the essence of the liberal position is easy to identify, its legitimate boundaries are far from clear. MacKinlay and Little's notion of 'compensatory liberalism' incorporates many of the adjustments that sensible 'liberals' have made to practical requirements over the years and, thereby, accommodates modest levels of interventionism, of 'Social Democratic' principles.[13] Unfortunately, an accommodation of a measure of governmental intervention in the economy and society seriously blurs the edges of the liberal position and establishes a significant overlap with economic realism.

Marxist theory is also thought by many to be a readily identifiable corpus of theoretical principles and analytical procedures. At one time, it would have been widely accepted that Marxism rested upon a dialectical materialism that gave overwhelming, if not unqualified, priority to the mode of production prevailing within any phase in the historical development of a society, or group of societies, and the deterministic implications of that basic 'reality'. All pre-socialist economic systems would have been analysed in terms of the labour theory of value; the 'exploitative' extraction of surplus value; and the consequential pattern of class conflict. The development of the capitalist economic system would then have been attributed to the dynamic of continuing class conflict; the progressive emiseration of the proletariat; the constant accumulation of productive capacity; an ever intensifying cycle of economic boom and recession; and a secular tendency for the rate of profit to decline.

Politically, 'traditional Marxism' would have viewed the state in advanced capitalist society as an instrument of the interests of the ruling (capitalist) class. However, the experience of repeated economic cycles, and progressive emiseration, would radicalize the proletariat and ready it for revolutionary activity, once the internal contradictions and cyclical crises within the capitalist system had reached unmanageable proportions. At this revolutionary stage, the proletariat would seize state power, transform the relations of production within the economy and, once the 'socialist' phase had been completed, orchestrate the 'withering away of the state' and the introduction of true 'communism'.

Such a model of Marxism is, however, challenged by many recent developments and departures within the ranks of self-proclaimed 'Marxists'. A straightforward form of determinism is widely rejected as a vulgar simplification; a rejection that is reinforced by the view of a number of 'Marxists' that the state may be more than merely the agent of the interests of the dominant capitalist class. Neo-Ricardian 'Marxists' have, moreover, repudiated the labour theory of value as erroneous, misleading and unnecessary.[14] Such developments, or deviations, within contemporary Marxist theory seriously undermine much that has been thought distinctive of the approach and much of its emotional appeal to former devotees. Moreover, they constitute substantial departures from the 'Marxist' ideal type propounded in this introduction and, hence, weaken the contribution to the wider polylectical debate.

The third main approach to political economy covered in this volume is rather more contentious than the other two approaches; contentious in its existence, nature and appropriate title. The label economic realism has been chosen to reflect its flexibility and responsiveness to the varying conditions encountered in the real world and the differing levels of governmental involvement in economic developments in various countries, from 'social partnership' through to systematic *dirigisme*. It also associates this approach to political economy with the 'realism' of those who acknowledge the general need for communities, and states, to ensure their own well-being in a world characterized by uncertainty and insecurity.[15]

The disposition inherent in economic realism rests upon modest, and often agnostic, assumptions. Great 'truths' about the human condition are treated with considerable caution, if not positively repudiated. Deterministic philosophies and determinate forms of analysis are both abjured. The world is seen to be far from perfect, probably incapable of perfection and in need of purposeful collective action if acceptable conditions are to be secured and maintained. Where governments are the primary agency for collective action, they have a legitimate, possibly decisive, but not unlimited role in economic developments. Where states seem to be the most effective means for maintaining a community's interests in a potentially hostile environment, then they too will have a legitimate and significant role.

The intellectual sources of economic realism are many and varied. It draws much from the long-standing tradition of mercantilism and neo-mercantilism.

Recent debates about the form and nature of suitable approaches to economic analysis have also generated ideas and schools of interpretation that make an invaluable contribution to an elaborated economic realism. Prominent amongst such sources and inspirations are the post-Keynsian disciples of extended and inherently radical Keynsian analysis; those, of a post-Keynsian or Marxist origin, who follow Piero Sraffa's 'neo-Ricardian' approach to value, distribution and class conflict; advocates of a new institutionalist form of economic analysis, be they inspired by earlier American institutionalism or the Continental institutionalism of Hayek and his disciples; and, finally, proponents of 'corporatist' views of many advanced industrial societies and a number of developing countries. At the level of international economic relations a significant contribution to economic realism is also made by those who have constructed structuralist, and similar, analyses of the global political economy from diverse intellectual sources, including post-Keynsianism, neo-Ricardianism and neo-institutionalism.

The three approaches to political economy, when presented as ideal types, can be readily differentiated from one another. The liberal and Marxist approaches contrast most sharply. Economic realism distinguishes itself more by its intellectual and methodological eclecticism and modesty of expectation. However, each approach throws an interesting, and quite distinct, light upon many of the major issues within the contemporary political economy and the intellectual questions that they generate.

Issues and perspectives

The liberal, Marxist and economic realist approaches to political economy present quite different views on many fundamental intellectual issues and contemporary empirical problems. On one issue they are, however, relatively united: that of casting doubt upon the simple and rigid distinction traditionally drawn between the domestic economy and the international economic system. Indeed, much of the renewed interest in political economy, in whatever form, has been prompted by the apparent permeability of the modern national economy and the growth of competitive pressures within the international economy.

FUNDAMENTALS

Beyond a common recognition of the intimate interrelationship between the domestic and the international in the modern global political economy there are, however, many areas of dissimilarity among liberal, Marxist and economic realist political economies. A range of differing philosophical and methodological dispositions underlies contrasting views on such basic issues as the most appropriate analytical and theoretical forms; the general association between politics and economics; the relationship between government and economy; the nature of, and interconnections among, such basic elements as states, communities and individuals; and, finally, the nature and reality of 'progress'.

METHODOLOGICAL INDIVIDUALISM, FORMALISM AND ANALYTICAL COLLECTIVISM

The methodological individualism and analytical formalism of liberal political economy sets it apart from both Marxism and economic realism. Methodological individualism is central to the wider philosophical and political concerns of liberalism and is compatible with, if not strictly necessary to, the basic analytical approach of liberal political economy.[16]

Marxist political economy opposes the methodological individualism of liberalism, generally, with an extreme form of intellectual and analytical collectivism. It also rejects the formalistic analysis of liberal political economy. Key notions, such as that of equilibrium, are entirely alien to a Marxist political economy that focuses upon conflict, crisis and radical change. Comparative static analysis is also notably absent from most Marxist studies.[17]

Economic realism is also highly dubious about the methodological individualism of liberal political economy. The contrary stress upon the historical and institutional framework within which economic developments take place, and by which they are largely conditioned, is incompatible with liberal philosophy. Many devotees of economic realism, in various of its forms, are also highly dubious about the formal analytical procedures that characterize much of liberal political economy, particularly in its neo-classical and proximate forms. Both the constrained vision provided by comparative statics and the great delusion of general equilibrium analysis are particularly deplored by the more vigorous critics of mainstream liberal economic analysis.

POLITICS, ECONOMICS AND THE ROLE OF GOVERNMENT

Analysis and prescription are intimately intertwined in the view adopted towards the relationship between politics and economics within liberal political economy. Conventional economic analysis has long been undertaken on the presumption that sensible statements can be made about an economy that is assumed to be discrete from the political realm. This exclusion of the political serves, partly, to ease the formal analysis that is the essence of modern mainstream liberal economics. However, it proceeds beyond mere analytical convenience to embrace an implicit illegitimization of the intrusion of political concerns into the operation and management of the economy. This is, in part, the result of a confusion between the artificial, stylized world of economic analyis and reality; it is also, however, a reflection of a long-standing liberal inclination towards the minimization of governmental activity in the economy, within society, or towards the individual. The result of this fusion of analytical and prescriptive dispositions is the view that governmental action rarely contributes constructively to economic and industrial performance and, if anything, is often harmful by suppressing individual initiative and distorting wider developments.

Marxism maintains an entirely different view of the relationship between economics and politics. In 'traditional Marxism', government within capitalist society was seen to serve the interests of the dominant, capitalist class. It acted, often forcefully, to preserve the interests and positions of the 'exploiting' class. Moreover, the forms of government, and the beliefs and ideologies that found contemporary political expression, were conditioned by the development of the capitalist order. Ultimately, however, the dimensions of the periodic, and deepening, crises of capitalism will prove unmanageable by bourgeois governments, and they and their capitalist masters will be swept away by the desperate, but now radicalized, proletariat. Thus, politics remains a function of economics; capitalism conditions bourgeois governments; and the ultimate disintegration of the capitalist system will usher in the Marxist-socialist revolution.

The contemporary revisions within 'Marxist' theory have done much to complicate and cloud the model suggested above.[18] However, even the substantially modified 'Marxisms' that find popularity today present a picture of political-economic relations, and of the role and functioning of governments, that is massively removed from that of liberal political economy and, indeed, liberal political theory.

Economic realism, for its part, recognizes the crucial influence exerted by the political order upon the economic realm. This role proceeds far beyond the simple establishment of basic law, order and propriety, as in the liberal vision. Politics sets the arena for economic activity and has a considerable role to play in creating, and sustaining, the foundations for effective economic and industrial development. Few, if any, economic systems will generate conditions that are widely acceptable and be able to sustain steady growth and progress, if left entirely to themselves.

A positive, and sometimes extensive, role for government and politics does not, however, mean that such a role will be either predetermined or unlimited. It is the flexible involvement of government, and its reponsiveness to the particular needs of the economy with which it has to deal, that marks the approach of economic realism. It is not, in short, a question of whether governments should act but of how they are acting, or should act, in different countries and under varying circumstances.

STATES, SOCIETIES AND INDIVIDUALS

Liberal political economy offers a highly distinctive view of states, societies and individuals, and of the proper relationships among them. Individuals, as has been suggested, are given empirical and normative priority. In the more extreme forms of liberalism, the individual is all but attributed with a consciousness, and a linguistic competence, prior to his or her experience of society. Certainly, societies are denied any practical, or moral, reality beyond that of mere aggregations of individuals.

Beyond society, the state is a much distrusted institution: a necessary instrument for certain purposes, but an instrument which must be constrained and guarded against at all times. The state, like society, is seen to be nothing more than a functional, voluntary and conditional creation of free individuals. The notion of a social contract, as the foundation of any state, is dear to many of liberal persuasions. Purer liberals accept no more than a limited number of state functions within the economy. It must ensure external security, preserve internal order and the sanctity of property, establish respect for contracts and maintain a stable monetary system. 'Compensatory liberals' may permit some limited extensions of state activity to enhance the opportunities of those who are unduly disadvantaged.[19] However, all liberals remain uneasy at the prospect of an extensive, and intrusive, state.

Marxist theory is unashamedly collectivist in its philosophical foundations and political perspectives. The individual's consciousness is seen to be profoundly conditioned by the ideologies generated by and for the dominant interests within the prevailing socio-economic system and the effects of the current stage of development of that system. In pre-socialist eras class conflict prevails and true society is impossible. States serve, and are largely the creation of, the dominant economic classes; to be opposed, and then seized for revolutionary purposes, by the exploited classes and their allies. Once the economic, social and political system has been transformed through the revolutionary use of state power, then the state will be encouraged to 'wither away' and give way to a new, more libertarian, communist order.

Economics realists are varied in their views of the state. Some have viewed it as the most important agency for communal well-being, and preservation, in an insecure world. Some, indeed, have deemed the state to be the ultimate form of political expression, and achievement, of human societies. However, there are many who entertain less doctrinal, and less eulogistical, views of the state; seeing it as more or less functional, given the requirements of communities under varying conditions.

The conditional view of the state, by some economic realists, is based upon a recognition of the need for governmental involvement in the support, and even direction, of many desirable domestic economic and industrial developments. It is further encouraged by a cautious view of the environment within which societies have to operate; an environment which is characterized by change, turbulence and many sources of potential damage to the well-being of the members of individual societies.

Economic realism is also distinct from both Marxism and the more extreme forms of liberalism in acknowledging and accommodating the possibility, and significance, of cohesion within societies. Marxism's emphasis upon class conflict requires a critical view of sentiments of collective, or 'national', identity as manifestations of a 'false consciousness' instilled into the exploited classes by those who wish to preserve their interests and their system. The more extreme forms of liberalism can accommodate cohesiveness only as a form of spontaneous, yet continuing, compact between rational individuals who recognize a common interest in common, or mutually regarding, activity. However, the imperative of self-interest, inherent within the liberal prescription, may engender a serious paradox of 'rationality'[20] and prove to be fatally damaging, to the practical foundations of cohesiveness.[21]

In contrast to the dismissiveness of Marxism, or the confused wishfulness of liberalism, economic realism pays considerable attention to the possibility, and the implications, of cohesiveness within society. It is able to acknowledge that no economic or social order can long survive, in an acceptable condition, without a significant measure of internal cohesiveness. It also accepts that many economic systems encompass the simultaneous existence of competitive struggle and mutual advantage; and that maintaining a tolerable balance between differing interests and classes may be a vital contribution of government to the preservation of a mutual advantageous social framework. Finally, economic realism is distinctive in its view that the moral imperative of governments must be focused primarily, if not exclusively, upon the needs of the communities that they serve; and that communities are composed of real human beings, not merely members of classes, disembodied 'consumers', 'producers', or other theoretical abstractions.

PROGRESS

A further fundamental upon which liberal, Marxist and economic realist political economies differ is that of progress. Both liberalism and Marxism are products of the European Renaissance and subsequent 'enlightenment'. Indeed both intellectual departures enshrine the notion, central to the enlightenment, that human beings, through the exercise of reason, can effect substantial change, promote fundamental progress and, ultimately, attain a new level of human self-realization and even perfection.[22].

Two notions are thus central to both liberalism and Marxism: that prescribed changes will constitute progress and that such progress will ultimately lead to a condition of perfection. Perfection for liberals would constitute a combination of minimalist political democracy, free markets and a world of free trade, peace and harmony. Marxists, in contrast, envisage a multitude of liberated communist societies coexisting harmoniously in a world purged of acquisitiveness, inequality, exploitation, oppression and the malign influence of states. The general condition envisaged by both liberalism and Marxism is thus perfect and, once achieved, would require no further changes of any substance. In an important sense, therefore, history, change and progress will end once the liberal or Marxist millennia are attained.

Economic realism, in contrast to liberalism and Marxism, rests upon no utopian vision. The world is, and will always remain, a turbulent, insecure and often messy realm. History is certainly a matter of constant change, but notions of progress are impositions of a simple judgement upon a far more complex reality. The achievement of perfection, or the attainment of a non-catastrophic 'end to history', are certainly not to be expected. Some conditions do improve for some of the people some of the time, but the notion that change is always progressive, or that there is general benefit from all major changes, is illusory and seriously misleading. All that can be expected, by an economic realist, is for individuals and societies to do the best they can, under prevailing constraints and conditions, while maintaining no more than modest expectations of what can be achieved through their actions.

GOLDEN AGES

Just as liberal, Marxist and economic realist political economies differ in their views of the nature and probability of progress, so, too, there are interesting differences over the nature, and existence, of 'golden ages' in the past. The late nineteenth century is often evoked as a near 'golden age' of laissez-faire, free trade and developing democracy, by those ultra-liberals who have furnished the intellectual rationale for the recently renewed popularity of neo-conservative politics and political philosophies. Marxism, too, identifies a primitive 'golden age' in the era before the emergence of hierarchical social orders, and their embryonic class conflicts, which humanity will recapture, at a higher level of development, in the attainment of true communism. Only economic realism is devoid of any notion of a 'golden age', seeing history in terms of gains qualified by losses, as a constant fluctuation between improvement and deterioration.

Central concepts and issues

Many of the terms that occupy a central position within the analysis of the contemporary political economy do not stand alone, as uncontested, neutral terms in description and analysis. The meaning, and significance, of most of the key terms is, in contrast, given by the theoretical structure within which they exist and of which they form a part. Many key terms are thus theory-dependent for their meaning and, given the contested nature of the governing theories, are also 'essentially contested'.[23] Indeed, if the governing theories are laden with political assumptions and implications, then many of the terms of which such theories are composed will also be inherently political.

The theory-dependent, essentially contested and inherently political character of basic terms is well illustrated in the field of political economy. Liberal, Marxist and economic realist perspectives give quite different meanings, and significance, to a range of important terms. Indeed, some concepts and terms are literally inadmissible within some approaches or admitted only to be refuted. Such diversity of meaning, and selectivity of admission, holds for many important concepts: 'markets'; 'class'; 'exploitation'; 'development'; and the popular notion of 'interdependence'.

MARKETS, EFFICIENCY AND EXPLOITATION

In the liberal vision, markets are a fundamental and benign agency for economic transactions, the satisfaction of human needs and wants, and encouraging the optimal employment of the world's productive resources. Markets are not merely benign, but actually exist in reality. A free market is unfettered by governmental control and undistorted by the actions of influential producers or consumers. A market that operates in such a free manner is, definitionally, fair and efficient. Efficiency is, indeed, the outcome of the operation of such a free market, by definition. Moreover, the exchanges generated by such a market cannot, again by definition, be exploitative; exploitation carries the implication of unfairness and, to the liberal, anything entered into within a genuinely free market, in which individuals freely choose the exchanges into which they wish to enter, cannot be unfair.[24]

Should markets encompass noticeable imperfections, liberal political economy will still accord them conditional approval. The test, here, is the net effect of such imperfections upon general welfare. If a restriction upon competition actually permits some goods to be produced more cheaply than under truly competitive conditions, then such restrictions will be tolerated. Unfortunately, it is impossible to establish the general consequences of any type of imperfection; the net effect will be a product of the specific, empirical conditions within which the imperfection exists.

Marxist theory is based upon a view of markets and exploitation that is diametrically opposed to that of liberal political economy. Markets, far from being neutral mechanisms for securing collective satisfaction and well-being, are the means through which capitalists realise the surplus value that they extract from their workers. Markets are thus a primary mechanism of exploitation, domestically and internationally.[25] Given the inequalities that are fundamental to all class societies, and to capitalism in particular, markets cannot be efficient, in any genuine sense of the term, for they satisfy the wants of the rich expropriators, at the expense of many of the needs and wants of the poor and exploited. They are, moreover, fundamental sources of human alienation: alienating producer from produce, producer from consumer, employer from employee and employee from employee.

Economic realists adopt a conditional attitude towards markets. The flexibility and potential freedom of market economies is acknowledged, but so, too, are the many potential distortions that can arise within the market economy and undermine its practical, and moral, force. A primary purpose of economic realism is to identify the many impediments to effective and equitable market functioning and the adverse effects that are frequently generated by markets under the conditions in which they actually operate. The prescriptions of economic realism then constitute proposals of domestic and international measures that might correct market impediments or damaging market effects. Communal and governmental action will play an important role in such recommendations, but will not necessarily be seen as a panacea for all problems.

INEQUALITY

Liberal political economy maintains an uneasy attitude towards inequality within the systems it addresses. The analysis of perfectly competitive markets, upon which mainstream liberal economics is based, takes the distribution of wealth, and command over productive resources, as given. Analysis is confined to an examination of market interactions, given that initial distribution. However, the functioning of the market will, in practice, be substantially affected by the prevailing distribution of wealth and control of productive resources. Substantial inequalities in disposable wealth will distort the pattern of effective demand within the market and draw productive resources disproportionately towards the satisfaction of the needs and wants of the wealthier members of society, at the expense of the requirements of the poor. Unequal command over productive resources will also limit the ability of some to contribute to the supply side of the market to their best advantage and may affect the range, quality or price of those goods and services that will be made available to the market.

The distorting effects of inequalities do not, however, lead many liberal political economists to condemn all economic conditions that include, or those policies that tolerate, a significant measure of inequality. Inequalities are defended on two grounds. First, the possibility of accumulating personal wealth might stimulate entrepreneurial activity which, in turn, creates new jobs and enhanced incomes for others, as well as bringing new goods and services to the market. Second, many beneficial economic developments require substantial investments which may most readily be supplied from the resources of those who enjoy disproportionately high incomes and wealth.

Marxists see the existence of inequalities as the fundamental reality of pre-socialist, politico-economic orders and the absolute demonstration of their fundamental deficiency. Economic inequalities are the inevitable consequence of a relationship of production in which the few, who own the means of production, expropriate 'surplus value' from those who actually operate the means of production. Such inequalities are progressive: capital is accumulated, on the one hand, while, on the other, the proletariat is increasingly emiserated. Such intensifying inequality is, however, at the heart of the political alientation of the proletariat from the capitalist order and its ultimate conversion to revolutionary socialism.

The ubiquity, implications and ultimate effects of inequality are not, however, the only bases of Marxists criticism of capitalism and liberal political economy. Even if it did not generate its own, and ultimately fatal, contradictions, a system founded upon gross inequalities would be deplorable. To Marxists, a society marked by substantial inequalities contaminates the lives of all its members: the rich being both fearful of the envious actions of the poor and morally diminished by toleration of the deprivations imposed upon others; the poor being exploited, alienated from the fruits of their labours and materially deprived. Only an egalitarian order holds the promise of practical stability, and moral acceptability, for Marxists.

Economic realists are agnostic in their attitude towards inequalities. They recognize the distorting effects of gross inequalities, but accept that entrepreneurial incentives may often be valuable in promoting desirable economic and industrial developments. However, they are also aware that inequalities and distributional conflicts may confront political authorities with some of their greatest difficulties and generate serious obstacles to desirable developments. Policies towards inequalities must therefore reflect the conditions prevailing within any given economy and the wider economic objectives being pursued.

Internationally, too, economic realists acknowledge that inequality constitutes a serious problem. It is the source of 'Southern' resentment against the rich 'North-West'. However, a sensitive diagnosis of its sources is essential if sound policies for the reduction of global inequality are to be adopted, and rhetorically appealing but often ineffectual policies adjured.

ADJUSTMENT

The concept of 'adjustment' is also associated with the liberal view and analysis of markets. Adjustment, in this context, is a relatively neutral term to describe those changes in demand, supply or policy conditions that will secure the changes signalled by market forces or, within formal economic analysis, the removal of imperfections identified through the 'comparative statics' analysis of stylized situations. The 'comparative static' of conventional liberal economic analysis ignores the time taken for such adjustments and allows their costs to be largely assumed away, a feature that has prompted many professional economists to doubt the methodology upon which such analysis is founded.[26]

Both Marxist and economic realist political economy are hostile to such formalistic and bland notions of 'adjustment'. Both view the economy as an arena of ceaseless change. For Marxian analysts, responses to economic changes are evolving struggles among dominant capitalist interests and between them and the subordinate classes. The management of 'adjustment', and the allocation of 'adjustment costs', is thus an intensely political matter, indeed the very stuff of movement and evolving conflict within the capitalist order.

Economic realists also view 'adjustment', and the allocation of 'adjustment costs', as a matter of central significance within the dynamic political economy. Prevailing structures and institutions will influence the kinds of costs generated by changing economic circumstances and their distribution amongst various groups, interests and classes. Government can, moreover, exert considerable influence over the extent to which a society will be willing and able to confront 'necessary' adjustment costs and in determining the extent and distribution of the costs that may have to be borne. Adjustment, then, is an intensely political matter for both economic realists and Marxists.

'SUPPLY–SIDE ECONOMICS', CORPORATISM AND INDUSTRIAL REGENERATION

In the promotion of economic 'adjustment', many analysts within the advanced industrial countries, and particularly those that have been experiencing a loss of international competitiveness or a deteriorating balance of payments, have turned their attention to 'supply-side' economics. Within the liberal camp, two strains of 'supply-side' thought are identifiable. First, there is the view that many of the problems of faltering advanced industrial countries stem from the excessive, and deleterious, interference of governments with the functioning of the laissez-faire economy. Their prescription is for the dramatic withdrawal of government and the repeal of 'meddlesome' legislation. 'Privatization', deregulation, balanced budgets and the 'roll-back of the state are the clarion calls of the disciples of such ultra-liberalism.

The second strain of liberal 'supply-side' economics is by no means incompatible with the first, but is focused, in contrast, on the activities that government might undertake to assist the competitive revival of the economy but which have hitherto been neglected or mismanaged. Legislation to constrain and control the activities of trades unions reflect one aspect of this approach; new industrial training schemes, vocational curricula within schools, and improved incentives and opportunities for entrepreneurial activity, exemplify another line of approach.

Marxists range from dismissiveness to fundamental hostility in their responses to all forms of 'supply-side' economics. Such policy prescriptions are deemed to be desperate attempts to sustain a disintegrating capitalist order, often assuming the worst features of class politics. The state is thus seen to be acting as the agent of the owning class, in its requirement for a more docile, suitable and pliable work-force as a means to the continued extraction of high levels of 'surplus value' and the sustained accumulation of capital.

Economic realism is more sympathetic towards the general notion of 'supply-side' economics. It is, however, rather more open to radical, interventionist, approaches than the mechanistic, often neo-conservative, prescriptions of 'liberal supply-siders'. Economic realists are thus quite receptive to proposals for improvements in the educational system but would also advocate wide-ranging governmental support for research and development, specific areas of industrial investment and general programmes of regional support and development. Such essentially interventionist prescriptions reflect the economic realists' recognition that the sources of desirable economic development, and of competitive industry, are more varied and complex than recognized in the free-market models of liberal political economy. Interventionist prescriptions also entail a rejection of the negative fatalism of Marxist political economy.

Interventionist economic realism produces a model of the desirable relationship between government and economy that is close to, if not identical with, *corporatist* models of many modern advanced industrial states and a number of developing countries.[27] Such models highlight the near fusion of interests, and sometimes personnel, between government and industry in many political economies. Such systems are quite unlike the state socialist systems of the centrally planned economies but are also far from the liberal vision of a clear separation between the economy and the political system, and of a government that merely ensures the broad, albeit minimal, framework for orderly economic activity. Such corporatist models are rejected or denied by both liberals and Marxists, each for their own reasons.

CLASSES AND CONFLICT

The political and intellectual divisions among liberal, Marxist and economic realist political economy are also well reflected in their respective treatments of class and conflict within the politico-economic system. In extreme forms of liberalism, a fusion of methodological individualism and political bias underlies a clear and explicit rejection of the very notion of class. In this view, class is a false, aggregate category imposed upon a reluctant reality by ideologically motivated, or misled, collectivist analysts. Moreover, notions of inherent conflict within a free-enterprise system are equally ideological or misconceived in their origin. Reality, to ultra-liberals, and indeed many less extreme liberals, is a potentially harmonious domain of freely interacting individuals in which conflicts among groups are a result of aberrant developments, misconceived 'interests', or malevolent leaders.

Marxists, in direct contrast, identify classes of a fundamental reality within pre-socialist society and class conflict as a primary mechanism through which the underlying dynamic of history is expressed. Individuals are shaped by the context within which they develop. They share interests with others in similar circumstances and are themselves able to pursue many of their purposes effectively only in company with their fellows. In a capitalist order, the group dynamic expresses itself through the fundamental antagonism between bourgeoisie and proletariat; an antagonism which will be resolved only with the socialist revolution.

Economic realists also acknowledge the powerful influence of the conditions within which individuals develop and operate. Class structures may develop and exert a decisive influence upon economic developments. However, economic realism acknowledges the existence and influence of other institutional arrangements within society. Moreover, many factors influence, modulate and modify class dynamics. Economic realism is not committed, therefore, to the invariable and fundamental role of classes, merely to their potentially significant, but always variable, influence and effects.

MONOPOLIES, OLIGOPOLIES AND TRANSNATIONAL CORPORATIONS

Few pheonomena better highlight the differences amongst liberal, Marxist and economic realist political economy than monopolies, oligopolies and transnational corporations (TNCs). Liberal political economy is thrown into some confusion by the possibility, and actual existence, of monopolies and oligopolies, in which one or a small number of producers dominate the supply of a given commodity, good or service. It is also embarrassed by the prevalence of TNCs, which transcend national frontiers and often enjoy oligopolistic market conditions. Standard textbooks of mainstream (liberal) economics treat monopolies and oligopolies as exceptional phenomena, relegating their discussion to later chapters. Discussion then follows the formal analysis developed, separately, by Joan Robinson[28] and E.H. Chamberlain,[29] which establishes that monopolies (and oligopolies) will generally supply goods at higher prices and in lower volumes, than would be the case in competitive markets. To the extent that the Robinson-Chamberlain expectation is fulfilled, the existence of monopolies and oligopolies signals a significant reduction in the well-being generated by the market.

The response of liberal political economy to the problems posed by monopolies, oligopolies and TNCs, is two-fold: first to deny the frequency of such phenomena, in practice; and second, to argue that where monopolies and oligopolies do, indeed, exist their detrimental effects may be more than compensated by advantages that arise from their exclusive, or large scale of, operation within any market. Thus, ensured profit levels might encourage a monopolistic or oligopolistic supplier to be more confident in initiating costly exploration, development or new investments than would be a supplier in a more competitive market. Again, a large scale of production and supply might enable a monopolist or oligopolist to secure economies of scale that could then be passed on to consumers as lower prices. Such arguments are central to the liberal toleration of TNCs, many of which enjoy oligopolistic market conditions. All such compensations are, however, conditional upon the specific conditions under which monopolistic or oligopolistic suppliers operate and cannot be assumed *a priori*.

Marixts often employ the term 'monopoly' to denote all forms of large-scale capitalist enterprise, and hence endow it with highly pejorative connotations. The use of the term 'monopoly', in this context, reflects the traditional Marxist view that the development of capitalism generates a steady concentration of capital and the increasing domination of society by a tacit alliance among major financial and industrial enterprises.[30] It is these same capitalist 'monopolists' that then metamorphose into the TNCs that, according to Lenin's version of Marxism, stimulated the late nineteenth-century phase of capitalist imperialism and subsequently generated the conflicts among the capitalist metropoles that led, ultimately, to the First World War. Latterly TNCs are seen to be the primary agents of a sustained neo-colonialist relationship between the richer and the poorer sections of the world. To some neo-Marxists, moreover, the monopolistic domination of the world has developed to a new stage in which tacit cartels of world-bestriding mega-corporations dominate the global economy to their own advantage: a latter form of 'ultra-imperalism'.[31]

Notions of monopoly and oligopoly are also of considerable importance within economic realism. Their significance lies in the introduction of 'power' and influence into the analysis of the political economy. Economic realists believe that differential endowments of such power and influence and characteristic of real-world political economies, with perfect competition being so rare as to be a virtual aberration or theoretical fantasy. Power and influence exist within many more economic situations and relationships than those normally covered by the terms 'monopoly' and 'oligopoly'. Such situations require analysis within any realistic political economy. However, actual monopolies and oligopolies often exert considerable influence on the functioning of the political economy. They may, moreover, be formed by groups of states as well as by coalitions of private corporations. Indeed, significant power and influence may also be exerted by groups of purchasers of some commodities, goods and services. Such monopsonistic or oligopsonistic power also requires careful examination within any realistic analysis of the contemporary political economy, whether it be exercised by private enterprises or nation-states.

Given the emphasis on monopoly, oligopoly and all other forms and patterns of power and influence within the political economy, it is natural for economic realism to pay particular attention to TNCs. These enterprises are often able to exercise considerable, and sometimes distinctive forms of, power and influence in their relations with other enterprises, governments or communities. Where TNCs are able to maintain themselves in monopolistic, oligopolistic, monopsonistic or oligopsonistic positions then their potential power and influence will be substantially enhanced. Economic realism is, however, sensitive to the complexities involved in the exercise of actual power and influence in the real world: the complex equations of autonomous capability, signalling skills, actual determination and the perceptions, expectations and calculations of others. The actual relationships of power and influence in the real political economy are expected and ascribed central significance within economic realism. Such configurations can be established only by empirical investigation, rather than deduced from *a priori* criteria. They must, moreover, be acknowledged to be changeable under a wide variety of influences and conditions.

INTERNATIONAL ORDER

Ultra-liberals are rarely interested in questions of order, beyond the construction of limiting 'constitutions'. 'Compensatory liberals' have recognized that a suitable framework for free-market activity is neither self-creating nor self-maintaining. Just as government is deemed to be desirable in order to create law and maintain order, by all but the most extreme of liberals, so, too, international arrangements are now viewed as essential for orderly interaction within a liberal, or relatively liberal, international economic system. Such arrangements, often loosely entitled 'regimes', are held to have been fundamental to the impressive speed and extent of post-war recovery and to the subsequent progress towards a prosperous, and relatively liberal, international order.[32]

Marxists, too, have a view of an international order but it is an essentially hierarchical, unequal and exploitative order. Whether in the form of earlier neo-colonialist ideas[33] or later notions of dependency structures,[34] world-wide accumulation[35] and a world system of capitalism,[36] the view presented of the prevailing order is far from benign. Indeed, the prescriptive thrust of most Marxian analyses is towards the fundamental transformation of the prevailing order by socialist revolutions within the capitalist metropoles or, increasingly, through the disengagement of the 'South' from the 'North' and its subsequent self-determination, economically and politically.

Economic realists are singularly interested in the existence and nature of any international order. Order, here, might be a matter of formal international arrangements, characteristic patterns of behaviour and outcome, or underlying structures of power and influence. The economic realist view of the international order is thus able to combine the discriminating approach of some 'regime liberals'[37] with insights derived from Marxist schools of analysis. The actual analysis of any given international configuration will, however, reflect its particular characteristics and conditions.

INTERDEPENDENCE AND THE DEVELOPMENT OF THE WORLD POLITICAL ECONOMY

Liberal political economy envisages the progressive development of a benign form of international interdependence. Indeed, free international trade is seen to be not merely the means of transcending the economic constraints imposed by geography, and national frontiers, but also of overcoming the political divisions generated by jealous state sovereignties. Free trade, in this vision, generates a mutually beneficial specialisation of production and mutually advantageous pattern of international trade. Societies increasingly appreciate the mutual benefit gained from their trade with one another and, in consequence, develop fellow feelings for those with whom they have such positive relationships. Moreover, it is possible that the patterns of productive specialisation will engender new mutual dependencies that make it difficult, if not impossible, for states to go to war with one another. Mutual benefit, and the eventual harmonization of all relations, are thus the products of a free international system of trade in this liberal, and essentially 'functionalist', view of the global political economy.[38]

Marxist views of contemporary international 'interdependence' are highly critical. The very concept, with its implication of mutuality, may constitute no more than ideologically motivated camouflage for something rather more pernicious.[39] What interconnections there are between the 'North' and the 'South' may, indeed, be systematically damaging to the well-being of the populations of the LDCs and the developmental prospects for their countries.[40]

Economic realists do not accept a simple view of contemporary interdependence—of its form, level or likely future development. The naive optimism of the liberal view is rejected, but so, too, is the unqualified criticism by many Marxist analysts. Moreover, economic realists focus upon the complex interrelationship between political decisions and developments within the economic realm of 'interdependence'. Thus, it is at least as possible that the growth of post-war 'interdependence' as a function of a prior commitment to maintain peaceful relations among the advanced industrial countries (and often wartime adversaries) has been the source of peace and relative harmony.[41]

Economic realists and Marxists also recognize the way in which much contemporary 'interdependence' actually reflects the development of transnationally integrated production by TNCs. In this new pattern, the TNC distributes its production amongst specialized subsidiaries located in different countries. Components, part assemblies and semi-finished products are then shipped between subsidiaries, but across national frontiers: 'intra-firm trade'. The resulting pattern of 'induced interdependence' alters the balance of 'power' between TNCs and nation-states substantially, if not always in one simple direction.

Political developments also lend their weight to the influence of economic conditions in shaping the future development of the global political economy. The combination of such influences will determine whether the future will lie in the direction of growing global 'interdependence'; the emergence of complex webs of bilateral association; the crystallization, as many believe possible, of mutually antagonistic regional economic and trading blocks; or a partial retreat into mercantilist national economic redoubts.[42]

DEVELOPMENT

The development of the LDCs divides liberal, Marxist and economic realist political economies as much as any other issue. Many of the concepts and issues discussed thus far indicate many of these differences of view about development. However, there are also some definitional issues which require clarification. Some, but by no means all, liberal political economists have tended to equate economic growth, as measured by aggregate Gross National Product (GNP), with development. Not merely is such a limited definition of development simplistic but it may be misleading. The growth an LDC's GNP can be made to appear impressive if much of its traditional non-market production is brought into the money economy. Indeed, a highly inflated view of growth may be presented where agricultural production for family consumption is replaced by the production of cash crops. The net addition to 'wealth creation' may be relatively small in such cases and, where luxury cash crops are produced for export, may actually reduce the nutritional standards of the rural population whilst actually increasing the economy's dependence upon imports of basic foodstuffs. Such possibilities indicate the complexities and controversies involved in the definition of 'development'.[43]

Marxists maintain a sceptical attitude towards most conventional perspectives upon development. The attempt to develop LDCs within the prevailing global capitalist order is held to be futile by many Marxist analysts. Genuine and sustainable development will arise, it is argued, only when socialism prevails within the capitalist metropoles, or the LDCs dissociate themselves from the world capitalist order and rely upon their own-resources for authentic development.

Economic realists share the view that development within the LDCs means something far more than the mere growth of their GNPs. They, too, are concerned with the domestic distribution of benefits from 'development', the sustainability of the process and the net effect upon the developing country's level and forms of external dependence. The location of a national economy within the prevailing international economic system will, economic realists acknowledge, have a considerable bearing upon the ease, or difficulty, of the development process. However, many domestic conditions also have a significant bearing upon development prospects; conditions that include the prevailing culture, the nature and effectiveness of the governmental system.

The actual capabilities of LDCs may be crucial to their development prospects. The 'need' of many LDCs for investment by TNCs often reflects a lack of significant capabilities. TNCs are endowed with precisely the financial resources, physical capital, skilled manpower, and knowledge of, and access to, distributional systems that many LDCs lack. This imbalance of capabilities provides the basis for the TNCs 'welcome' in many LDCs and underpins the bargaining advantages that such enterprises often enjoy in their negotiations and relationships, initially at least, with their weaker hosts.

The possibility of non-revolutionary progress is acknowledged by economic realists, despite some scepticism towards the more naive of expectations. Moreover, economic realists recommend a cautious attitude towards the apparent successes of the NICs, given their continued dependence upon markets in the established advanced industrial countries and their relatively narrow technological and industrial bases.

AID

Differing views of development, and its prospects, are reflected in varying attitudes towards international economic aid. Pure liberals regard such aid as an unnecessary, and often damaging, form of welfare payment from the rich countries to their poorer neighbours. Such aid, it is argued, stimulates a form of welfare dependence within the poorer countries; underwrites wasteful, and possibly detrimental, policies; distracts attention from necessary changes in official policy and improvements in private entrepreneurship; and is often an unnecessary substitute for local savings and investments.

Compensatory liberals, in contrast to their purer cousins, recognize that many LDCs face formidable obstacles to development; obstacles that can sometimes be overcome through the judicious provision of development aid.

Marxists condemn much of the past and present flow of aid as, at best, a sop to liberal consciences within the rich countries and, at worst, a means of preserving the economic subordination of the LDCs.[44] Far from being welcome, aid should thus be rejected as constituting a mechanism for preserving the continued attachment of LDCs to the prevailing world economic order and, hence, their continued exploitation and subordination.

Economic realists are discriminating in their overall view of international economic aid. Its strategic utility to donors is acknowledged: its use as a 'payment' for political support, strategic services and economic alignment.[45] Aid may, moreover, be particularly welcome to many within the recipient countries: furnishing many benefits from personal wealth to resources for the recruitment and maintenance of domestic political support. However, a programme of economic aid may, if sensitively directed and judiciously administered, significantly assist many forms of development within LDCs, from the enhancement of basic conditions of life, to the encouragement of profitable initiatives and investments.[46] The 'power' relationships that underlie aid relationships, and the political implications of many aid programmes, must, however, be acknowledged within any sensitive analysis.

Conclusions

The discussion within this chapter highlights the diversity of viewpoints on many central ideas and issues within the contemporary political economy. The liberal and Marxist approaches, in their purer forms, stand in diametric opposition to one another. Economic realism sometimes appears to offer a compromise position between the other two 'ideal types'. However, economic realism is also founded on distinctive intellectual foundations, including a rejection of determinate and deterministic theory, a post-Sraffian theory of value, and a recognition of the positive, and often decisive, contribution that governmental action can make to the economic well-being of communities.

The debate among the contrasting and contending perspectives constitutes a polylectic of considerable value. Advances in the analytical methods and insights of each perspective are stimulated as much by criticisms from contending perspectives as by problem identification within each perspective. The argument of each perspective is certainly sharpened through debate with contending approaches. If 'truth' is not to be secured through the perfection of any one approach, nor divined through some subtle and all-illuminating synthesis, then truth is to be approximated through a continuing polylectic.

The continuing process of mutual criticism and self-improvement among the contending approaches also constitutes a *critical* project.[47] In the realm of political economy, as elsewhere within the social sciences, no one approach can monopolize the title of 'critical' theory. All worthwhile theories of human activity penetrate beneath the apparent 'realities' of daily experience and develop concepts and arguments that, in some respects, appear counter-factual, such statements about underlying reality do not accord, simply, with 'ordinary' experience. Claims to exclusive tenancy of 'critical theory' are thus presumptive, when all approaches challenge some commonplace assumptions and are contestants in the ceaseless competition among contending, necessarily partial 'truths'. It is an awareness of this partiality of all proposed 'truths' that forms the real basis of a critical approach to political economy. Thus it is in their relationship with popular 'orthodoxies', and received wisdoms, that some approaches are more critical than others.

Students of political economy, however, often require a clear starting point from which to initiate their investigations. Criteria are therefore desirable for selecting from among the range of attractive, albeit incomplete, analytical approaches. Criteria for choice can be developed, although their satisfaction does not guarantee the ultimate suitability, or 'truth', of the approach selected. Approaches that oversimplify reality, or even seek to explain it in terms of a severely limited number of factors, are to be doubted as sound perspectives on a complex, and inherently dynamic, area of human activity. The power of an approach may also be assessed, power being defined in terms of the range, exclusivity and capacity for self-explanation.

The range of an approach is a measure of the variety of phenomena that can be accommodated and the number of major insights from alternative approaches that can readily be incorporated. If a wide variety of clearly pertinent developments, or aspects of reality, must be excluded by a theoretical approach then its effectiveness may be doubted. Again, if it indiscriminately rejects insights from alternative approaches, then it may be unduly rigid or misleadingly 'pure'.

The capacity for self-explanation also indicates the value of an analytical approach. The nature of such self-explanation is, however, illuminating in its indication of an approach's epistemological implications. Simple notions about the possibility and nature of 'truth' might be seriously suspect in a world clear of complexity, variability and considerable malleability. An approach that is modest in its claims upon the 'truth', but is yet able to provide a plausible account of its own existence, may thus be preferred to one that is overambitious, existentially silent or offers a suspiciously simple explanation of its own existence. Whichever approach is adopted initially it remains important, however, that its partial character is recognized. Such partiality also highlights the existence of, and the insights provided by, alternative perspectives upon reality.

Whichever 'corner' is occupied in the ceaseless debate amongst contending approaches, it is clear that political economy is a field of intense debate, continuing development and profound significance. It remains an arena of *political* economy by virtue not only of the policy implications which always attend upon the analytical enterprise, but also the contestation over the essentially political values that lie at the heart of the contending approaches. In the study of complex, and often elusive, realms of human activity, views of what 'ought' to be invariable condition assertions about what 'is': a duality that lies at the heart of *political economy!*

Notes and references

1. See, for instance, Ch. 1 of Martin Staniland, *What is Political Economy: A Study of Social Theory and Underdevelopment* (New Haven, CT: Yale University Press, 1985).
2. See, in particular, Rendigs Feis (ed.), *The Second Crisis of Economic Theory* (Morristown, NJ: General Learning Press 1971); and Daniel Bell and Irving Kristol, *The Crisis in Economic Theory* (New York: Basic Books, 1981).
3. See, for example, Susan Sovengey 'International Economics and International Relations: A Case of Mutual Neglect', *International Affairs*, 46, no. 2 (April 1970), pp. 304-15; and Christopher Brown, 'International Political Economy: Some Problems of an Inter-Disciplinary Enterprise', *International Affairs*, Vol. 49, no. 1 (January 1973), pp. 51-60.
4. See, for example, Ralph Milliband, *The State in Capitalist Society: The Analysis of the Western System of Power* (London: Weidenfeld and Nicolson, 1969).
5. See, in particular Fred Northedge, *The International Political System* (London: Faber, 1976).
6. See W. F. Ilchman and N.T. Uphoff, *The Political Economy of Change* (Berkeley: University of California Press, 1971); N. Frohlich and J.A. Oppenheimer, *Modern Political Economy*. (Englewood Cliffs, NJ: Prentice-Hall, 1978); N. Frohlich, J.A. Oppenheimer and Oran R. Young, *Political Leadership and Collective Goods* (Princeton, NJ: Princeton University Press, 1971); and, to an extent, C.K. Rowley, 'The Political Economy of the Public Sector' in R.J. Barry Jones (ed.), *Perspectives on Political Economy: Alternatives to the Economics of Depression* (London: Frances Pinter, 1983), pp. 17-63.
7. See, on the continuing problems of simple 'testing', and 'corroborating', theories, Hilary Putnam, 'The "Corroboration" of Theories' in T. Honderich and M. Burnyeat (eds.), *Philosophy As It Is* (Harmondsworth: Pelican Books, 1979), pp. 353-80.
8. See the discussion in John Maclean, 'Marxist Epistemology, Explanations of "Change" and the Study of International Relations', in Barry Buzan and R.J. Barry Jones (eds.), *Change and the study of International Relations: The Evaded Dimension* (London: Frances Pinter, 1981) pp. 46-67.
9. For an early discussion of the political character of 'political economy', see Gunnar Myrdal, *The Political Element in the Development of Economic Theory*, trans. Paul Streeten (London: Routledge and Kegan Paul, 1953).
10. Fred Hirsch, *Social Limits to Growth* (London: Routledge and Kegan Paul, 1977).
11. See, for example, J.W.N. Watkins, 'Ideal Types and Historical Explanation' in J. O'Neill (ed.), *Modes of Individualism and Collectivism* (London: Heinemann, 1973), pp. 143-65, esp. pp. 144-6.
12. See the discussion of liberal political economy by R.J. Barry Jones, in Chapter 2 of this volume.
13. See Robert W. Cox, 'Ideologies and the New International Economic Order: Reflections on Some Recent Literature', *International Organization*, Vol. 33, no. 2 (Spring 1979), pp. 257-302, esp. pp. 261-6 and 274-80.
14. See Andrew Gamble's contribution to this volume (Chapter 3).
15. For a further discussion see R.J. Barry Jones's contribution on international economic

realism in Chapter 8 of this volume.
16. See the discussion in Chapter 2 of this volume.
17. Ibid.
18. See Chapter 3 of this volume; Nicos Poulantzas, 'The Problem of the Capitalist State' in Robin Blackburn (ed.), *Ideology in Social Science: Readings in Critical Social Theory* (London: Fontana, 1972), pp. 238-253; J. Holloway and S. Picciotto (eds), *State and Capital: A Marxist Debate* (London: Edward Arnold, 1978); and Ian Steedman, *et al., The Value Controversy* (London: Verso, 1981).
19. See R.D. MacKinlay and R. Little, *Global Problems and World Order* (London: Frances Pinter, 1986), esp. pp. 26-41 and 45-8.
20. See the brief discussion in Chapter 2 of this volume.
21. See the illuminating discussion in Hirsch, *Social Limits to Growth*, esp. Chapter 5.
22. See, Sidney Pollard, *The Idea of Progress: History and Society* (London: C.A. Watts, 1968), esp. Chapter 2 and 3.
23. See the discussions in Richard Little, 'Ideology and Change', and R.J. Barry Jones, 'Concepts and Models of Change', both in Buzan and Jones, *Change and the Study of International Relations: The Evaded Dimension.*
24. See the clear expression of this view in Robert Nozick, *Anarchy, State and Utopia* (Oxford: Basil Blackwell; and New York: Basic Books, 1974), esp. Chapter 7.
25. For a general discussion, see Robin Jenkins, *Exploitation: The World Power Structure and the Inequality of Nations* (London: McGibbon and Kee, 1970).
26. See the discussion in Chapter 2 of this volume.
27. See the discussion in Staniland, *What is Political Economy?* esp. pp. 73-98; and also Colin Crouch, 'Corporative Industrial Relations and the Welfare State' in Jones, *Perspectives on Political Economy,* Chapter 6.
28. Joan Robinson, *The Economics of Imperfect Competition* (London: Macmillan, 1933).
29. E.H. Chamberlain, *The Theory of Monopolistic Competition: A Reorientation of the Theory of Value* (Cambridge, MA: Harvard University Press, 1933).
30. See, for a classic exposition of this thesis, V.I. Lenin, *Imperialism: The Highest Stage of Capitalism* (1916).
31. See, for instance, Robin Murray, *Multinational Corporations and Nation States* (London: Spokesman Books, 1975); and the introduction to Robert B. Stauffer (ed.), *Transnational Corporations and the State* (Sydney: University of Sydney, Transnational Corporations Research Project, 1985).
32. See the discussions in R.O. Keohane and J.S. Nye, *Power and Interdependence: World Politics in Transition* (Boston: Little Brown, 1977); Stephen D. Krasner (ed.), *International Regimes* (Ithaca, NY: Cornell University Press, 1983); Robert O. Keohane, *After Hegemony: Cooperation and Discord in the World Political Economy* (Princeton, NJ: Princeton University Press, 1984); and Richard L. O'Meara, 'Regimes and Their Implications for International Theory', *Millennium*, vol. 13, no. 3 (Winter 1984), pp. 245-64.
33. See Jack Woodis, *Introduction to Neo-Colonialism* (London: Lawrence and Wishart, 1967).
34. See, for example, Andre Gunder Frank, *On Capitalist Underdevelopment* (Bombay: Oxford University Press, 1975).
35. See, especially, Samir Amin, *Accumulation on a World Scale, Vols 1 and 2,* trans. B. Pearce (Hassocks: Harvester Press, 1974).
36. See, especially, Immanuel Wallerstein (ed.), *World Inequality* (Montreal: Black Rose, 1973).
37. See Keohane and Nye, *Power and Interdependence*, esp. Chapter 3.
38. See A.J.R. Groom and P. Taylor, *Functionalism: Theory and Practice in International Relations* (London: University of London Press, 1975), esp. pp. 1-6.
39. See John Maclean, 'Interdependence — An Ideological Intervention in International Relations' in R.J. Barry Jones and P. Willetts, (eds), *Interdependence on Trial: Studies in the Theory and Reality of Contemporary Interdependence* (London: Frances Pinter, 1984), pp. 130-66.
40. See the review of such ideas in R.J. Barry Jones, 'The Definition and Identification of Interdependence', in Jones and Willetts, *Interdependence on Trial*, pp.17-63; Frank, *On Capitalist Underdevelopment*; and Amin, *Accumulation on a World Scale.*
41. See, in particular, the argument of Barry Buzan, 'Economic Structure and International Security', *International Organization*, vol. 38, no. 4 (Autumn 1984), pp. 597-624.

42. See, in particular, D.P. Calleo and B.J. Rowland, *America and the World Political Economy: Atlantic Dreams and National Realities* (Bloomington: Indiana University Press, 1973); Robert Gilpin, *US Power and the Multinational Corporation: The Political Economy of Foreign Direct Investment* (New York: Basic Books, 1975; London: Macmillan, 1976), esp. pp. 253-8; and Dudley Seers, *The Political Economy of Nationalism* (Oxford: Oxford University Press, 1983), esp. Chapter 11 and 12.
43. For a number of interesting discussions, see the contributions to Section 1 of Gerald M. Meier (ed.), *Leading Issues in Economic Development* 3rd edn (New York: Oxford University Press, 1976).
44. See, for example, Teresa Hayter, *Aid As Imperialism* (Harmondsworth: Penguin, 1971.
45. See, particularly, Joan M. Nelson, *Aid, Influence and Foreign Policy* (New York: Macmillan, 1968); and David Wall, *The Charity of Nations: The Political Economy of Foreign Aid* (New York: Basic Books, 1973).
46. See, especially, Robert Cassen, *et al.*, *Does Aid Work?* (Oxford: Oxford University Press, 1986).
47. On 'critical political economy', see Dwayne Ward, *Toward a Critical Political Economics: A Critique of Liberal and Radical Economic Thought* (Santa Monica, CA: Goodyear Publishing Co. Ltd, 1977).

PART II PERSPECTIVES ON POLITICAL ECONOMY

Chapter 2

Liberal political economy

R.J. Barry Jones

Introduction

The 'liberal' approach to political economy exerts a profound and continuing influence throughout the modern world. Liberal political economy, in one guise or another, constitutes the orthodoxy of the world's free-market nations. It has also crystallized into a highly elaborated, sophisticated and intellectually beguiling theoretical system. Moreover, ideas born in the minds of the classical forefathers of liberal political economy have continued to form the basis of both Marxist and neo-Ricardian political economy.

The inherent appeal of the wider corpus of liberalism is undeniable. It proclaims the virtues of a free-market mechanism that has, in many respects, proved the most dynamic economic system in human history. It justifies the possession of private property and self-seeking acquisitiveness. It also advances the principles of individual political freedom and liberal democratic institutions. Its appeal has been further enhanced by the frequent intertwining of these three principles of free markets, private property and liberal political democracy.

The power and effectiveness of the liberal perspective has not, however, been attained without significant costs. As with all theories of human activity, it rests upon prior value preferences, simplifying assumptions, in its 'purer' forms, and the exclusion of unmanageable aspects of reality. Moreover, the liberal position also incorporates a number of insecure arguments and many unwarranted conclusions about 'reality'. However, an informed judgement upon such a complex and influential perspective, whether ultimately favourable or critical, clearly requires a careful review of its general propositions, its analytical foundations and its possible shortcomings.

The basic liberal position

The liberal position rests upon a small number of basic propositions: the rationality of human beings, conceived of as *individuals;* the generally benign mechanism of the free market for goods, services and all productive resources; the practical and moral desirability of private property; and the primacy of individual freedom within a framework of law, as enacted by responsible and democratic political institutions.[1] These notions are often presented as a complex whole, as an inextricably intertwined set of ideas and propositions.

The intimate association of such a set of nominally distinct notions is as much a product of the historical origins of the liberal disposition as it is a matter of analytical necessity. The liberalism of John Locke, Adam Smith and myriad European and North American theorists and political activists of the seventeenth and eighteenth centuries was forged in opposition to many of the institutions, policies and practices of the autocratic governments of those times. To liberals (and other radicals of the time), arbitrary and despotic government appeared to be chronically prone to expropriate property, dictate economic activity, proscribe dissent and preserve itself through undemocratic institutions. The pursuit of liberty was thus as much a matter of defending the individual's right to the possession and disposition of his[2] property as it was of enshrining individual freedoms of belief, speech and assembly, or of establishing democratic forms of government. Individual property rights would enshrine a diffusion of economic power and, by extension, contribute to a dispersal of political power.

The subsequent development of the liberal paradigm lent increasing sophistication to its analytical components and their purported interconnections. Individuals that were self-interested *and* rational would provide the foundation for both an efficient and benign market economy and a responsible, democratic political system. Rationality was the vital key for it would moderate rampant self-interest by revealing, to each individual, the need to consider the requirements of orderly and cohesive interaction and association with others. The democratic political order would require such 'enlightened self-interest' if individuals were to support those laws and regulations that might actually restrain their own future behaviour, albeit in a manner conducive to general harmony and stability.

Rational self-interest would also be central to the development and functioning of an efficient market economy. As will be seen in the subsequent discussion, rational self-interested individuals would constitute the consumers in the market, to be supplied by rational self-interested producers of goods and services. The market's price mechanism would allow such rational self-interested individuals to bring consumption desires and production possibilities into balance.

Any arbitrary interference with the possession or disposal of individuals' property would necessarily distort developments in the market. Morally, the ability of governments to interfere with the property of individuals would constitute a fundamental violation of their basic human rights. Practically, too, the ability of men to assert their political liberties, and to promote their legitimate political purposes, would be undermined by a system that denied them the right to possess and dispose of their property freely. Free and vigorous men required a state that protected their property rights rather than one that arrogated undue power, and property, to itself, thereby spawning a corrupt and corrupting Leviathan.

The basic assumptions and arguments of liberal political economy

It is possible to view liberal political economy from a political or an economic starting point. Politically, liberal political economy constitutes a normative theory of political institutions and activity which has strong implications for the conduct of economic affairs. Economically, liberal political economy may be seen as an analytical theory (albeit firmly grounded in prior values) of economic activity, with many implications for the policies and practices of governmental authorities. The 'economic' model of liberal political economy rests upon a number of assumptions and arguments that have emerged during its long process of evolution.

From an analytical (rather than political) point of view, the purposes of the classical forefathers of liberal economic theory turned around a relatively small number of basic questions, of both practical and philosophical implication. Commerce comprised the production and exchange of a variety of goods and services. How, however, did the production and exchange of such goods and services come about and expand with time? Such goods and services had sometimes been bartered for one another or exchanged through the medium of some form of money. How, in such exchanges, were various goods and services to be valued against one another and, hence, how were the efforts of those who produced such diverse goods and services also to be valued?

Classical liberal economic theory, as it evolved via Adam Smith, David Ricardo, John Stuart Mill and their many followers, located the sources of 'modern' economic *growth* in the twin foundations of accumulated profits and the increasing productivity of labour.[3] For Smith, the development of the division of labour, within the market economy, provided the central source of increasing labour productivity.[4] Should the possibilities of technical innovation prove inadequate to satisfy the requirements of a growing population, and overcome the exhaustion of cultivable land, then growth would come to an end and a stationary or stagnant state would result.[5]

Given the philosophical and moral concerns of classical economic theorists, the nature of *value* was also a matter of considerable interest and importance. Central questions concerning the fundamental nature of economic activity, and the equity of various patterns and process of economic life, turned upon the sources of value in the goods and services that were exchanged in the market-place. The equation of value with market price seemed too trite and ephemeral a proposition for the classical theorists. A long-term 'natural price' might exist for goods,[6] but such a notion shaded into metaphysics. If the intrinsic value of a good was to be established then the idea of *use value*, or the value of a commodity to its actual user, had more potential merit but could not, in itself, discriminate between 'free goods' and those commonly bought and sold in the market. Such difficulties encouraged the notion that the real value of goods and services derived from the amount of human labour that had to be devoted to their production.[7] The theory of *labour value* thus flourished only to be supplanted ultimately in mainstream liberal economic doctrine by the notion of marginal utility. However, it remained at the heart of the great economic 'heresy' of Karl Marx, and his numerous disciples.[8]

In their investigations of the nature and significance of that most peculiar of all commodities — money — the classical theorists identified and elaborated its role as a vital facilitator of complex economic exchanges. 'Bullionist' doctrines of money, which identified issued forms of money with the stocks of precious metals held by issuing institutions, however, held sway and encouraged the development of a fully-fledged Gold Standard doctrine for national and international monetary management.[9] Moreover, a rather simplistic notion of interest rates was developed which deemed them to be primarily a function of levels of demand for, and supply of, capital within an economy. The supply of and demand for capital were also held to be determined by factors other than the level of interest itself.[10]

Classical liberal political economy thus focused upon the basic issues of economic life, retaining a continuing concern with the souces of value, growth and the distribution of well-being among the members of an economic community. The classical tradition was to be split and deflected by developments during the second half of the nineteenth century, however. The central concerns of classical economics persisted in its Marxian offshoot, but were to be largely eclipsed within the liberal tradition by the triumph of marginal analysis, and theories of general equilibrium, from the early 1870s onwards. The centrality of such issues was not to be acknowledged again, within liberal political economy, until the Great Depression of the 1930s impressed itself upon the more responsive of liberal thinkers.

The neo-classical paradigm

The elaboration of the notions of marginal utility and general equilibrium, and the development of sophisticated techniques of marginal analysis, characterized the main thrust of liberal economic analysis during the late nineteenth and early twentieth centuries.[11] The question of intrinsic value was to be dissolved in the notion that the value of things could be determined by consumers' marginal choices among available goods and services: an idea that achieved its apogee with the indifference curve analysis of Sir John Hicks and R.G.D. Allen.[12] With rational consumers maximizing their personal satisfactions by choices that equalized the utility to them of the marginal (or last chosen) unit of every good or service purchased, one side of an overall market equilibrium had been established.

The other side of a market equilibrium could then be established if rational producers produced those levels of goods and services at which their marginal costs (costs of the last unit produced) just equalled their marginal revenues (price obtained for the last unit sold) and when time had been allowed for production decisions to adjust to market signals regarding the pattern of relative demand within the range of available goods and services.[13] The elaboration of a notion of general equilibrium, and its mathematical analysis, were the outstanding theoretical achievement of a lineage of economic thinkers from Jevons and Walras through to the great synthesis and popularization of Alfred Marshall's *Principles of Economics*.[14]

The neo-classical paradigm was to be undermined by a number of theoretical developments during the twentieth century. The theories of imperfect competition and monopolistic competition, developed by Joan Robinson and E.H. Chamberlain respectively,[15] undermined the practical and theoretical security of analysis based upon assumptions of perfect competition within markets. J.M. Keynes's macro-economic theories then challenged earlier presumptions that automatic mechanisms would ensure that a free economy would ultimately attain stability in a condition of full employment.[16]

However, neo-classical orthodoxy has preserved itself in the face of such potentially fundamental intellectual and theoretical challenges. While the empirical existence of monopolies and oligopolies cannot be denied, nevertheless, in Phyllis Deane's view: 'Whenever problems of the optimal allocation of resources are paramount economists have tended to revert to the assumption that the market is competitive in the sense that there is no overriding monopoly power on the market.'[17] Keynesian challenges to many of the central tenets of neo-classicism have also been evaded by economists. Keynes's repudiation of the presumption of benign and mechanistic general equilibrium tendencies had been discarded[18] and his rejection of the 'quantity' theory of money reversed by the modern proponents of 'monetarist' doctrine.[19] Far from accepting such potentially profound challenges, the neo-classical paradigm has been protected by efforts to graft Keynsian concepts and techniques of aggregate analysis onto its established armoury of theories and techniques.[20]

While a wide diversity of views exists amongst those who fall under the general title of liberal political economists, the neo-classical paradigm remains a dominant force within the liberal camp. Moreover, it constitutes a theoretical position which distills, and exemplifies, many of the assumptions that continue to lie at the heart of many liberal views.

The persistence of the neo-classical paradigm, and its relative primacy among liberal economists, thus encourages a closer, critical consideration of its basic assumptions and central arguments. The purpose of this body of liberal theory and analysis is to reveal something fundamental about economic life. However, an important corollary of this vision, always implicit and sometimes explicit, is to establish the moral effectiveness of a laissez-faire economic system.

Some of the basic ideas of the neo-classical economic paradigm formed a fundamental part of the liberal persuasion from the outset. Philosophically, human beings are seen to act *as individuals*; society, and all other human collectivities, being no more than aggreggations of such self-willed individuals. This philosophical individualism has informed the liberal approach, in politics as well as economics, throughout its evolution.

The market is also fundamental to both classical and neo-classical economists. It is the market that permits the division of productive activity and labour; the increase of productivity; and the accumulation of investable capital resources to which classical liberals attributed economic growth. The market is also the arena in which politically and economically free individuals can interact to the advantage of themselves and, ultimately, of everyone.

The development of techniques of 'marginal' analysis heralded the crystallization of the neo-classical paradigm. Such techniques allowed the market mechanism to be displayed in a more formal and precise manner than had previously been possible. With such a market, a rational individual, equipped with finite resources (of barterable goods and services, or, more commonly, money) purchases a range of goods and services. The quantity of any one good or service purchased will be determined by the marginal utility of that good or service. In other words, when the cost to the individual of the last unit of any good or service purchased just equals the satisfaction (utility) that it will provide then that will, indeed, be the final unit purchased of that particular good or service. Overall, the individual will purchase a set of goods and services such that the marginal utility (*to him or her*) of each good and service is equal.

Those who have productive resources (labour, skills, equipment, accumulated savings, etc.) to deploy in the generation of goods and services that can be exchanged in the market, will make decisions comparable to those made by the purchasers of goods and services. All such resources will be committed to production to the extent that the rewards generated by the last unit committed are just equal to the costs of making that commitment. Thus, the limit of time and effort that a worker will contribute to production will be reached when the wages received for any one hour worked just equal the costs, in terms of exhaustion, foregone leisure time, or whatever, incurred by working that last hour. Decisions about the commitment of all productive resources will be determined in an analogous manner.

On his or her side, an entrepreneur will employ additional labour up to the point at which the contribution of the last labourer hired (or last hour worked by existing employees) just equals the value of the additional product generated by that labourer's efforts. Moreover, any over - or under-supply of any productive resource (including labour) will reflect itself in the relative price paid for that resource (wage rates in the case of labour), with the principle of diminishing marginal returns continuing to prevail.

The market provides the appropriate signals with regard to the specific goods and services that might be produced. Once a good or service has been introduced into the market, any price movements that are necessary to sell the available stocks (or consume all the time of those providing services), without the formation of queues of unsatisfied would-be customers, will signal any necessary changes in the volume of supply of that good or service. If demand is too high at the price initially charged, some of the potential purchasers can be dissuaded from their intended purchases by increasing the unit price of the good or service. Increasing prices will thus bring demand and supply back into balance. Under the contrary conditions, where demand is inadequate at the initial price, and stocks remain unsold, then the unit price can be reduced to persuade purchasers to buy more of the given good or service. Whichever situation prevails, the price adjustment generates a condition of market, or *partial equilibrium*.

The corollary of price adjustments will be changes in the rates of return (profits) secured by the producers of various goods and services. Those who find themselves supplying goods and services for which there is high relative demand, and have therefore been able to raise their prices, will be making greater than average profits. Equally, those who find themselves supplying low-demand goods and services may have had to reduce prices to clear stocks and will thus be securing less than average profits.

Adjustments in the production and supply of goods and services will be stimulated by such variations in profit levels. Rational producers will identify the signals that are generated in the market and switch their productive resources from the production of low-profit goods and services into the production of higher-profit goods and services. However, as rational producers continue to respond in this manner, the volume of previously low-profit goods and services supplied to the market will decline, until reductions in supply generate an increase of their prices to a level at which producers make more or less normal levels of profit. Equally, as the supply of previously high-profit goods and services increases, that very increase in supply will necessitate progressive reductions in market prices to ensure continued sales of available supplies. This, in turn, will gradually reduce the profit levels secured by suppliers of these goods and services towards the 'normal' level.

The equalization of profit levels throughout the supply side of the market will generate a stable condition in which no producer has an economic incentive to move productive resources from their current occupation, unless circumstances are changed by some external disturbance. This condition of *general equilibrium* in the market is both stable and 'efficient'. Given the prevailing availability and distribution of both income and productive resources, the market has ensured the optimal employment of productive resources and the maximum possible level of satisfaction of the needs and wants of consumers.

The supposed ubiquity, and force, of the market mechanism allowed the earlier neo-classicists to overcome many of the objections that things were, in reality, rather more complex, and indeterminate, than envisaged within the simple general equilibrium model. Implicit adherence to a loose variant of Say's Law[21] sustained the belief that there were no inherent obstacles to the full utilization of all productive resources in a free-market system. While presented as a 'straw man' for analytical debunking, by John Maynard Keynes, Say's Law did suggest that there would be a tendency for any production that was undertaken to result, reasonably swiftly, in the generation of demand sufficient to absorb that which had been supplied to the market.

More specifically, the early neo-classicists' view of money and interest rates also encouraged the belief that a condition of equilibrium would automatically be achieved, thereby ensuring the full employment of all productive resources. The savings of thrifty, or better-off, members of society might constitute a serious source of leakage of demand from the economic system. Moreover, the level of such savings was held to reflect a wide variety of independent influences. However, there were many entrepreneurs who were constantly seeking profitable opportunities, for which they often required additional financial capital. The savings of the thrifty, and the demands for funds by the enterprising, were matched in a market for financial capital with the rate of interest playing the role performed by prices in the market for goods and services. Interest attracted savers to lend their resources; the higher the level the more savings that were offered for loan or investment. Interest was the price that entrepreneurs were prepared to pay for additional capital; the lower the rate of interest the more that was acquired from lenders and investors. When allied to the 'quantity' theory of money, such a notion of the role and functioning of the interest rate also provided the early neo-classicists with a satisfactory (to them) overall view of money and the financial sector.[22]

The effect of self-equilibrating finance and capital markets was, once more, to ensure that productive opportunities were not overlooked and productive resources left idle. The later contribution of Keynes would be to demolish all vestiges of confidence in Say's Law and to replace the neo-classicists' simplistic approach to the financial system with a far more discerning view of its considerable complexities, of the potentially decisive role of interest rates and a wholly new insight into the mechanisms of the macro-economy. However, the neo-classical paradigm has proved resistant to change or extinction.

Neo-classicists, and a variety of 'liberals', have managed, successfully in their view, to accommodate many of the concepts and insights introduced by Keynes. The neo-classical paradigm remains a dominant force within liberal economics and, with its continued emphasis upon the virtues of the free market, a major source of support for international free trade.

Comparative advantage

In its view of an international free trade system, contemporary neo-classicism has allied general equilibrium theory with the earlier notions of comparative advantage enunciated by the classical theorists in general, and by David Ricardo in particular. The effect of a world laissez-faire system should be the optimum exploitation of the world's productive resources and, in turn, the maximum satisfaction of the needs and wants of the world's population. The source of this benign outcome is held to lie in the varying efficiencies with which the populations of various countries are able to produce goods and services. The policy condition that will permit the full exploitation of the opportunities provided by comparative advantage is the minimization of governmental interference with, and restraint of, free trade among societies.

The principle of comparative advantage takes liberal political economy beyond the boundaries of the domestic economic system and its corresponding analysis. However, the international economy is intimately interrelated with the domestic economies of all but the most unusual of modern nation-states. Moreover, the principle of comparative advantage is both one of the major propositions of liberal political economy and a central part of the argument that associates laissez-faire with the well-being of *all* the inhabitants of the world. A brief consideration of the principle of comparative advantage (despite its extensive discussion elsewhere[23] is thus necessary in any review of liberal political economy.

The need for the principle of comparative advantage arose from the clear inadequacy of simpler explanations of international trade. Trade had initially been explained in terms of *absolute advantage*, whereby societies were believed to export only those goods and services in which they had a clear, general productive advantage over other societies. Imports would equally be confined to those goods and services in which other societies had a clear overall productive advantage. Unfortunately, for such a straightforward theory, international trade actually exhibited a rather more complex pattern. In particular, it was observed that some societies which were generally more productive than all others still continued to import some goods and services from abroad.

The principle of comparative advantage provided a solution to the apparent puzzle posed by the realities of international trade and productive specialization. The decisive factor in encouraging trade, it was argued, was not the overall levels of productive efficiency existing between any two (or more) societies, but the relative efficiency with which a given set of goods and services were produced *within* one society when compared with the relative efficiency with which the same set of goods and services were produced *within* the other society.

The above proposition can be illustrated by some highly simplified examples. If two societies (A and B) produce only two commodities (Wheat and Wine) then it is possible that society A and society B are equally efficient and both are able to produce six bottles of wine *or* two kilograms of wheat with the same amount of time and effort. The ratios of productive efficiency within both societies are thus as below:

Society A	Society B
6 bottles wine : 2 kg wheat	6 bottles wine : 2 kg wheat

In such a situation there is no basis for specialization of production and trade between society A and society B. Equally, however, there will be no basis for specialization and trade if the following situation prevailes:

Society A	Society B
6 bottles wine : 2 kg wheat	3 bottles wine : 1 kg wheat

In this second example, society A produces twice as much wine and wheat as society B with the same expenditure of effort, and is therefore twice as 'efficient'. Here, there is no basis for specialization of production and bilateral trade. Society A would have to stop producing 2 kg of wheat for every six additional bottles of wine that it produced domestically (or, in the same ratio, 1 kg of wheat for every additional three bottles of wine). If it then sought to replace the wine no longer produced domestically by exchanging its additional wheat for wine from society B, it would find that society B (if it was at all interested in trade) would offer only three bottles of wine for every kilogram of wheat on offer from society A. Society A would find itself back where it started; obtaining through trade exactly what it had given up in domestic production. Any costs involved in switching productive resources from wine to wheat would therefore have been wasted. Society B, for its part, would also find that it lacked any incentive for engaging in trade and, hence, specializing in the production of one commodity at the expense of the other. Society A's general superiority in productive efficiency over society B is not therefore a basis for international trade and specialization.

Societies A and B, in our example, will specialize and trade only if wine and wheat *are not produced with the same relative efficiency* within their two societies. The illustration below indicates one such case.

Society A	Society B
4 bottles wine : 1 kg wheat	2 bottles wine : 1 kg wheat

In this third example, the ratio of productive efficiency of wine and wheat within society A is 4:1. However, the ratio in society B is now 2:1. This provides a basis for mutually advantageous productive specialization and trade. If society A gives up producing wheat domestically, and shifts its productive resources into the production of wine, then it obtains four additional bottles of wine for every kilogram of wheat forgone. In the case of society B, if it switches productive resources from wine to wheat it gains one kilogram of wheat for every two bottles of wine forgone.

If societies A and B now look to international trade to compensate for the wine and wheat no longer produced domestically, they will find that a mutually advantageous bargain can be struck. If, for example, it is decided that an exchange of three bottles of wine for one kilogram of wheat would be fair then a mutually beneficial outcome will have been achieved. Society A will have produced four bottles of wine for every kilogram of wheat forgone in domestic production, but now obtain 1 kg of wheat from society B for only three of those additional four bottles of wine. It thus ends up with the same quantity of wheat for domestic consumption but with one extra bottle of wine. On its side, society B finds that it can secure three bottles of wine from society A for every kilogram of wheat it exports, but has had to give up producing only two bottles of wine domestically in order to produce the extra kilogram of wheat which it is now trading. Its population is now also able to consume the same quantity of wheat but additional quantities of wine as a result of specialization and trade. Wine production has been increased, and wheat production sustained, in this miniature international trade system, with an undoubted enhancement of satisfaction for consumers in both societies!

The sources of the comparative advantage enjoyed by various societies was held, by later theorists, to lie in the varying endowments of the wide range of relevant *factors of production* required for the generation of possible products and exports.[24]

As was indicated earlier, the liberal argument suggests that global well-being can be maximized if an international free-trade system is permitted to function and general equilibrating tendencies realize themselves. Such conditions will allow all societies to specialize in the production of those commodities, goods and services in which they find they have a comparative advantage (as well as a simpler absolute advantage). Indeed, the persistence of free international trade should encourage the equalization of profit levels globally and the 'prices' of all factors of production, thus overcoming the inequalities generated by constraints upon the mobility of labour in the modern world. The policy imperative following from this view is that governments should endeavour to interfere with free international trade as little as possible, given the constraints of security and similar concerns.

Criticisms of the basic neo-classical model

The outline of the neo-classical paradigm provided above is a considerable simplification of a complex and multi-faceted body of theory and analysis. Moreover, such a neo-classical model is by no means accepted by all those who might legitimately be entitled economic liberals. The outline offered at this stage of the discussion is, however, intended to highlight a number of ideas that have been central to the evolution of modern mainstream liberal economics and which continue to underlie, albeit implicitly, the basic attitudes and dispositions of many who adopt a generally liberal approach. The neo-classical model, by its very clarity and simplicity, also facilitates sharp and orderly criticism. Such criticism, moreover, provides clear keys to many of the debates and developments that have arisen during recent years both within the liberal persuasion and between it and contending approaches to political economy.[25]

Specific criticisms of the neo-classical paradigm arise from numerous sources and operate at various levels of the argument. Some of these criticisms, though not all, are also germane to the wider liberal perspective. A number of significant criticisms may, however, be directed at assumptions which are acknowledged, by its own advocates, to play a central role in the basic neo-classical model.

INTRINSIC CRITICISMS

Methodological ambiguity

Contentious, and highly insecure, assumptions about economic behaviour remain central to the neo-classical paradigm.[26] However, effective criticism of these assumptions requires a prior consideration of their methodological status. The difficulty here is that the status attributed to such assumptions is not always entirely clear in the arguments of many neo-classicists. Highly simplistic and simplifying assumptions may always be made, and defended, on purely heuristic grounds. Here, the intention is no more than to make a few clear and precise assumptions which, while acknowledgedly unrealistic, nevertheless facilitate the development of arguments and models of greater precision and clarity than is usually possible within studies of human activity. The objective is hypothetical models of reality based upon the analytically legitimate question: 'what would be the consequences *if* certain assumptions were to be true?'

Such an essentially heuristic model of economic activity would, of necessity, remain extremely modest in its claims to empirical correspondence, and hence, practical relevance. Empirical correspondence could be hypothesized only if a number of demanding tests and conditions had been satisfied. It is, however, clear from many statements by devotees of neo-classical economics that such assumptions have often been attributed with a high degree of empirical veracity; that such assumptions are accepted as 'true', as an act of faith, because of the many services that they perform for both theoreticians and policy advocates.

Rationality

The concept of rationality is central to the neo-classical paradigm, but remains rather more problematical than is often acknowledged. The basic difficulty here is that an undifferentiated notion of rationality cannot generate a determinate analysis of economic behaviour. If rationality is to be taken to be any course of action that maximizes the full range of needs, wants and desires, entertained by any individual, then it is impossible to know, in advance, whether one 'rational' individual will devote time and energy to solitary contemplation, revolutionary activism, or the ceaseless pursuit of greater material wealth. Moreover, it is difficult, if not impossible, to know what any individual is likely to do in response to the appearance of a commodity, service or behavioural opportunity not previously available, save to assert that if it proves to be desirable then it will be pursued by a rational individual.

A concept of rationality that is useful to neo-classical economic theory (and to liberal economics generally) thus has to be highly constrained. Rationality must be confined to those ends that can be secured through market exchanges; exchanges, moreover, involving only those goods and services that are currently available in the market. 'Non-economic' needs, wants and desires must be excluded from the calculus of rational choice and behaviour. Needs, wants and desires for which there is no current means of satisfaction can also be ignored unless the unsatisfied have some means of impressing their requirements on potential suppliers.[27]

Given such constraints upon the 'acceptable' range of relevant needs, wants and desires, then a number of additional and inherently unrealistic assumptions must be fulfilled if consumers are to be able to maximize their satisfactions. Moreover, consumers must be endowed with roughly equivalent disposable incomes if the satisfactions of the better-off are not given scarce productive resources, to be secured at the expense of the poorer members of society.

Current and potential producers alike must be equipped with perfect information about all possible consumption choices and production opportunities. Moreover, the market within which consumers and producers interact must be perfectly competitive, and must certainly not be distorted by the existence of oligopolies or monopolies. No producer, whether current or potential, must face any barriers to entry to any area of production in which their productive resources could be more profitably employed. As a special extension of this latter proposition, it must also be possible to switch all factors of production between alternative commodities, goods and services with relative ease.

To make the choices that will actually maximize personal satisfaction, given limited means for making purchases, the individual must be equipped with perfect information about what is available in the market, of what quality and at what price. Unless consumers do possess such information they may well remain ignorant of products that they would have preferred to those actually purchased and may find themselves paying more than the lowest available prices for purchases that are made. Unfortunately, this assumption of perfect information, which is just acceptable for purchases made in the much-quoted small village market, has little relevance in the diffuse marketplace of complex, modern and increasingly global society.[28]

The desirability of a roughly equitable distribution of wealth and diposable income within society is not commonly considered in discussions of the mechanisms of competitive markets. It is, however, a vital condition if the needs and wants of the community as a whole are to be satisfied at the highest possible level and if one of the primary moral claims of liberal political economy is to be fulfilled. The central point here is that the market is deemed to be the mechanism which guides the employment of scarce productive resources. Unless all consumers have roughly equal opportunities to express their demands in the market — broadly similar amounts of money with which to support their consumption demands — then productive resources will be drawn disproportionately towards the satisfaction of the needs of those who have more money to support their market demands. Given 'scarce' productive resources, it is a further consequence that inadequate resources will be devoted to the production of those goods and services that are desired by the less well-off. There is, in this view, a form of short-term zero-sum game, in the language of game theoreticians, at work in a market characterized by an unequal distribution of disposable wealth and income.

It is clear that an unequal distribution of disposable wealth and income has been the exception, rather than the norm, throughout the history of the more complex and developed economies. Liberal political economy is, therefore, confronted with a serious moral dilemma to which there are three possible solutions. The first solution, and one which often hovers close to the surface of many pronouncements, is that the qualitative character of the needs and desires of the better-off, and often more educated and 'refined', members of society are so superior to those of the 'lower orders' that their satisfaction more than compensates for some loss of satisfaction of the needs and wants of the less advantaged! Such, indeed, was one of the implications of J.S. Mill's famous argument, in *On Utilitarianism*, challenging the unqualified utilitarianism of Jeremy Bentham and the implication that mass 'tastes' might prevail at the expense of 'higher' values.[29]

The second strategy for dealing with the problematical consequences of an unequal distribution of wealth and income is to devise a technical means for its evasion. This, essentially, is what is achieved within conventional liberal economic analysis by the employment of the term 'revealed preferences'. The effect of such a notion is to declare, to all intents and purposes, that the demand actually expressed in the market is all that will, and indeed can, be of concern to technical economic analysis. The moral claims of the liberal free market, assumed *a priori,* have been relegated to a dark and distant cupboard, well shielded from further illumination and critical interrogation.

The third response to the problem of inequalities of wealth and disposable income is to argue that the resultant distortions, which are not denied, are nevertheless acceptable in the short term because of the long-term benefits that they generate. The disproportionate rewards secured by the entrepreneurs and other innovative members of society are viewed as necessary incentives and rewards for their productive efforts. Such entrepreneurial and innovative vigour will, in time, generate greater wealth for society, create more and better-paid jobs for the working population and, hence, distribute wealth and well-being generally throughout society: the 'trickle-down' process so beloved by both earlier development economists and more recent 'supply-side' polemicists.[30]

For the market to generate the maximum satisfaction of consumer wants, and the most efficient deployment of productive resources, it must operate flexibly and competitively. Any impediments to full competitiveness will result in higher prices for at least some of the goods and services purchased by consumers. This, in turn, will reduce their consumption of other goods and services below the level that would otherwise have been purchased. This under-consumption of some goods and services will reduce the aggregate level of satisfaction enjoyed by consumers, overall, and constitute a significant loss of efficiency within the economic system.

In practice a variety of 'barriers to entry' may impede the movement of resources into the production of goods and services for which there is unsatisfied demand and/or in which higher than normal profits are currently enjoyed. Many areas of production and supply require specialized knowledge and experience which may be difficult to acquire by those currently outside the given industry. Moreover, the various *factors of production* are far from perfectly mobile and flexible in practice. Enterprises with a capital stock and work-force that is specialized in one area of production may find it difficult, to the point of impossibility, to switch into a quite different area of production. The relative immobility of enterprises and their work-forces may also inhibit the rapid exploitation of new, but geographically specific, opportunities for production, or more competitive production.[31]

A major source of restraint upon the movement of resources into a profitable area of production and supply may be the domination of a given area of economic activity by monopolies or oligopolies. Here one, or a few, enterprises are so prominent in a given industry that they are, by their own decisions and actions, able to influence, if not dominate, conditions in the market; they are not, in the jargon of economic analysis, merely 'price takers' in a competitive marketplace. Two problems are created by the existence of such monopolies or oligopolies. First, formal economic analysis suggests that rational monopolists and oligopolists will supply lower levels of the product at higher prices than would be the case under competitive market conditions.[32] Second, the behaviour of oligopolists will be coloured by strategic considerations, in which non-price forms of competition alternate with periods of predatory price warfare, at times and under circumstances which cannot be predicted with any certainty.[33] The relative prevalence of oligopolistic conditions in the real world thus creates a considerable problem for the claims of the laissez-faire economic system to efficiency, and hence to the maximization of consumer satisfactions.

The insecure assumptions considered thus far, constitute some of the corner-stones of the liberal economic perspective in general, and the neo-classical paradigm in particular. Other conditions must also be satisfied if a liberal political economy is to fulfil its claim to maximize the well-being of its consumers. These conditions are, however, ancillary to the fundamental assumptions of the liberal model.

If a laissez-faire market system is to maximize the satisfactions and general well-being of the people then adverse side-effects must not be generated by activities undertaken within that system, or, in some sense, by the system itself. A benign laissez-faire system must not, therefore, be marked by the production of *negative externalities*, or, if generated, there must be satisfactory mechanisms for countering or compensating these adverse effects. A considerable range of economic activity actually generates negative externalities and thus confronts liberal political economy with a significant problem.

Two strategies have been prominent in the response of liberal economists to the problem of negative externalities. Many economic 'purists' have sought to deal with the problem by simple evasion. Analysis, it is contended, must be confined to market exchanges and is both bound and entitled to ignore non-market phenomena. The alternative strategy has been to conjure up mechanisms for ensuring that those who suffer such negative externalities are compensated by those who secure the benefits generated by the relevant economic activity. Unfortunately, this 'solution' owes more to rationalistic analysis than to empirical observation. Far too many members of many modern societies have, in sharp contrast to the fantasies of economic metaphysicians, discovered a complete absence of any practical procedures for ensuring adequate compensation for planning decisions, and resultant developments, that impose severe adverse consequences upon themselves or their property.

A special form of negative externality arises where the pursuit of personal satisfactions necessarily involves the denial of the same, or similar, satisfactions to others. Game theoreticians term such situations 'zero-sum games', where, in essence, 'what I win you loose, and vice versa'.[34] Formal economic analysis generally evades this problem by identifying the market mechanism as a morally neutral means of rationing those commodities, goods or services, for which demand exceeds current levels of supply. In short, liberal economic theory is content with the notion that those who can pay will secure those satisfactions that are in short supply, and those who cannot pay the necessary price will have to go without and pursue alternative (and necessarily less agreeable) satisfactions.

Many zero-sum situations may be relatively temporary. It may be possible to increase the supply of many commodities, goods and services in response to high demand. Indeed, the market provides the very mechanism by which many temporary shortages can be overcome. Those who most desire the given item(s), and who have the means to bid up the price, will increase profits made by suppliers. This, in turn, will attract new suppliers, or encourage existing suppliers to devote additional resources to increase levels of supply. The result will be a general improvement in supplies and an increase in the number of consumers whose desires can now be satisfied. Unfortunately, not all zero-sum situations can be resolved by the simple expansion of supply.

A special, and singularly intractable, form of zero-sum situation arises where there are goods whose supply is necessarily limited, or strictly finite. One type of such 'goods' is 'positional goods' in which satisfaction is secured only because others are being denied the opportunity to secure that same satisfaction. All matters concerning status are definitionally 'positional' in this sense. Expensive motor cars are thus, in part at least, desired by some people precisely because others cannot afford them. If others could afford such motor cars then a significant part of their distinctive appeal would be lost. Worse still, where valued resources, commodities or conditions are necessarily limited, the desirable will be enjoyed by some only when others are denied such satisfactions. Thus, in a seaside town which has a limited sea frontage, some will enjoy a sea view only when others, and probably the majority, are denied such a rewarding aspect.[35]

It is not only zero-sum situations, and positional goods, that undermine the degree to which a market system can deliver the maximum satisfaction to all the consumers in any society (in other than the restricted and essentially tautological manner in which liberal economic analysis often covers its ethical retreat). Many of the goods and services which are consumed by the members of complex modern economic systems may not, in themselves, actually constitute real sources of satisfaction. They may actually be little more than *intermediate goods* — of little instrinsic value to the consumer, but significant, if not essential, to the achievement of primary satisfactions.[36] Thus, many inhabitants of rural areas may not be particularly enthusiastic about the ownership or use of motor vehicles *per se*, but merely find them essential when living at some distance from places of work, shopping centres and other necessary services.

The possible existence of intermediate goods raises questions about the level at which any economic system is generating the satisfaction of needs, wants and desires. There are arguments about the nature and extent of such goods, but if they do exist, it is questionable whether their value should be considered as a contribution to consumers' satisfactions and society's wealth creation or, in contrast, a burden on the former and a detraction from the latter. Moreover, the functioning of the modern laissez-faire economy may well generate an increasing need for intermediate goods and impose that need upon a growing number of the members of society.

The functioning of a market economy *may* encourage the movement and diffusion of the locations of employment; spread housing to new, and more remote, districts; bring private forms of transport within the reach of a growing proportion, but not all, of the population; and consequentially generate increasing road congestion whilst also weakening popular demand for effective public transport. The net effect of such developments will be to impose upon those living anywhere but in the centres of the town a growing 'need' to acquire a motor vehicle and to require the public authorities to provide more and better roads to accommodate the growing numbers of vehicles in regular use. In such a case, many of the cars purchased and the roads built are no more than intermediate goods and have not in themselves contributed positively to human satisfaction. Moreover, their costs should properly be subtracted from the benefits arising from the ends that they serve, whether those ends be the better distribution of industry or increased numbers of those living in aesthetically pleasing rural locations.

The problems confronting liberal political economy do not, however, end with intermediate goods. It is essential to the liberal model that rational self-interest does, through the operation of the market-based 'hidden hand', actually secure the best for the members of society, both individually and collectively. If the notion of rational behaviour that lies at the heart of all liberal analyses of economic life, encounters any significant difficulty in this respect, then the claims of the approach are seriously, if not fatally, weakened.

A serious problem does, indeed, confront liberal political economy with respect to rational behaviour. The difficulty arises when the focus of attention moves beyond those commodities, goods and services that can be produced in relatively easily varied quantities and consumed by one individual, exclusively, and in small quantities. Such goods, *private goods*, contrast sharply with the *public* or *collective goods* which generate considerable difficulties for the notion of rational self-interested behaviour.

Collective goods are marked by number of characteristics. Primarily they are conditions, facilities or other 'goods' of value which, when once produced, are enjoyed by all the members of a group or collectivity for which they have been produced. Members of the collectivity cannot be excluded from enjoying the benefits of such a good, or can be excluded only with extreme difficulty. The benefits generated by such a collective good are, moreover, enjoyed more or less equally by the members of the collectivity. It may also be the case, although it is not a definitional requirement, that a given proportion of the members of a collectivity has to make some form of contribution if the collective good is to be generated.

Liberal political economy traditionally assumed that no intrinsic difficulties attached to the notion and provision of collective goods. There were clearly things that were beneficial to societies, as a whole, and thereby to their individual members. If individual members of a society perceived that the benefit secured from any collective good exceeded the costs involved then they would, as rational self-interested beings, accept those costs in order to secure the collective good's benefits. Unfortunately, as Mancur Olson has demonstrated,[37] it is even more rational for an individual to save the costs of contributing to a collective good if it is possible that the collective good will be produced by other members of the society, irrespective of the missing contribution. If, in other words, a collective good can be produced for a society with less than universal contributions, then it becomes irresistibly tempting for the rational, self-interested individual to 'free ride' on the efforts and contributions of others, thereby enhancing his or her ultimate cost-benefit outcome. However, liberal political economy is necessarily committed to a notion of homogenous human rationality and must therefore accept the equal temptation of all rational self-interested members of a collectivity to attempt to 'free ride' on the contributions of others. If all try to 'free ride' simultaneously, there will be no contributions, whatsoever, and no subsequent collective good.

The argument outlined above depicts a situation in which the members of a set of rational self-interested individuals have each sought maximum personal value satisfaction by withholding contributions while hoping that others will produce a beneficial collective good. Unfortunately, the result of all trying to 'free ride' has been to deny the collective good, and the attendant benefit, to all. Each member of society has thus helped to bring about a situation in which each has been denied an outcome that would have brought positive benefits and, indeed, benefits that would have exceeded any costs involved in producing the beneficial collective good. The pursuit of greater self-interest has thus reduced the level of satisfaction that all the members of society have secured below that which would have been achieved had behaviour been a little less 'self-interested'.

Extensive analysis of the 'free-rider' problem has revealed a number of paths to its practical resolution. There is, in the view of some analysts, one specific condition in which each individual believes that his or her contribution is marginally decisive to the production of a desired collective good. In such circumstances, a contribution should be made by the rational self-interested individual.[38] Other solutions involve the identification of conditions which will, in practice, encourage individuals and other actors to overcome their temptation to 'free ride', conditions which range from social rewards, ideological values, and 'side-payments', to compulsion by 'governments'.[39] In effect, such conditions amount to sets of *associated* costs and benefits; associated in the sense that they are not the benefits arising from the collective good, itself, or the direct costs of its production, but are costs avoided and benefits enjoyed as a by-product of having made the necessary contribution to the collective good.

The problem generated by paradoxes of rationality, particularly in the area of collective good, is that they are likely to reduce the overall benefits secured by individuals and communities operating in purely laissez-faire systems. Where voluntary contributions cannot be generated by the one unique and psychologically unstable condition in which all necessary contributors are convinced of the marginal decisiveness of their contributions, then 'free-riding' will undermine aggregate well-being. The practical mechanisms for overcoming such 'free-riding' are thus costly in themselves, as with side-payments or governmental compulsion, and/or elements which formal liberal economic theory has sought to exclude or relegate firmly to the analytical sidelines: ideology, belief systems or the activity of government. Liberal purists can evade the dilution of their basic analytical model, necessitated by such paradoxical forms of 'rational behaviour' and the resultant problems of generating of collective goods, only by hoping for the resolution of 'free-riding' by contributors' convictions of marginal decisiveness or by denying the very existence of significant collective goods.

General equilibrium and the methodology of comparative statics

The issues considered thus far are specific assumptions and necessary conditions which must be satisfied if liberal economic theory's claim regarding the production of general well-being generated by a laissez-faire system is to be realised. The practical insecurity of many of these assumptions, and the impossibility of many theoretically essential conditions, underlie the rejection by many of the liberal economic model or its substantial modification, by Keynes, 'post-Keynsians' and 'neo-institutionalists'. Most of these assumptions and conditions have, however, remained central to the neo-classical version of the liberal approach. The neo-classical paradigm has, moreover, reinforced reliance upon the methodology of *comparative statics* and enshrined the beguiling, yet highly contentious, notion of *general equilibrium*.

Comparative statics is an analytical technique in which the 'motion' of real life is reduced to a limited number of 'frozen images' for analysis and comparison.[40] The 'frozen images' are, moreover, images constructed upon the highly simplifying assumptions, and under the highly constricting constraints, of mainstream economic analysis. The practice of such comparative statics analysis is to compare a pre-adjustment with a post-adjustment situation. Given the objective of economic optimization, the analysis demonstrates the preferability of the post-adjustment to the pre-adjustment situation and/or highlights the changes in determining conditions which must be effected if the desirable adjustment is to be achieved. The analysis itself usually assumes that the necessary adjustments and changes in governing conditions will take place relatively automatically once their desirability has been demonstrated.

The methodology of comparative statics dovetails with the characteristic equilibrium models of much of mainstream liberal economic theory, including neo-classicism. The post-adjustment condition in such comparative statics analysis is invariably an equilibrium condition, however temporary or partial; it is the result of adjustments that eliminate the imperfections identified in the pre-adjustment situation. Stated briefly, the methodology of comparative statics (usually in a mathematical or graphical form) facilitates the analysis and revelation of 'optimalising' behaviour, and, in the words of John D. Hey: 'Under conventional methodology, if we require our agents to behave optimally, then we are restricted (at the market or economy level) to analysing equilibrium: whether it be equilibrium states, equilibrium adjustment processes, equilibrium adjustments of adjustment processes, or whatever.'[41]

Originating in the idea of equilibrium within a specific market for a limited period of time — *partial equilibrium* — the concept expanded into an analytical notion of a system-wide condition in which all markets achieved, or were tending towards, overall and simultaneous balance — *general equilibrium*. The latter condition necessarily constitutes the optimal employment of productive resources and practical maximization of consumer satisfactions. Moreover, the mechanisms of the free market should make this condition of perfection self-restoring if the system is subject to any disturbances from without. However, general equilibrium has refused to reveal itself within the real world and has retained a marked measure of ambiguity within the domain of theory. It remains unclear whether general equilibrium is to be viewed as a realisable condition or a mere tendency underlying, but not immediately manifest in, the somewhat chaotic realm of everyday economic experience, or as nothing more than a mathematical abstraction.

Characterized in a slightly different manner, the idea of equilibrium is used in a manner akin to the notion of aiming artillery at an immobile target. Once the target has been hit, the artillery piece will require no further attention from the gun crew, save for correction of any minor errors that might arise from changing wind conditions or heat effects upon the gun. The methodology of comparative statics is, in turn, akin to the maps that show the gun crew the relative positions of their target and the current point of impact of their artillery shells and thus indicate the degree and direction of necessary corrections to their aim. Such notions of equilibrium, and the associated methodology of comparative statics, have, however, been widely criticised as unrealistic, unwarranted and ultimately misleading.[42]

Comparative statics techniques are commonly employed in the analysis of particular situations in which misallocations of productive resources, erroneous consumption conditions or misconceived official policies generate sub-optimal conditions and outcomes. The correction of such 'distortions' in the directions indicated by the analysis then establishes a desirable condition of partial equilibrium.

The methodology of comparative statics is not, however, limited to the analysis of partial equilibrium and disequilibrium conditions. It also sustains a notion of general equilibrium and facilitates its mathematical analysis. The precise status of the notion of general equilibrium is, however, often unclear within mainstream liberal economics, and particularly within neo-classical analysis. Conceived at its most simple, a state of general equilibrium would be one of universal static perfection. No possible improvements in the allocation of productive resources, consumer choices or governmental policies would be identifiable. No sources of, or motives for, change could be discerned within a system characterized by such general equilibrium. Indeed, such a system would 'respond' to disturbances by reversing any changes induced by moderately disturbing influences.

Many practitioners of general equilibrium analysis, including some of its eminent forefathers, clearly ascribe no more than heuristic value and status to such exercises. Such analysis is intended to reveal no more than the general results of simultaneous interactions among a set of factors and variables within a highly stylized 'economy'. Unfortunately, attractive ideas have a tendency to escape into wider and less discriminating pastures and notions of general equilibrium are all too common as implicity and sometimes explicity bases of statements and arguments about conditions and policy options within the real world.

The notion of general equilibrium as a static condition can, however, be no more than a theoretical fiction in a world of such clear dynamism and change and can be of pertinence only to a highly abstracted and rarefied form of analysis. However, a notion of general equilibrium need not be restricted to cases of static and universal perfection. The concept might well be applied to systems that move through time and space and that are subject to change. This wider notion of general equilibrium is more suited to the real world but also encounters some serious theoretical and methodological difficulties.

Theoretically, the identification of the conditions that are actually to be sustained (or equilibrated) are far more problematical for a moving and changing system than for one that is static. To establish that the system is still the same system, given the passage of time and the occurrence of some 'change', its essential features (parameters) have to be specified and the limits of their 'permissible' change have to be identified. However, the specification of the system's parameters, in this manner, has to draw upon existing theoretical notions. Such notions will be contentious and controversial, to some degree. Moreover, in the case of notions of general equilibrium the theories involved are likely to presume the existence of the condition *prior* to its empirical investigation and identification.

The methodological difficulty confronting the notion of general equilibrium is a function of the points made in the previous paragraph. With regard to a system in the real world of time and change, general equilibrium can be specified only of the basis of prior theory. An interest in general equilibrium thus requires the use of theoretical approaches that permit, and probably encourage, the notion that general equilibrium might actually exist, in some sense, in the real world. Self-fulfilling theory is thus an inherent problem in general equilibrium analysis.

The actual character of the general equilibrium that is envisaged in much analysis is also uncertain and philosophically problematical. The need to specify the system's parameters in terms of prior theory itself challenges simple, albeit common, views about the relationship between observation and theory in 'scientific' endeavours. It also compromises the claim, dear to at least some mainstream economists, to be practitioners of a 'positive' and 'objective' analytical enterprise. However, there is also serious doubt about the existential and analytical status of a condition of general equilibrium for a system, the essential nature of which has to be specified in such a theoretically based manner. The question here is how real, in a simple and directly observable manner, are the tendencies that draw the system towards, or return it to, equilibrium. Broadly defined system parameters will accommodate considerable turbulence and variation before the system is seen to have changed and equilibrating tendencies deemed to have been overwhelmed. Considerable 'disequilibrium', in practice, might thus be tolerated before the presumption of equilibrium is finally abandoned.

It is possible, however, that many studies of specific issues, processes or developments will not involve the precise specification of the system's parameters, but merely take the system, and its essential characteristics, as given. Such studies, when confronted by a dynamic, turbulent and constantly changing world, might deem 'general equilibrium' to be no more than an immanent tendency within, or underlying, the chaos of the visible world.

Devotion to the notion of general equilibrium will now have added a 'non-observable' to the earlier necessity for prior theory. Aspirations to a 'positive science' are thus doubly compromised and a methodological position adopted which, if fully appreciated, is far closer to that of contemporary Marxist approaches than many liberals would find comfortable.[43]

Unsurprisingly, the notion of general equilibrium has been criticised from various positions, including many 'liberals' who believe it to be a serious diversion from real progress in economic analysis and understanding. Rather more realistic, to many minds, is an economics founded upon the notions of uncertainty and ceaseless change; an analogue of the aerial 'dog-fight' rather than static artillery sighting. Time and disequilibrium are fundamental to such a vision of the economic world. Optimalising assumptions, and preoccupations, are obstacles to the analysis of such a realm which requires, in contrast, stochastic models of development and a vision of individuals as 'rules of thumb' calculators of their conduct.[44]

Comparative advantage and factor endowments

As liberal economic theory extends its vision to international trade, and reiterates its injunctions to minimize governmental interference with free trade, the principle of *comparative advantage* returns to the centre of the stage. Critical discussions of this principle belong to reviews of liberal international political economy. It has, however, been summarized earlier in this discussion and it is worth noting that the practical application of the idea of comparative advantage encounters two serious difficulties.

The first difficulty is that there is a strongly tautological flavour to the concept of comparative advantage. It purports to explain why one state is competitive in the production and export of any given good in terms of a condition which can be established, in practice, only by the existence of the competitiveness which it purports to explain. The 'explanation' of comparative advantage by varying endowments and 'prices' of factors of production amongst different economies merely adds an additional step in the overall tautology. The practical significance of any given pattern of factor endowments,[45] given the variability of 'factor mixes' possible in the production of most goods and services, cannot be established independently of the existence or absence of the competitiveness that the given set of factor endowments is supposed to explain.

The second overwhelming problem with the notion of comparative advantages is that it is of surprisingly little use to those who seek to anticipate future trade patterns or to those charged with the determination of national economic and industrial policy. The problem here is that it is only the more obvious opportunities and constraints under which societies operate (and which are often rather close to earlier notions of absolute advantage) that are truly immutable. Most of the more significant 'factors of production' in the modern world are, in an important sense, *created* by human beings. Educated work-forces are produced by the educational systems of societies. Dynamic and enterprising entrepreneurs arise from sympathetic cultures and social systems. The general momentum of vital and competitive industries owes much to the past history of that industry within a society and to the economic and industrial context within which they thrive. However, the principle of comparative advantage, and its explanation by factor endowments, can tell the policy-maker nothing beyond the relatively obvious and remains necessarily silent on the great questions of whether today's policies for industrial development will meet with success in the future.[46]

EXTRINSIC CRITICISMS

Liberal political economy has also been subject to a range of criticisms from sources external to the liberal perspective. A range of philosophical and methodological doubts have been expressed. Specific and vigorous opposition has been expressed by Marxist of many varieties. Moreover, the positions of 'post-Keynsians', 'neo-institutionalists' and 'neo-Ricardians' are such substantial developments of, and departures from, liberal orthodoxy as to constitute a transformation, and ultimate repudiation, of that body of theory and analysis.

Methodological individualism versus holism

There is widespread criticism of the *methodological individualism* upon which liberal political economy is firmly founded.[47] Methodological individualism rests upon a philosophical presumption that individual human beings are the only ultimate reality, or causal agency, in human affairs. The resulting methodological imperative then, is not only that individual actions should be explained in terms of individual volition, but 'that large-scale social phenomena like inflation, political revolutions, etc., should be explained in terms of the situations, the dispositions and the beliefs of *individuals*'.[48]

Such methodological individualism has been criticized as a prior assumption which denies *holistic* forms of analysis. Ensnared by individualistic presumptions, the analyst is obliged to explain collective life in terms of aggreggations of individual motives, understandings and consequential behaviour. Analysis cannot, therefore, accommodate the notion that, at many times and under a variety of conditions, the 'whole may be greater than the part'.[49] Such individualism constitutes a form of *reductionism* which obscures the collective context within which individuals act and which shape the effects of their actions. It also neglects the historical context within which all human beings are formed and their dispositions shaped.[50]

Marxism versus liberalism

Marxist views constitute a particularly critical rejection of the philosophical foundations, methodological imperatives and analytical perspectives of liberal political economy.[51] Methodologically, Marxists reject the claims of liberal political economy to universal objectivity and argue that its propositions do not hold true at all times and under all conditions. Liberal political economy is, like all other (non-Marxist) forms of knowledge, seen to be contextually constrained and necessarily imperfect. Pre-Marxist knowledge is essentially a product of the socio-economic system within which it is generated and constitutes an ideological support for the dominant groups (ruling class) of that system.[52]

The contrast between liberal and Marxist political economy is sharp.

Modern liberal political economy focuses upon utility, commodity exchange and equilibrium. The primary concerns of Marxist political economy are with the sources of value, the social relations of production, patterns of wealth distribution, capital accumulation and instability within the capitalist economy.[53] The classical labour theory of value is retained and enshrined within a doctrine of the long-term accumulation of capital, overproduction of consumable goods, cycles of boom and slump, decline of profitability, progressive emiseration of the working class, and ultimate collapse of the capitalist system, with its replacement by socialism (and later communism).[54]

Marxism is not only identifiable 'school' of political economy that occupies a critical stance towards contemporary 'mainstream' liberal political economy. The roots of many of these approaches lie firmly within the liberal tradition. The developments and departures that are central to such 'heresies' are, however, such as to throw serious doubt upon their continued membership of the liberal camp.

Keynes versus neo-classical liberalism

The contribution of John Maynard Keynes can be interpreted in one of two contrasting ways. Many within the mainstream of liberal economics view him as having contributed new and powerful tools for the analysis of the macro-economy to the body of liberal, and neo-classical, theory and analytical techniques.[55] To post-Keynsians and neo-institutionalists, the work of Keynes and his immediate associates constitutes a sharp challenge to mainstream liberal economics as it existed in the mid-1930s, and as it has evolved subsequently.[56]

The starting point for Keynes's distinctive contribution lay in the recognition that a condition of full employment of all productive resources, including human labour, would not automatically arise within a laissez-faire economy. Say's Law, by which the mechanisms of the free market were thought to be capable of generating sufficient demand to absorb all the output arising from productive activity, was forcefully refuted. In practice, the circular flow of money from business to workers and back to businesses was prone to a number of potentially critical sources of leakage: personal savings; purchases of imports; and the payment of governmental taxes.[57] Governmental spending and new investment might remedy the deficiency of demand within the domestic economy, but such stimuli were far from self-generating. Moreover, the rate of interest did not function as an automatic balancer of savings and investment; savers' decisions to lend, rather than hoard, money were prompted by different considerations from those that motivated the decision to borrow by those who might invest in new machinery and production.

While the vigour of a fully-employed economy might be sustained by propitious conditions, it was quite possible for a recessionary cycle to become established. If business cuts back output and pays out lower total wages then domestic demand for consumer goods will be reduced fairly rapidly and domestic demand for new machinery will eventually be depressed. Reduced demand for consumer goods will encourage further reductions in output; reduced demand for new or replacement machinery will subsequently prompt substantial reductions in production and employment by the manufacturers of capital equipment and hence compound the reduction of general demand within the economy.

A recessionary spiral is unlikely to continue indefinitely and the economy will probably come to rest eventually. Unfortunately, stability might be achieved at a level of substantial unemployment of labour and idle manufacturing capacity. Until the expectations of entrepreneurs are improved, no simple lowering of interest rates or abundance of investable funds will be sufficient to stimulate the increased output, and eventual revival of orders for capital equipment, that are necessary if unemployed labour is to be brought back into work and demand restimulated within the domestic economy. Moreover, the money wages of the work-force of advanced industrial societies are rarely, if ever, sufficiently downwardly flexible to stimulate substantial reductions in the numbers of unemployed.

If advantageous external conditions develop, or stimulating government policies are adopted, then a benign cycle of expanding production, investment, demand and employment can result. However initiated, a growth of employment expands disposable income and, hence, demand in the economy (multiplier effect). Increased demand will eventually stimulate additional orders for capital equipment, increase employment in the capital goods sector of the economy and further stimulate demand (accelerator effect).[58]

Many of the analytical techniques introduced in Keynes's work were fully acceptable to mainstream liberal economists and, indeed, came to form the foundations of modern macro-economic analysis and national accounting. The narrowly mechanistic vision of much of this work has not, however, been concordant with Keynes's approach. A number of essentially psychological variables — the propensity to consume, liquidity preference, and, most significantly, the expectations of entrepreneurs[59] — assumed a critical role in Keynes's analysis. Liquidity preference and entrepreneurial expectations were, moreover, variables that were conditioned by an inherent and pervasive uncertainty[60] that has remained extremely problematical for mainstream liberal economics.[61]

Keynes's theoretical challenges have been evaded by many mainstream liberal economists, acknowledged by many Marxist political economists and formed the basis of a loose, if clearly identifiable, constellation of unorthodox political economists falling under the various titles of 'post-Keynesians', 'ultra-Keynsians' and 'neo-institutionalists'. All share a renewed interest in the 'institutional' framework within which economic activity takes place in any society or international arena.

Post-Keynsians, ultra-Keynsians and neo-institutionalists draw their inspiration from many and varied sources. Keynes, and his Cambridge collaborators and students, are one corner-stone.[62] The American institutionalist school of economics constitutes a second, major, influence.[63] The Austrian school of 'radical subjectivist' economics, identified with F.A. Hayek and his associates, has also made a contribution.[64]

Joseph Schumpeter's seminal study, *Capitalism, Socialism and Democracy*,[65] is both an inspiration for many of those working within this diffuse 'school' of political economy and a model of the kind of 'institutional' analysis that is undertaken. Schumpeter identifies the inherent dynamic within capitalism, its cycles of vitality and decline and the central significance of a loss of entrepreneurial vigour as business becomes increasingly bureaucratized and the 'capitalist ethos' dissipated.[66] Economics, as an activity that occurs within real time and concrete and historically influenced socio-economic conditions, is thus a central concern of the post-Keynsian/neo-institutionalist critics of mainstream liberal political economy.

Overall, the post-Keynsian/neo-institutionalist school is concerned centrally with such heterodox issues as: uneven growth within a capitalist economy and world; varying income distributions within, and between societies; the possibility of 'equilibrium' and/or economic growth at many levels of employment or unemployment; the existence and effect of advanced credit and monetary institutions; the often critical influence of interest rates in governing the level of economic activity; the role and impact of differences of power and influence within the economy; the existence and structural impact of multinational corporations; the possibility of 'administered prices', rather than price setting by competitive markets; and, last but by no means least, the generally dynamic character of real economic systems.[67]

Contemporary extensions of liberal political economy

Liberal political economy has remained a vibrant and fecund analytical perspective, spawning many developments and diversions. Three such departures are, however, of particular interest to an examination of the contemporary political economy. Ultra-liberals of many varieties have mounted a spirited counter-attack against economic interventionism generally, and against post-war 'Keynsian' macro-economic demand management in particular. Others, highly impressed with the power and precision of mainstream economic analysis, have sought to apply its ideas and analytical tools to previously non-economic arenas of human activity, including government and politics.

Two strands of ultra-liberalism are of particular interest here. The first accepts that there are intractable difficulties with the notion of 'efficiency' within a laissez-faire economy and its achievement. The achievement of efficiency is particularly problematical in respect of collective goods and could be used to justify a substantial, and essentially interventionist, role for government. However, ultra-liberals of this persuasion argue that such extensions of governmental activity are still to be resisted as sources of undue restraint upon free individuals and, in all probability, sources of other inefficiencies and even corruption.[68] Indeed, some go so far as to advocate, and detail, a 'Constitution of Liberty' to be enshrined in all societies.[69]

The second branch of ultra-liberalism seeks to demonstrate that the post-war habits of intervention and economic management are at best futile and at worst positively harmful to economic stability, growth and prosperity. One of the latest variants on this theme — the 'rational expectations school' — argues that popular understanding, expectations and consequential behaviour develop in such a manner as to negate the stimulating effects that 'Keynsian-type' measures are intended to have upon the economy.[70]

Such ultra-liberals argue that, far from being benign and beneficial, the effects of the modern extension of governmental control of, and intervention in, the economy are generally bad. Governments have been tempted, by their new-found powers, to manipulate economic development to their own interests of those of their supporters.[71] Periods of economic 'boom' have been engineered to enhance the electoral prospects of incumbent governments and thus established a 'political business cycle'.[72] Inflation has, in turn, been generated by the combined effects of such economic 'gerrymandering', the 'appeasement' of potentially troublesome domestic economic groups, the accumulation of a governmental deficit that has also 'crowded out' potentially productive commercial investments, and the remorseless growth of the 'money supply'.[73]

An enterprise distinct from that of the ultra-liberals is the attempt by an identifiable group of analysts to apply some of the basic concepts and tools of formal economic analysis to the study of various aspects of political and social life. The central notions here are an extended concept of economic rationality, cost-benefit analysis and maximizing choices.[74] Much of this work, by being clear, internally rigorous and novel in its perspective, has succeeded in throwing an interesting light upon aspects of politics and governmental activity. The empirical veracity of the economic analysis of politics is, however, an inherently controversial matter. Much of its intrinsic appeal may reflect its origins in the United States of America and the markedly entrepreneurial character of the political system and politicians of that country. Moreover, the economic theory of politics shares with all other significant theories a strongly self-fulfilling flavour; with familiar matter being systematically reinterpreted in terms of an internally coherent, and externally all-encompassing, perspective. This feature is reinforced by the extended notion of rationality employed within the approach. As was argued earlier in this chapter, a concept of rationality that is extended very far beyond the restricted, market-orientated form employed in economic analysis, soon dissolves into tautology.

Conclusions

Liberal political economy may be all manner of things to all manner of men and women but it has never, in any form, been trivial or uninteresting. Indeed, concepts born within the liberal tradition continue to play a significant, if not central, role in virtually all the prominent approaches to political economy. Something of the real world is clearly apprehended by such a powerful and prolific perspective. The extent of the reality that is effectively accommodated and illuminated by any discernible 'liberal' approach is, however, a more contentious matter.

Liberal political economy is, in fact, a widely diverse theoretical and analytical disposition. Proponents of a revived classicism vie with determined neo-classicists. Post-Keynsians and neo-institutionalists sustain an analytical perspective, and an attitude towards governmental intervention in the economy, that is profoundly at variance with those ultra-liberal economists and political theorists who are content with the policies (if only declaratory) of President Reagan in the United States or Prime Minister Thatcher in the United Kingdom.

The boundaries of liberal political economy are difficult to define precisely in the face of such internal diversity. Indeed, the ideas of many post-Keynsians and neo-institutionalists shade away from liberalism into the distinct camps of economic realism, neo-mercantilism, structuralism and socialist economics.

Some notions are, however, generally characteristic of a distinctly liberal political economy. Methodological individualism prevails at the philosophical level. Politically, there is a restrictive view of the desirable range of governmental action. Free markets are generally favoured as a means to economic efficiency and individual freedom. Private ownership of property in general, and of the means of production in particular, are also advocated, although this owes more to the historical origins of modern liberalism than to the conditions that are analytically necessary for the functioning of an effective free-market system, which could equally be sustained by an economy of collectively owned or worker-controlled enterprises.

Beyond such basic dispositions, it is difficult to define liberal political economy in a simple manner; as MacKinlay and Little's concern to differentiate 'compensatory liberalism' from 'pure liberalism' exemplifies.[75] The neo-classical paradigm occupies a central position within contemporary discourse and underlies much 'mainstream' economic theory and analysis. It can be employed as a stylized target for criticism and debate from outside, and indeed from within, the broad liberal church. Other variants of liberal political economy can also be subject to critical examination but few exhibit the clarity, in their current development, with which the neo-classical paradigm has been endowed by its simplifying, but facilitative, assumptions.

The arguments advanced within liberal political economy, whatever their sources and targets, remain consistently vigorous and constructive, informing and encouraging the further development of both liberal and non-liberal perspectives. Liberal political economy would have more than justified itself if its contribution had been limited to that of a major stimulus to the polylectical development of thought about the contemporary political economy. Liberal political economy, in one or other guise, has remained an outstanding source of knowledge and understanding in its own right; a source which none who would understand the contemporary world can safely afford to neglect. In its criticisms of statism, and opposition to extreme forms of collectivism, liberal political economy also sustains a view of continuing moral and practical importance.

Notes and references

1. For an admirable documentary summary, see E.J. Bramsted and K.J. Melhuish (eds), *Western Liberalism: A History in Documents from Lock to Croce* (London: Longman, 1978); and for a classic critical review, see C.B. Macpherson, *The Politcal Theory of Possessive Liberalism* (Oxford: Clarendon Press, 1962).
2. These were, it must be recalled, overwhelmingly pre-feminist times!
3. For a discussion of classical growth theory, see Phyllis Deane, *The Evolution of Economic Ideas* (Cambridge: Cambridge University Press, 1978), Chapter 3; and David Simpson, *The Political Economy of Growth* (Oxford: Basil Blackwell, 1983), pp. 33-57.
4. See Simpson, *The Political Economy of Growth* esp. pp. 52-5.
5. See, Deane, *The Evolution of Economic Ideas*, pp. 37-8 and 191.
6. See ibid., pp. 23-4.
7. See William J. Barber, *A History of Economic Thought*, (Harmondsworth: Penguin Books, 1967), pp. 30-8; and Deane, *The Evolution of Economic Ideas,* pp. 26-8 and 64-9.
8. See Karl Marx, *Capital* (various editions, originally 1867) Vol. 1, especially Part 1; and for a commentary, see: M.C. Howard and J.E. King, *The Political Economy of Marx* (Harlow Longman, 1975), esp. Chapter 5.
9. For a brief discussion of the 'bullionist' position, see Deane, *The Evolution of*

Economic Ideas pp. 48-9. For a discussion of the 'Gold Standard' see ibid, pp. 55-6; and for a more elaborate discussion, see P.T. Ellsworth, *The International Economy* (New York: Collier-Macmillan, 1964), esp. pp. 339-50.
10. See, Deane, *The Evolution of Economic Ideas*, pp. 53-4 and 164.
11. Ibid., Chapters 7, 8, 10 and 11.
12. For an introduction to indifference curve analysis, see H. Speight, *Economics: The Science of Prices and Incomes* (London: Methuen, 1960), Chapter 6.
13. For formal analysis, see ibid., Chapter 6, 7 and 8. See also other textbooks on economic analysis, such as R.G. Lipsey, *An Introduction to Positive Economics* (London: Weidenfeld and Nicolson, 1963, and subsequent editions) Chapter 5, 6, and 7.
14. A. Marshall, *The Principles of Economics* (1890); on which, see, Deane, *The Evolution of Economic Ideas,* pp. 117-22 and 149-51.
15. See Deane, *The Evolution of Economic Ideas*, pp. 153-7; and Joan Robinson, 'Imperfect Competition Revisited' in Joan Robinson, *Contributions to Modern Economics* (Oxford: Basil Blackwell, 1978), pp. 166-81.
16. Deane, *The Evolution of Economic Ideas* Chapter 12.
17. Ibid., p. 156.
18. Ibid., esp. pp. 181-2 and 208.
19. Ibid., pp. 208-9.
20. Ibid., pp. 207-8.
21. Ibid., pp. 177-9; and see, also, the entry on Say's Law in G. Bannock, R.E. Baxter and R. Rees, *A Dictionary of Economics* (Harmondsworth: Penguin Books, 1972).
22. Deane, *The Evolution of Economic Ideas,* Chapter 11.
23. See, for instance, R.J. Barry Jones, *Conflict and Control in the World Economy: Contemporary Economic Realism and Neo-Mercantilism* (Brighton: Wheatsheaf, 1986), pp. 30-5; and, for textbook introductions, see C.P. Kindleberger, *International Economics* 5th edn (Homewood, II: Richard D. Irwin Inc., 1973) Chapters 2 and 3 and esp. pp. 17-20; and, Ellsworth, *The International Economy* Chapters 4 and 5.
24. On which, see Ellsworth, *The International Economy*, pp. 144-59; Romney Robinson, 'Factor Proportions and Comparative Advantage' in R.E. Caves and H.G. Johnson (eds), *Readings in International Economics* (London: George Allen and Unwin, 1968), pp. 3-23; and H.G. Johnson, 'Factor Endowments, International Trade, and Factor Prices' in Caves and Johnson, *Readings* pp. 78-89.
25. See the discussion in Jones, *Conflict and Control in the World Economy*, esp. pp. 36-60.
26. C.P. Kindleberger, *Power and Money: The Politics of International Economics and the Economics of International Politics* (New York: Basic Books, 1970), p. 19.
27. Ibid., pp. 36-9.
28. Ibid., 39-40.
29. J.S Mill, *On Utilitarianism* (1861) (London: Fontanta, 1962), esp. pp. 258-62; and also Bramstead and Melhuish, *Western Liberalism,* pp. 275-6.
30. On 'trickle-down', see W.W. Rostow, *The Stages of Economic Growth* (Cambridge; Cambridge University Press, 1960) and on 'supply-side economics', see the entries by Ronald Reagan, Donald T. Regan, George Gilder, Edward Meadows, Arthur Laffer and George Perry, and Irving Kristol in *Economic Impact,* no. 35 (1981-3), pp. 8-35.
31. Ibid., pp. 40-2.
32. See, Joan Robinson, *The Economics of Imperfect Competition* 2nd edn (London: Macmillan, 1969); and E.H. Chamberlain, *The Theory of Monopolistic Competition: A Reorientation of the Theory of Value,* (Cambridge, MA: Harvard University Press, 1933).
33. See, Alfred S. Eichner, *The Megacorp and Oligopoly: Micro Foundations of Macro Dynamics* (White Plains' NY: M.E. Sharpe, 1976), esp. pp. 40-4; and on the dynamics of price wars, see K.E. Boulding, *Conflict and Defense: A General Theory* (New York: Harper and Row, 1962) Chapters 2, 7 and 10.
34. For an introductory discussion, see Stephen Brahms, *Game Theory and Politics* (New York: Free Press, 1975), Chapter 1.
35. For a discussion of 'positional goods', see Fred Hirsch, *Social Limits to Growth*. (London: Routledge and Kegan Paul, 1977), Chapter 3.
36. Ibid., esp. pp. 56-67.
37. For a general introduction to the issue of collective (public) goods, see Mancur Olson Jr., *The Logic of Collective Action*, (Cambridge, MA: Harvard University Press, 1965);

N. Frohlich and J.A. Oppenheimer, *Modern Political Economy*, (Englewood Cliffs NJ: Prentice-Hall, 1978), esp. Chapter 2 and 3; Michael Laver, *The Politics of Private Desires* (Harmondsworth: Penguin Books, 1981), Chapter 2.
38. Frohlich and Oppenheimer, *Modern Political Economy*, pp. 53-5.
39. Ibid., pp. 64-5, and Chapter 4; Laver, *The Politics of Private Desires*, pp. 62-9; and see also N. Frohlich, J.A. Oppenheimer and Oran R. Young, *Political Leadership and Collective Goods* (Princeton, NJ: Princeton University Press, 1971).
40. See John Hicks, *Causality in Economics* (Oxford: Basil Blackwell, 1979), Chapter 4; and Jones, *Conflict and Control in the World Economy*, pp. 46-50.
41. John D. Hey, *Economics in Disequilibrium* (Oxford: Martin Robertson, 1981), p. 243.
42. See, for extended criticisms: John Hicks, *Causality in Economics,* Chapter 4; N. Kaldor, 'The irrelevance of Equilibrium Economics,' *Economic Journal*, vol. 82, (December 1972), pp. 1237-55; Joan Robinson, 'History versus Equilibrium', and 'A Lecture Delivered at Oxford by a Cambridge Economist', both in Robinson, *Contributions to Modern Economics* pp. 126-45, respectively; and T.W. Hutchinson, *Knowledge and Ignorance in Economics* (Oxford: Basil Blackwell, 1977), pp. 74-87.
43. See, J. Maclean, 'Marxist Epistemology, Explanations of Change and the Study of International Relations', in Barry Buzan and R.J. Barry Jones (eds), *Change and the Study of International Relations: The Evaded Dimension* (London: Frances Pinter, 1981) Chapter 3.
44. See, in particular, the conclusions of Hey, *Economics in Disequilibrium* pp. 198-200 and 242-3.
45. For a fuller discussion, see Kindleberger, *International Economics,* Chapter 2.; and see also Paul A. Samuelson, 'International Factor-Price Equalization Once Again', *The Economic Journal,* vol. 59, no. 234 (June 1949), pp. 181-97, reprinted in Caves and Johnson, *Readings in International Economics*, pp. 58-71; T.M. Rybczynski, 'Factor Endowments and Relative Commodity Prices', *Economica*, vol. 22, no. 84 (November 1955), pp. 336-41, reprinted in Caves and Johnson, *Readings*, pp. 72-7; and Johnson 'Factor Endowments, International Trade and Factor Prices'.
46. For a fuller discussion of these issues, see Jones, *Conflict and Control in the World Economy*, pp. 50-4; and see also Robert Gilpin, *The Political Economy of International Relations* (Princeton, NJ; Princeton University Press, 1987), p. 178.
47. See, John O'Neill, (ed.), *Modes of Individualism and Collectivism* (London: Heinemann, 1973), esp. Part 3.
48. J.W.N. Watkins, 'Methodological Individualism: A Reply' in ibid, p. 179.
49. See, O'Neill, *Modes* Part 4 and, especially, E.A. Gellner, 'Explanations in History', pp. 248-63.
50. See, for example, Sue Himmelweit, 'The Individual and Basic Unit of Analysis' in F. Green and P. Nore (eds), *Economics: An Anti-Text* (London: Macmillan, 1977), pp. 21-35; and, in the different context of international relations Kenneth N. Waltz, *Theory of International Politics* (Reading, MA: Addison-Wesley, 1979), Chapter 2.
51. See, in particular, the contributions of Andrew Gamble and Chris Brown in this volume; Andrew Gamble, 'Critical Political Economy', in Jones *Perspectives on Political Economy* pp. 64-89; Deane, *The Evolution of Economic Ideas*, Chapter 9; E.K. Hunt, *Property and Prophets: The Evolution of Economic Institutions and Ideologies* 5th edn (New York: Harper and Row, 1986); and Howard and King, *The Political Economy of Marx.*
52. See Howard and King, *The Political Economy of Marx*, Chapters 2 and 3; Gamble, 'Critical Political Economy', pp. 71-5; Norman Geras, 'Marx and the Critique of Political Economy', Martin Nicolaus, 'The Unknown Marx', and Maurice Godelier, 'Structure and Contradiction in Capital', all in R. Blackburn (ed.), *Ideology in Social Science: Readings in Critical Social Theory* (London: Fontana/Collins, 1972).
53. Edward Nell, 'Economics: the Revival of Political Economy', in Blackburn, *Ideology in Social Science*, pp.. 76-95.
54. Howard and King, *The Political Economy of Marx*, Chapters 5 and 6.
55. See Deane, *The Evolution of Economic Ideas*, pp. 205-8.
56. Inasmuch as these two approaches are actually distinct. On the various approaches of 'post-Keynsianism', 'ultra-Keynsianism', and 'neo-institutionalism', see Alfred S. Eichner (ed.), *A Guide to Post-Keynsian Economics* (London: Macmillan, 1979); Robinson, *Contributions to Modern Economics*, Joan Robinson and John Eatwell, *An Introduction to Modern Economics* (London: McGraw-Hill, 1973); John Knapp, 'Economics or Political Economy', *Lloyds Bank Review* (January 1973, pp. 19-43; Warren J. Samuels

(ed.), *The Economy as a System of Power*, Vols I and II (New Brunswick, NJ: Transaction Books, 1979); Richard N. Langlois (ed.), *Economics as a Process* (Cambridge: Cambridge University Press, 1986).

57. For accounts of Keynes's economics, of varying detail, see A.H. Hansen, *A Guide to Keynes* (New York: McGraw-Hill, 1953); Joan Robinson, *Economic Philosophy,* (London: A.C. Watts, 1962), Chapter 4; Eric Roll, *A History of Economic Thought,* revised edition (London: Faber, 1973), Chapter 11; and E.K. Hunt, *Property and Prophets: The Evolution of Economic Institutions and Ideologies,* 5th edition (New York: Harper and Row, 1986), Chapter 12.
58. For discussions of the multiplier and accelerator effects, see Bannock, Baxter and Rees, *Dictionary of Economics.*
59. For a general account, see Deane, *The Evolution of Economic Ideas*, Chapter 12.
60. Ibid., esp. pp. 181-2 and 188. See also the discussion in Hansen, *A Guide to Keynes.*
61. See, in particular, Hey, *Economics in Disequilibrium*, G.L. Shackle, *Imagination and the Nature of Choice* (Edinburgh; Edinburgh University Press, 1979); and C.F. Carter and J.L. Ford (eds), *Uncertainty and Expectations in Economics: Essays in Honour of G.L.S. Shackle* (Oxford: Basil Blackwell, 1972).
62. See, in particular, Eichner, *A Guide to Post-Keynsian Economics*; and Paul Davidson, 'Post-Keynsian Economics: solving the Crisis in Economic Theory' in Daniel Bell and Irving Kristol, *The Crisis in Economic Theory* (New York: Basic Books, 1981), pp. 151-73.
63. See, for example, Samuels, *The Economy as a System of Power*, esp. Vol. I.
64. See, Richard N. Langlois, 'The New Institutional Economics' in Langlois, *Economics as a Process*, pp. 1-25.
65. Joseph A. Schumpeter, *Capitalism, Socialism and Democracy*, 5th edn (London: George Allen & Unwin, 1976).
66. Ibid., esp. Chapter 14.
67. See Eichner, *A Guide to Post-Keynsian Economics*, esp. pp. 11-16; and Davidson, 'Post-Keynsian Economics'.
68. See, in particular, the discussion by Charles K. Rowley, 'The Political Economy of the Public Sector', in Jones, *Perspectives on Political Economy*, pp. 18-63.
69. See ibid., pp. 55-61, and, especially, F.A. Hayek, *The Constitution of Liberty,* (London: Routledge and Kegan Paul, 1960).
70. For a brief outline of 'rational expectations' theory, see 'Expecting the Future', *The Economist,* 20 October 1984, pp. 19-20; and, at greater length, 'Rational Expectations as a Counterrevolution' in Bell and Kristol, *The Crisis in Economic Theory,* pp. 81-110.
71. See many of the papers and discussions in *The Economics of Politics,* Institute of Economic Affairs Readings no. 18, (London: IEA 1978).
72. See Bruno S. Frey, 'The Political Business Cycle: Theory and Evidence' in ibid., pp. 93-115. See also Paul Whiteley, *The Political Control of the Macroeconomy: The Political Economy of Public Policy Making* (London: Sage, 1986).
73. See, variously, J.A. Trevithick, *Inflation: A Guide to the Crisis in Economics* (Harmondsworth: Penguin Books, 1977), esp. Chapter 5; Tim Congdon, *Monetarism: An Essay in Definition,* (London: Centre for Policy Studies, 1978); and Milton Friedman and Rose Friedman, *Free to Choose* (London: Secker and Warburg, 1980), Chapter 9.
74. For an admirable introduction and survey, see Frohlich and Oppenheimer, *Modern Political Economy.*
75. R.D. MacKinlay and R. Little, *Global Problems and World Order* (London: Frances Pinter, 1986), pp. 26-41 and 45-8.

Chapter 3

Marxist Political Economy

Andrew Gamble

The critique of political economy

Marxism has long been regarded as an important perspective within the political economy, and at times political economy has even been used as a synonym for a Marxist approach. Marx himself, however, described his work as a critique of political economy rather than a contribution to it. In a similar way he also claimed to offer a critique of ideology rather than a new ideology. Yet in the course of critique he laid the basis for a new perspective in political economy and provided the materials for a new ideology.

There has always been a tension in Marxism between its status as a doctrine and its status as a scientific analysis of society. If it had been just the latter it seems unlikely that it would have escaped absorption into the mainstream of modern social science. The identity of Marxism as the theory of a political practice, however tenuous the connection has sometimes been, has nevertheless enabled Marxism to maintain its isolation and periodically renew itself as a distinct paradigm for research and analysis.

Whether Marxism is still a distinctive paradigm and, if it is, whether it should remain so are often debated. Marxism has been declared dead and refuted by its critics in every decade since Marx's death, yet it still acts as a powerful magnet for many intellectuals. There are certain questions which are difficult to ask except within a Marxist framework of analysis. Marxism has failed to found an alternative science of society, but as a critique of orthodox approaches and as a source of novel insights it remains an important stimulus to research and new thinking.

This view is in contrast to the common conception of Marxism as a dogma which demands rigid adherence to the concepts and conclusions of Marx and Engels. If Marxism had been only that it might have survived as the creed of various political groups, but it would have had no intellectual vitality and would have disappeared entirely as a serious intellectual perspective.

The source of Marxism's ability to renew itself lies in its use of the method of critique. The notion of critique is a complex one and is used in at least three senses by Marx.[1] It means, first of all, criticism of established authority. Here it follows the Enlightenment tradition of oppositional thinking aimed at challenging established views in order to uncover the truth about society. Second, critique involves reflection on the conditions for possible knowledge, in order to determine what kind of claims could be legitimately held. Third, critique means identifying those areas of social life where the fulfillment of human potential is limited by constraints produced by human actions themselves.

Marxism shares with many other variants of radical social thought an urge to oppose established power and authority and expose abuses. But it differs from most of them in the range and level of its criticism. This made possible the construction of an alternative theoretical system, but one which was forged through a detailed critique of liberal political economy, and which therefore recognised the strength of the liberal case. Marx is perhaps the greatest single critic of liberalism and this required a thorough knowledge of its assumptions and claims. The popular appeal of Marxism may have had much to do with its association with simple oppositional thinking, but its intellectual appeal and fascination has rested on Marxism's paradoxical relationship to the system of thought it criticizes. In order to provide a critique it has to absorb and ingest the liberal view of the world.

Marx's critique of liberal political economy in the 1840s had two main strands. In the first place he criticized the premises on which liberal political economy is based. He recognised from the outset the importance of the analyses produced by the early classical economists like Quesnay, Adam Smith and Ricardo. They had developed categories for a scientific study of how modern civil society was organized.

Classical political economy was limited, however, in Marx's view because it contained ideological assumptions which restricted its range and its development, and prevented a fully scientific analysis of the anatomy of civil society.[2] The two assumptions which Marx criticized most were the timelessness of the categories of political economy and the necessity of private property.

The first criticism is the foundation of Marx's view of the historical basis of capitalism. Political economists, argued Marx, treated the capitalist mode of production as though it were the culmination of historical development. As he put it: 'For the political economists, there was history but there is no longer any.' The relationship between capitalism and previous modes of production is obscured because the latter are understood simply as imperfect realizations of capitalism. The possibility that capitalism is one mode of production among several in history is not recognized.

One consequence of this for liberal political economy is that its categories were universal categories designed to apply to all societies at all periods in history. Capital was held to exist in primitive tribes as well as in modern industrial economies. Marx did not deny the existence of universal categories of analysis. What he criticized in the liberal political economists was their failure to distinguish between what was common to all modes of production and what was specific to capitalism. This reliance on universal rather than historical categories of analysis has become one of the distinguishing features of modern economics.

Marxist political economy has encouraged a historical, comparative approach to the study of capitalism. Because Marxists distinguish the capitalist mode of production from other modes of production, a central research question has been the analysis of non-capitalist modes of production in different historical periods and within capitalist social formations. This has opened up many fruitful areas of enquiry, including the role of domestic labour and migrant labour, uneven development, and the character of state expenditure.

The second assumption Marx criticized in the theories of the political economists was the idea that the modern economy must be founded upon private property of the means of production. The effect of this, he argued, was to treat capital as a thing, rather than as a social relation, and to obscure the nature of production and distribution of the social product in a capitalist economy. Capital was instead treated simply as a stock of money, tools and raw materials, ownership of which was rewarded by an income (profits). The existence of private property and its unequal distribution were not questioned but accepted as basic parameters of the analysis of political economy.

For Marx, capital is a social relation between the owners of the means of production and the owners of labour power. Without wage labourers there can be no capital and no capitalists. Marx argued that private property, far from being a natural or inevitable feature of human societies, was created and recreated through human beings alienating their most precious capacity — the capacity to labour. The importance of this conception, and the theory of surplus value which Marx develops from it, is that it directs attention to the struggles between capital and wage labour and to the analysis of the labour process.

Marx wanted his critique of political economy to remove the obstacles he saw to a fully scientific analysis of the modern capitalist economy. But he also intended his work as a critique in a second sense, a reflection on the humanly produced constraints which were obstacles to the creation of a free society. Demystifying the social world by criticizing the categories through which it was understood and lived was one of the conditions for the emergence of a revolutionary consciousness and a revolutionary movement.

For Marx, the existence of private property destroys the basis on which liberal thinkers proposed that the individual and the general interest could be reconciled, a community of independent owners of commodities who were equal both as producers and as consumers. Private ownership of the means of production depends on wage labours alienating their labour power to capitalists. This creates a social system not controlled by its individual members but controlling them, and so denying freedom, autonomy and the realization of the potential of each human being.

This critique is rooted in Marx's concepts of the human species, labour and nature, which form the premises for his analysis of history. He rejects the claims of bourgeois society to be the first classless society, and attempts to prove that capitalist society is a new form of class society, despite the formal freedom and equality enjoyed by its citizens. He presented his critique as written from the standpoint of the working class, the class which potentially represented the general interest because overcoming its subordination would mean the abolition of all classes.

Such alienation occurs even in an ideal liberal society of independent producers in which all producers own property and work for themselves, because although no one is exploited in such a society the individuals relate to one another through a process of buying and selling. This creates a social system which is not controlled by its individual members but on the contrary controls them through the impersonal forces of supply and demand. Marx counterposes to the liberal vision the ideal of a society in which human beings achieve conscious control over the conditions of their lives.

The liberal ideal of the society of independent commodity producers bears little relation to the actual inequalities in property ownership in capitalist societies. For the great majority their only significant property is their labour power, which they are obliged to sell to the owners of the means of production in return for wages. In the society of independent commodity producers, alienation of labour involves dependence on an impersonal and arbitrary process which governs prosperity and life chances. In the society of capital, alienation of labour power involves dependence of the great majority of the population on capital, whose agents organize the process of production in the pursuit of private profit.

For Marx, the limits of classical political economy are shown by its adherence to a model of the economy which assumes that everyone is an independent commodity producer. When this model is then applied to the analysis of modern economies, the substantial inequalities in wealth and power which the distribution of property confers are left unexamined.

What distinguished Marx's critique from other criticisms of political economy was the specific weight he gave to liberal political economy. For purposes of argument he accepted the market economy in its ideal form — the society of independent commodity producers. Such a community lacks control over the conditions of its own existence since the labour process is co-ordinated and resources allocated through the operation of the forces of demand and supply. But, as Marx conceded, in such a society based on individual production and exchange of commodities, there is no exploitation, injustice or fraud that is inherent in the social relations themselves. Commodities are exchanged according to their values whose measure is the socially necessary labour time required for their production, and which finds expression in money, the commodity that greatly facilitates exchange because it is the universal equivalent of all commodities. Where fraud and injustice do exist it is because the rules of a market order are being broken.

The enduring strength of Marx's critique lies in his ability to see capitalism as a historically specific mode of production. The manner of organising the labour process — the interaction between human communities and the natural physical world — is for Marx what differentiates human societies. Labour is a nature-imposed necessity, but in class societies the labour process is organized to produce a surplus which is appropriated by the class owning the means of production. For Marx the crucial question in analysing capitalism was explaining how a surplus arose and how it was appropriated in an economy which claimed to have abolished exploitation and oppression and to be founded upon the principle of exchange of equivalents between independent sovereign individuals.

Marx's purpose in *Capital* is to show how, in an economy founded on the exchange of value equivalents, capital and surplus value can arise. He argues that it depends on certain preconditions — the accumulation of money by various means in the hands of particular individuals and the availability of labour power as well as all other elements of the production process as commodities traded in markets. Purchase by capitalists of the one commodity whose unique use value is the creation of more value gives them control over the labour process.

Marx contrasts the freedom and equality which commodity owners, including the owners of labour power, enjoy in the marketplace, with the coercion and exploitation they are subject to at work. The equal nature of the wage bargain contrasts with the unequal nature of the relationship at work. This was the reason why Marx saw the production process as potentially a battleground between the owners of labour power and the owners of capital, for the interest of the capitalist was to extract as much surplus labour from the work-force as possible while the interest of the worker was to give back to the capitalist only that amount of labour that is equivalent to the wage that has been received.

Marx conceives capital as a process of self-expanding value, possessed of an inner drive to expand. This dynamism of capitalism arises directly from the central social relationship on which this mode of production is founded — the relationship between owners of capital and owners of labour power. The constant struggles between them over the organisation of the labour process — the length of the working day and the introduction and deployment of machinery — are conflicts over how surplus value is extracted and determine the way in which capitalism develops.

What drives these struggles is the necessity for capital to extract ever greater quantities of surplus labour from the work-force. Raising the productivity of labour through investment in new machinery has in the long run proved more important to capital in its quest to accumulate than extending the working day. The limits to the latter are soon encountered in the physical capacities of the work-force. The limits to raising labour productivity are, however, much less immediate. Marx speculated that they would only be reached when the production process had been automated and living labour expelled from it, and the capitalist mode of production had come to dominate the whole world.

Marx argued that, long before this limit was reached, attempts to raise the productivity of labour would encounter a tendency for the rate of profit to fall. To overcome it capitalists would be compelled to manage their affairs in ways which greatly increased the productivity of labour and brought nearer a fully automated production process. Competition compelled them to concentrate production on larger plants and centralize it in fewer hands, to introduce new technological innovations to cut costs, and to create a world market by searching for areas of the world economy where the structure of costs was significantly lower.

The tendency of the rate of profit to fall is a theoretical concept which points to the problem of maintaining profitable accumulation except by means which give short-term relief at the expense of making the long-term problem worse. Marx believed that he could demonstrate theoretically that the process of capital accumulation would be highly unstable and uneven. It would create poverty and a surplus population, and make every member of civil society dependent upon capital.

Marx's critique of liberal political economy provided an alternative standpoint for judging public policy and analysing the historical development of modern societies. On the basis of his analysis a political economy of the working class can be derived which challenges the political economy of the bourgeoisie. The former is concerned with the emancipation of labour which meant a political programme that pointed to an eventual abolition of wage labour and individual market exchange. The latter is concerned with maintaining the conditions under which the market order could be preserved and extended. Marx believed that the struggles to limit the working day, to secure trade union rights, and to win universal suffrage, were essential steps in the creation of a socialist movement capable of overthrowing the role of capital and transforming industrial society.

Recent developments in Marxist political economy

The continuing relevance of Marxism as a theoretical perspective is much disputed. There are naturally many aspects of it which root it very firmly in the nineteenth century. But there are other elements which continue to stimulate and inform a wide range of work in the social sciences. This is partly because Marx provided a way of thinking about the historical development of capitalism which is not easy to dispense with even when specific judgements or aspects are questioned. Marx did not foresee several of the long-run developments of capitalism as a world system. Considering how little developed capitalism actually was at the time he was writing (even in England), the accuracy with which Marx charted some of its basic tendencies, such as its drive to create an ever wider and more interdependent world market, is remarkable.[3]

Against this must be set his major failures of analysis, in particular the revolutionary potential of the proletariat and the institutional organization of a socialist society. He believed that the inability of capitalism to resolve its internal contradictions except by violence and wars would generate a revolutionary consciousness and a revolutionary movement centred on the industrial proletariat. Marx was right to see the relationship between labour and capital as a key political relation, but he failed to foresee how the very success of the political programmes of the working class and their allies in tightening the limits within which capital could operate, would then become one of the major obstacles to the emergence of a revolutionary socialist consciousness. Continuing ideological hostility to capitalism came to be joined with pragmatic accommodation to it.

The continuing insights offered by the theory of capital accumulation into the long-run development of capitalism could not compensate for the evident political passivity and in some cases increasing marginality of the Western proletariat. The disjunction between Marxism as a theory and as a political practice first became acute in the 1950's. It has become still sharper in the 1970's and 1980's.

During the 1950s it became clear to Western Marxists that capitalism had not only survived the slump and depression of the 1930s and the tremendous economic and social upheaval of the Second World War, but had also emerged stronger and more united and had entered into the fastest period of expansion in its history. Marxism as a doctrine and a theoretical perspective had become closely tied to the fortunes of the Soviet Union. The increasing recognition of the totalitarian character of Stalinism became combined with the new resilience of the capitalist economy and democratic institutions to raise fundamental questions about the Marxist analysis.

Was the capitalist economy still subject to crises or had state intervention succeeded in permanently moderating them? Was the working class in any sense revolutionary? Was it gradually disappearing as a coherent social category and as an organized movement? Was the state still a class state or did the achievements of social democracy mean that it had been transformed into a neutral instrument which was capable of implementing reforms and maintaining prosperity? Together these questions contributed to one central doubt — was the economy still capitalist? Did it make sense to analyse it any longer in class terms or as a process of capital accumulation, founded on the antagonism between wage labour and capital[4]

Many of these doubts appeared to have been stilled by the re-emergence of political radicalism in the 1960s and the outbreak of a major world economic crisis in the 1970s. It helped to stimulate much new writing within a Marxist framework. Fundamental debates were initiated on how Marxist political economy should be utilised in analysing modern capitalism. Apart from the debate on the world economy which is considered elsewhere in this volume, three debates have been of particular importance - on value, on crisis, and on the state.

VALUE THEORY

The first of these controversies has concerned the status of Marx's concept of value.[5] This is a debate that never seems to die away, partly because the concept is so central to the whole of Marx's theory of capitalism, partly because it is the value theory which more than anything else distinguishes Marxist economics from orthodox economics. The rejection of the labour theory of value and its replacement by the marginal utility theory became one of the corner-stones of modern economic analysis. Economists ever since have tended to treat the labour theory of value as a rejected theory, and by extension Marxist economics, if it appears at all, does so as a survival from a pre-scientific era. Samuelson once referred to Marx as an 'autodidact' and a 'minor post-Ricardian', while others have talked of Marxism as a degenerating research paradigm.

Marxist economists have been face with the problem of either finding a way to justify the labour theory of value, or trying to reconcile it with modern neo-classical concepts. Models of considerable mathematical complexity have been erected to demonstrate how under certain assumptions labour-time measures of value can be transformed into prices. But even if Marx's theory could be rescued in this way its utility as a method of analysis of how prices were formed would be highly questionable, because it would be so cumbersome.

A different approach has come from those Marxists influenced by the work of Sraffa and his school at Cambridge. They have been labelled by their opponents the neo-Ricardians,[6] and although the label is not entirely accurate it does indicate that their concern is to return to the formulations of the labour theory of value held by Ricardo and other classical political economists, and find solutions to some of the problems Ricardo could not solve. The ideas that emerge are neither Ricardian nor Marxian but they are closer to both than they are to neo-classical economics whose theoretical foundations in the subjectivist theory of marginal utility they reject.

What several of the neo-Ricardians wish to do is to find an alternative way of theorizing capitalism as a surplus-producing economy without embracing what they see as the theoretical shortcomings of Marx's work. They reject the concept of the economy that is to be found in neo-classical economics which sees production as the result of mutual co-operation between the owners of the various factors of production. Instead they share with classical political economy the notion of an economy that produces a surplus which is appropriated as profit, interest, and rent, and they put forward a class analysis of the way in which production is organized and the product distributed.

Where this approach differs from Marxism is that they argue strongly that the whole framework of value analysis is redundant for producing this analysis. Labour-time values are irrelevant for explaining prices. They favour instead a cost-of-production theory derived from Sraffa, which sees prices determined by the socially necessary conditions of production. These are the actual physical quantities of machines and raw materials employed, combined with the wages paid to the work-force. Prices emerge as a mark-up on these costs.

The neo-Ricardians are anxious to point out that their theory does not exclude the possibility of exploitation or coercion in the labour process. They see no reason to alter Marx's analyses of the working day and machinery in *Capital*. Rather, they argue that for the first time a genuinely scientific account of capitalism can be developed which does not rest upon 'metaphysical foundations'. Obsession with value, they argue, has been one reason why Marxism has made such little progress. As Ian Steedman puts it:[7] 'The project of providing a materialist account of capitalist societies is dependent on Marx's value magnitude analysis only in the negative sense that continued adherence to the latter is a major fetter on the development of the former.'

Many of the Neo-Ricardians regard themselves as developing Marx's theory in the most fruitful manner, discarding only what is theoretically suspect, but retaining many important features, including class analysis and the analysis of the labour process. But what is discarded is the analysis derived from value theory of the tendency of the rate of profit to fall, and any conception of long-run tendencies of development of the capitalist mode of production based upon the value analysis.

The argument against the neo-Ricardians has concentrated on two themes. The first is expressed most clearly by Erik Olin Wright[8] who argues that there is a basic complementarity between the two approaches. He argues that value analysis is concerned with establishing the structural limits within which the accumulation of capital develops, while the Sraffian analysis shows how specific outcomes are selected. The range of possible outcomes is not infinite but is limited by the forms in which value is expressed, such as the commodity, money and capital. This provides an ingenious reconciliation but leaves unsolved the problem of determining how precisely the two levels of analysis are related.

A second argument is more uncompromising. It rejects the neo-Ricardian analysis on the grounds that it misunderstands the methodology that is involved in value analysis. It rejects claims that it is impossible to derive a coherent theory of prices from Marx's theory of value, arguing that value and prices are not treated by Marx as separate categories. Values cannot be calculated or observed independently of prices — prices are the necessary form through which values are expressed but it is impossible to measure both separately and then theorize about the relationship between the two. This approach sees Marx's theory as providing an integrated set of concepts which makes knowledge of a complex structure like capitalism possible by identifying the basic forms whbich compose it.[9]

Form analysis, as it has become known, allows both theoretical and historical analysis of the forms which social relations take under capitalism. These forms are deduced from the categories of value analysis.[10] What is analysed, therefore, is, for example, the commodity-form, the wage-form, and the money-form. Capital is conceived as 'circulating', passing through a number of stages or circuits during which it buys the means of production including labour power, organizes the production of goods and services, and sells what is produced in a way that preserves and extends the original capital. By such means capital reproduces itself.

Form analysis can lead to a fatalistic and at times reductionist emphasis upon the logic of forms in the circuits of capital which has produced some ingenious but rather arid expositions. When it is combined with historical analysis, however, it encourages a focus on how the legal, political, and social forms that are necessary for a capitalistic economy are imposed and sustained, and the conflict that this creates.

The debate on value has often been conducted at a fairly high level of abstraction but it has implications for most other areas of substantive research within Marxist political economy, particularly the debates on the labour process and the debates over the state. There is a lot at stake in the controversy. Rival conceptions of the capitalistic economy, disputes over the correct method of analysis, and the problem of the normative basis of socialist political economy are all involved.

The strength of the neo-Ricardians is that they wish to develop concrete analysis of the contemporary capitalist economy. They find much of the conceptual apparatus of Marxist political economy an encumbrance. They particularly dislike the way in which value analysis is often used to suggest that capitalism follows an inevitable sequence of development, arguing that this promotes political fatalism. The neo-Ricardian future is much more open because they reject the idea of necessary trends. Each situation has to be analysed afresh.

Some of the critics of neo-Ricardianism share its dislike of the fatalism and determinism with which Marxism has often been associated but doubt that neo-Ricardianism provides an alternative theoretical basis for a socialist political economy. Marx gave central importance to the labour process and pinpointed the structural conflict between labour and capital as the centre of his analysis of capital. Neo-Ricardians also assert the primacy of the labour process. But it is difficult to see why they should insist on this while rejecting the theoretical analysis which first established this primacy. They wish to remain on the terrain Marxism established while disowning the means by which it was constructed.

A more radical move is made by those like Barry Hindess and Paul Hirst who reject the entire apparatus of Marxist concepts, starting with the concept of value, on the grounds that it springs from a rationalist and essentialist methodology which is quite incapable of grasping the real relations of capitalism.[11] These must be understood empirically, by researching the concrete circumstances which shape and define them. The universal rationalist concepts of Marxism and of all similar social science, including theoretical economics, are rejected as inadequate for the purpose that is set — to provide a concrete analysis of the capitalist economy. This leads to historically specific studies of institutions and their evolution. Some very interesting work has come from this school but the connection with theoretical tradition of

Marxism is now extremely tenuous.

CRISIS

The divide over method runs right through the substansive debates on the nature of contemporary capitalism. This is particularly evident in the debates over capitalist crisis and over how to analyse inflation, recession and the activities of the modern state. Four major approaches may be distinguished.

The first is the orthodox value analysis of capitalist crisis advanced by classical Marxists like Ernest Mandel.[12] This focuses on the long-run tendencies of capital accumulation. Mandel makes use of a modified version of Kondratieff's long-wave theory to provide an analysis of how the conditions for renewed capital accumulation arose after 1945, and then how the boom was curtailed and the world economy plunged back into recession when these conditions became exhausted in the late 1960s. Mandel's grasp of the long-term development of capitalism is impressive, but this kind of classical Marxist approach has been criticized because it offers only general explanations of the novel elements of the crisis of the 1970s, particularly the combination of rising unemployment and rising prices, the growth of state activities, and the increasing domination of the world economy by multinational capital. Crisis tendencies are understood in terms of the developing conflict between the forces and relations of production and political and idealogical developments are accorded no real autonomy but treated as expressions of this conflict.

The neo-Ricardian position, in sharp contrast to this, emphasizes specific institutional features of modern capitalism, in particular the oligopolistic structure of markets. In this it tends to converge with other formulations in non-Marxist radical political economy.[13] At the heart of its explanation of inflation, for example, is the idea of continual bargaining between different groups over the basic costs of the production process, the outcome of which is determined by the degree of monopoly each side can exercise. Inflation is seen as a result of a power struggle between organised capital and government. The individualist foundations of economic analysis are rejected. Economic relations are conceived as relations of power as well as relations of exchange.[14] Power and coercion are treated as integral rather than aberrant elements of markets and economic relations.

One influential application of these ideas is found in the work of Andrew Glyn, Bob Sutcliffe and John Harrison.[15] They have argued in favour of a model of the capitalist economy which gives most importance to class conflict between capital and labour. They interpret both the long boom and the recession in the 1970s in terms of the balance of power between labour and capital. They see the profits squeeze of the 1970s as brought about by a combination of increasing industrial militancy and intensified international competition. The fundamental barrier to renewed accumulation on an expanded scale is a class barrier, the stalemate between the two major classes. Until the balance of power shifts decisively in favour of either labour or capital no resolution of the crisis is possible.

Andrew Glyn ignores many features of the classical Marxist theory of crisis, such as the tendency of the rate of profit to fall and the rising organic composition of capital. The neo-Ricardians actively reject them. But among Marxists who continue to accept classical value analysis there has also been considerable dispute about the classical Marxist theory of crisis. Some of these criticisms are technical. There is dispute over whether the organic composition of capital did in fact rise during the 1960s and 1970s:[16] over whether the crisis in the 1970s was a classic crisis of overproduction, an expression of the tendency of the rate of profit to fall, or the result of more immediate and transient causes.[17]

More general criticisms have also been directed at reductionist and functionalist presentations of the Marxist theory of crisis. In such accounts the laws of capital accumulation are conceived as the reproduction of an economic system. A crisis is an interuption in this process of reproduction, caused by the appearance of barriers to further accumulation. Social and political crises are conceived as symptoms and effects of economic crisis.

One important new approach in crisis theory which rejects both neo-Ricardian and classical theories of crisis has been the analysis of regimes of accumulation.[18] This focuses on the problem of regulation — the way in which the structure of a society is reproduced. A regime of accumulation involves a specific set of production techniques, a specific structure of the working class in terms of skills, education and patterns of consumption, a specific pattern of labour relations and industrial management, and a specific industrial structure. Such regimes of accumulation involve also particular political structures and relationships between state and economy.

The regime of accumulation can be interpreted too rigidly, but it does permit an interesting periodization of capitalism. It is centred around the concept of Fordism and the break-up of this regime of accumulation in the 1970s. It has stimulated work on organized and disorganized capitalism.[19] It requires capitalist social formations to be grasped as functioning wholes, and does not reduce everything to the laws of motion of capital considered abstractly.

The classical approach, however, is by no means exhausted. It has recently received a major restatement and elaboration by, among others, David Harvey, and Ben Fine and Laurence Harris.[20] They have pointed out that Marx's theory of crisis has often been conceived far too narrowly in terms of only one of the circuits of capital, that of productive capital. Attention has as a result usually been focused on the rate of profit. But what is also required for a theory of crisis is a consideration of the circuits of money capital and commodity capital, and how they interact.

Harvey argues that there are three theories of crisis in *Capital,* and that they exist not as alternatives to one another, but at three different levels of abstraction. Much previous debate on crisis theory counterposed, for example, a theory of underconsumption to a theory of the tendency of the rate of profit to fall. Harvey argues that this mistakes the level of analysis. The theory of the tendency of the rate of profit to fall, so often presented by classical Marxists as *the* theory of crisis, is shown by Harvey to be only the first and most abstract formulation of the theory. There are two further stages, the financial and monetary aspects of crisis formation, and the spatial aspects. The third is the most concrete level of analysis since it deals with the obstacles that arise to capital accumulation from the uneven development of capitalism and the rigidities which are created by the distribution of plant, population, capital and resources, and the character of political systems and social structures.

Harvey presents a theoretical framework in which many of the problems that have prevented the fruitful development of a Marxist theory of crisis are overcome. But other Marxists have become increasingly sceptical of the conceptual approach of classical Marxism, believing that the value analysis of Marxist political economy needs replacing by a historical analysis which puts the emphasis on social and political factors.[21] This perspective gives up the last vestiges of Marxist fatalism, the belief that in some sense the eventual advent of socialism is guaranteed because of the laws of motion of the capitalist economy. Capitalist crisis is viewed not primarily as an economic crisis, but as a political and ideological crisis, a crisis of legitimation at the level both of public policy and personal identity. These ideas, which are prominent in the writing of Jürgen Habermas and James O'Connor, ultimately point away from the Marxist political economy tradition, however much they have enriched Marxism conceived more broadly.

THE STATE

The classical Marxist approach has also been fundamentally challenged within Marxism by much of the recent work on the theory of the state. Crisis theory and state theory have become inextricably connected. Until recently the analysis of the state and of politics has always remained relatively undeveloped within Marxism. *Capital* has long been treated as a book about economics rather than politics, and within the Marxist tradition — and still more among the critics of Marxism — there has been a deep-rooted tendency to interpret Marxism as a form of economic determination and to approach the study of ideology and politics from the side of economics. In this way the traditional division between politics and economics, promulgated by liberal political economy and fundamental to its understanding of the relation of economics and politics, was restated within Marxism. The liberal idea of the self-correcting and self-sufficient market was echoed by the Marxist notion of capitalism as a self-contained economic system, governed by its own inexorable laws of motion. In both conceptions the state hovered uneasily outside as an external and largely passive guarantor of the conditions needed to maintain and reproduce the social order. Much early Marxist writing on the state reflected this notion.

Yet one of the fundamental points of Marx's critique of political economy was the denial of the separation between politics and economics. The consequences of this were not worked out in Marx's own writings. He never lived to write the book on the state that he planned, and his formulations are often ambiguous and capable of many different interpretations. The questions that he posed, however, and some of his remarkable and arresting insights have fuelled the modern Marxist debates on the state.[22] These debates have centered around the relationship between the state and the economy and have led to some fundamental re-evaluations of Marxist political economy.

Two major strands in the literature will be discussed here. The first derives from those theorists, in particular Nicos Poulantzas, who have challenged explanations that treated the state as an instrument of the ruling class and have emphasized instead its relative autonomy from economic class interests.[23] The state is conceived instead as an arena of conflict between diverse political and social forces. Political institutions such as legislatures, the civil service, and parties are not seen as direct representatives of classes, and classes themselves are recognized as being composed of many fractions. The hegemony of the ruling class has to be forged and maintained politically. This involves a programme and tactics that can unify the power bloc while dividing and outmanoeuvring all opposition from the dominated classes.

This approach owes much to Gramsci. He saw the key role of the state as unifying the bourgeoisie and organising its political and ideological domination. This is achieved through particular forms of organization and representation like political parties, interest groups and legislatures. These are always specific to particular societies and periods and cannot be reduced either to particular class interests or to economic laws of motion.

This approach underlines the relative autonomy of the state. Its main weakness is identifying precisely the limits of the autonomy which the state enjoys. One solution is to modify the idea of economic determination by defining the limits in terms of class struggle. The laws of motion of capital appear, then, not as some inexorable force external to politics, but the result of a continual contest between the forces of labour and capital, and the state becomes not just an arena for conflict but a set of policies and agencies which are not orchestrated by a single will and are not subordinated to a single class interest.

Another solution is to get rid of the idea of economic determination altogether.[24] One influential perspective draws a sharp divide between competitive and monopoly capitalism. Under competitive capitalism, it has been argued, the economy did operate according to the laws of capital accumulation, but as a result of several major transformations this is no longer the case. State and economy have become closely interlinked — the boundaries are increasingly hard to determine, the state, moreover, has assumed responsibility for crisis management, steering the economy so as to minimize the social and economic impact of disturbances in the accumulation process. States have assumed this role partly in response to the needs of the giant corporations which increasingly dominate markets and industries and whose operations span the world, and partly because of the industrial and political strength of subordinate classes, particularly labour movements.

It is often argued that changes such as these mean that a qualitatively new stage in capitalist development has arrived — one in which the former laws of motion of capital accumulation no longer function as before. This requires a major redirection of analysis. For if political intervention is sufficient to displace crisis tendencies, then politics has become dominant over economics, and Marxist political economy becomes transformed into political analysis. Economic factors become just one aspect of any political situation, but they are not necessarily central to it.[25]

This perspective has been challenged by the state derivation school. The starting point of this approach was stated very clearly by the Russian legal theorist, Evgeny Pashukanis, when he wrote: 'why does the state take the form of an impersonal mechanism of public authority isolated from society?'[26] Pashukanis and those who have followed him have attempted to derive the forms of the state from the catergories of Marxian political economy.

The weakness of this approach is that it can easily lapse into an uncritical functionalism, identifying functions which the state must fulfil if the system is to survive, but not analysing the actual history of the circumstances which determined whether they were fulfilled or not. Its great strength is that, although its starting point is the way in which the economic and political are divorced, it works towards demonstrating their fundamental unity.

This unity is not something which has been only recently achieved, because the theory does not suppose that there was ever a time when the economy was independent or self-sufficient, powered by its own internal laws of motion. Instead the form the state assumes is derived from the functions that must be performed if the economic system is to be maintained and reproduced and which cannot be performed by market agents themselves. Security of contract, the enforcement of competition, the rights of property, and acceptability of money, are all shown to be necessary conditions for the existence and reproduction of an economy based on the production and exchange of commodities. Appropriate institutions and agencies are organized to maintain them. But the sale of labour power as a commodity and the coming into being of the relations between capital and wage labour further require that the state extends its activities to secure the profitability of accumulation. This means confronting the obstacles that periodically arise to continued profitable accumulation, chief among which is the organized working class.

The state derivation approach removes the need to see state policy as the expression of identifiable class interests or as an ideal collective capitalist which can intervene omnisciently to prevent crisis, or as a power suspended above society. It forms the basis on which political analysis of the state can be integrated with the value analysis of capital accumulation. The pitfall of mistaking levels of abstraction and substituting the logical categories for detailed historical research, or mistaking functional explanations for causal ones, remains. But it does open the way for a political economy that neither reduces politics to economics nor substitutes political analysis for economics but instead treats both economics and politics within the framework of value analysis.[27]

This was Marx's own procedure in *Capital*. He developed the logical structure of his argument out of his empirical researches, but he did not mistake this logical structure for the actual pattern of reality. In *Capital,* for example, having already discussed the specific form the labour process takes under capitalism, he shows how the capitalist mode of production depends on the extraction of surplus value. The actual extraction of surplus value, however, is by no means a smooth functional process, as he shows in his discussion of the struggles over the length of the working day. For Marx nothing was ever automatic or inevitable about the reproduction or continuation of capitalism. He never viewed it primarily as a system of economic production but rather as a system of social and political domination.

Important contributions to a modern Marxist state theory which attempts to combine the insights of the capital logic school with the emphasis on the historical specificity of the state, have been made by Nicos Poulantzas, Stuart Hall, Claus Offe and Bob Jessop. In different ways they have focused attention on the contradiction between the state's economic role and its role in maintaining order and organizing consent. In his last major book Poulantzas discussed the structural limits to the state's autonomy in a capitalist society.[28] It cannot intervene in relations of production; it cannot ignore the process by which surplus value is produced and realized; and it has to ensure the prosperity of the economy in order to extract the taxes to fund its activities.

Claus Offe has focused in his writings on the complex relation of state intervention to capital accumulation.[29] In seeking policy solutions to the problems of advanced capitalist economies, the administrative means which states have adopted create new problems. Governments find themselves involved in permanent crisis management. They can do enough to avoid a breakdown but the problems persist. Policy reaches an impasse. Corporatist representation and economic intervention are discredited, and neo-liberal plans for state disengagement flourish. But disengagement in its turn threatens the return of many of the problems for which state intervention was originally advocated. Mapping the constraints and the field of pressures within which modern governments have to operate becomes the goal of this kind of Marxist political economy. The apocalyptic tone of much classical Marxism has disappeared, and the analysis is much closer to other perspectives in social science and political economy.

Conclusion

Marx's critique of political economy remains powerful because of its ability to inspire new insights into the way capitalist economies are organized and are developing. Although there have been attempts to develop a self-contained Marxist tradition, Marxist political economy has generally been strongest when it has renewed itself as a critique of political economy and engaged in dialogue and interaction with other schools of political economy.

Marxist political economy may have made little contribution to price theory but it has given an impetus to studies in many other fields: the analysis of the capitalist mode of production as a world system (reviewed in Chapter 7); its interrelationship with other non-capitalist modes of production; the organization of the labour process and the composition of the labour force; the analysis of crisis and the stages of capitalist development; and the theory of the state and the formation of policy.

Many unresolved questions remain and new doubts and uncertainties have been created. But in the past twenty-five years Marxist political economy has renewed itself as a critical and open study.[30] The controversies over value and the state may not have resolved the disagreements, but they have helped to sharpen Marxist concepts. The theory of the state has been more firmly grounded than before in the theory of value. This has not convinced many critics, but classical Marxism has been able to demonstrate that certain problems can only be posed within the framework of value analysis.

A great deal of work in political economy consists of historical and institutional analyses of policy. Relating these to the major theoretical frameworks and concepts is not always easy. But the frameworks are indispensable for defining facts, identifying problems, and providing criteria for evaluation.

They are also important in indicating new lines of research. There has been important work in a number of areas: the nature of the present crisis, the role of debt and credit, the public sector, and new technology; the policy process of the modern state, the political response to the slump, and the limits of state involvement in the economy; the world market and the changing world division of labour, the internationalization of financial markets and production, the character of the Soviet economy and the feasibility of socialism, and the rise of the new centres of accumulation in the Third World;

the labour process, the impact of new technology and the implications of mass unemployment, the changing character and composition of the labour force.

Marxist political economy has become a very diverse tradition, but also a lively and productive new one. It has proved able to renew itself and to generate new lines of enquiry and new knowledge.

Notes and references

1. I have drawn here on the introduction to Paul Connerton (ed.), *Critical Sociology* (Harmondsworth: Penguin, 1976).
2. See B. Parekh, *Marx's Theory of Ideology* (London: Croom Helm, 1982).
3. See, for example, J. A. Schumpeter *Capitalism, Socialism, and Democracy* (London: Allen & Unwin, 1950), and the assessment by Krishan Kumar, *Prophecy and Progress* (Harmondsworth: Penguin, 1978)
4. The most important work of Marxist political economy produced in these years was P. Baran & P. Sweezy *Monopoly Capital* (New York: Monthly Review Press, 1964. See also John Strachey, *Contemporary Capitalism* (London: Gollancz, 1956).
5. Two useful collections of articles on value theory are Diane Elson (ed.), *Value* (London: CSE Books, 1969), and Ian Steedman *et al., The Value Controversy* (London: Verso, 1981).
6. See the important essay by Robert Rowthorn, 'Neo-Classicism, Neo-Riocardianism, and Marxism' in Rowthorn, *Capitalism, Conflict, and Inflation* (London: Lawrence & Wishart, 1980).
7. Ian Steedman, 'Ricardo, Marx, Sraffa' in Steedman *et al., The Value Controversy*. See also the contributions of Hodgson in the same volume. The best statement of the neo-Ricardian position can be found in Ian Steedman, *Marx after Sraffa* (London: Verso, 1977).
8. Erik Olin Wright, 'The Value Controversy and Social Research', in Steedman *et al., The Value Controversy,* pp. 36-74. His position is set out more fully in Erik Olin Wright, *Class Crisis and the State* (London: New Left Books, 1979).
9. Three different approaches are M. Itoh *Value and Crisis* (London: Pluto, 1980); Ben Fine and Laurence Harris, *Re-Reading Capital* (London: Macmillan, 1979); and Geoffrey Kay, *The Economic Theory of the Working Class* (London: Macmillan, 1979).
10. See J. Holloway and S. Picciotto (eds), *State and Capital: A Marxist Debate* (London: Edward Arnold, 1978).
11. A Cutler *et al., Marx's Capital and Capitalism Today* (London: Routledge 1976). Paul Hirst's work is reviewed by Gregory Elliott in 'The Odyssey of Paul Hirst', *New Left Review,* no. 159 (September-October 1986), pp. 81-105.
12. Ernest Mandel, *Late Capitalism* (London: New Left Books, 1975); and Ernest Mandel *The Second Slump,* (London: New Left Books, 1978). See also Itoh, *Value and Crisis;* Paul Mattick, *Marx and Keynes* (London: Merlin, 1970); David Yaffe, 'The Marxian Theory of Crisis, Capital, and the State', *CSE Bulletin,* no. 1 (1972); and David Yaffe, Value and Price in Marx's Capital', *Revolutionary Communist,* no. 1 (January 1975).
13. See, for example, Stuart Holland, *The Socialist Challenge* (London; Quartet, 1975).
14. See Joan Robinson and John Eatwell, *An Introduction to Economics* (Cambridge: Cambridge University Press, 1973).
15. Andrew Glyn and Bob Sutcliffe, *British Capitalism, Workers, and the Profits Squeeze* (Harmondsworth: Penguin, 1972); and P. Armstrong, A. Glyn and J. Harrison, *Capitalism since World War II* (London: Fontana, 1984).
16. See, for instance, Robert Rowthorn's criticisms of Mandel, in Rowthorn, *Capitalism, Conflict and Inflation,* pp. 95-128.
17. See the transcript between Ernest Mandel and Bill Warren, 'Recession and its consequences', *New Left Review,* no's 87-8 (September-December 1974), pp. 114-24.
18. See M. Aglietta, *A theory of Capitalist Regulation* (London: New Left Books, 1979); A. Lipietz, 'Towards Global Fordism', *New Left Review,* no. 132 (March-April 1982), pp. 33-47; and C Driver's review article on Aglietta in *Capital and Class* (Autumn 1981), pp. 150-68

19. Claus Offe, *Disorganised Capitalism* (Cambridge: Polity Press, 1985). Scott Lash and John Urry *The end of Organised Capitalism,* (Cambridge: Polity Press 1987).
20. D. Harvey, *The Limits to Capital* (Oxford, Blackwell 1982); Ben Fine and Laurence Harris, *Rereading Capital* (London: Macmillan, 1979).
21. J. O'Connor, *Accumulation Crisis* (Oxford: Blackwell, 1984); J. Habermas, *Legitimation Crisis* (London: Heinemann, 1976).
22. The major work on the Marxist theory of the state is Bob Jessop, *The Capitalist State* (Oxford: Martin Robertson, 1982).
23. Nicos Poulantzas, *Political Power and Social Classes* (London: New Left Books, 1973); *State, Power, Socialism* (London: New Left Books, 1978); Bob Jessop, *Nicos Poulantzas* London: Macmillan 1985).
24. See Habermas, *Legitimation Crisis;* O'Connor, *Accumulation Crisis;* and J. O'Connor *The Meaning of Crisis* (Oxford: Blackwell, 1987).
25. See Cutler *et al., Marx's Capital and Capitalism Today.*
26. E. Pashukanis, *Law and Marxism* (London: Ink Links, 1978); Holloway and Picciotto *State and Capital*
27. See Fine and Harris, *Rereading Capital.*
28. Poulantzas, *State, Power, Socialism*
29. Claus Offe, *Contradictions of the Welfare State* (London: Hutchinson, 1984); Offe, *Disorganised Capitalism.*
30. In Britain one of the main arenas for these debates remains the Conference of Socialist Economists, established in 1970, which holds an annual conference and publishes a journal, *Capital and Class.* Work in Marxist Political economy is flourishing in many countries, particularly Japan, West Germany, The Netherlands, France, Italy and the United States.

Chapter 4

Political Economy of Industrial Policy

Wyn Grant

This chapter focuses on the debate about the desirability and possibility of an industrial policy. This is a broad topic, and the treatment presented here will necessarily be selective. Attention is focused on three main themes, two of which have received extensive treatment in literature, and one of which has been relatively neglected by political scientists.

The efficacy of industrial policies has received considerable attention in the literature from both economists and political scientists. Many Western nations are retreating from attempts at systematic intervention in industry, having spent large sums of money in the 1970s with apparently little impact on underlying structural problems. Even so, the persistence of problems of competitiveness which do not appear to be resolved by allowing free play to market forces has led to a continuing argument about whether Western governments should endeavour to develop some kind of industrial policy. In particular, the size of the American trade deficit points to underlying structural problems in the economy of the United States, problems which have formed the focus of a debate about whether that country should have an industrial policy. That debate is renewed here.

One option that has emerged from the industrial policy debate in the United States is the idea of flexible specialization, involving a rejection of standardization, and an emphasis on the importance of being able to shift quickly from the production of one specialized product to another. These ideas are reviewed here in relation to Italy, West Germany and Scotland, as well as the United States. The debate on flexible specialization focuses our attention on the firm as a crucial actor, albeit firms located within a network of social institutions. However, in the debate on industrial policy there has been a relative neglect of the study of the firm as a political actor which both helps to shape, and is the target of, industrial policy. Industrial policies in Western countries have essentially relied on persuading firms, through a variety of incentives (rarely penalties) to modify their decisions on investment, employment, locations, and so on in accordance with the objectives of government policy. Many policies are, of course, formulated at a sectoral level, and intermediary organizations such as trade associations can play an important role in implementation. However, policies ultimately depend on their adoption by firms. Hence, it is important to understand how firms perceive themselves in relation to the political system. Should they have a systematic relationship to the policy and, if so, how should that relationship be conducted?

Thus, in pursuing these three themes, the chapter starts with an analysis of industrial policy at the macro level in terms of the options facing a country with serious problems of international competitiveness. It then shifts to the 'meso' level of firms in particular sectors and/or geographical locations bound together by the mix of formal institutions and informal networks which provide a propitious context for flexible specialization. Finally, the analysis focuses on the micro level of the individual firms.[1] Before proceeding to the discussion of the three substantive themes chosen for examination, it is necessary to explain how the term 'political economy' is used in this chapter, and to explore what the distinctive contribution of political science might be to a political economy of industrial policy.

Political science and political economy

There is an increasing recognition among political scientists that they have got to make a sustained effort to provide a distinctive and worthwhile contribution to the study of political economy if their subject is going to have anything to say about some of the most pressing problems of Western societies. However, if such a contribution is going to be made, political scientists need to be clear both about what they mean by 'political economy' and what the nature of their contribution to its study might be.

Political economy is a much used and much abused term. It means different things to different people. It has been used by some writers to promote a programme of intellectual colonization by economists, centring on the application of the methodology of formal economics to various aspects of human behaviour, not least political action. It has also been used by neo-Marxists to recognize fellow analysts seeking creatively to apply the ideas of Marx to the circumstances of the late twentieth century. There is also an ill-defined group of non-Marxist economists and political scientists interested in the interaction between economic and political phenomena, represented, for example, by the new institutional economists,[2] or by political scientists interested in the study of the economic policy-making process.

The term 'political economy' does at least represent a recognition that there is a vital symbiotic interaction between economic and political phenomena. However, the recognition of this interaction still leaves open the question of *how* it should be studied — from what disciplinary perspectives; with what conceptual frameworks; and with which methodological tools. There is a danger of political economy degenerating into a kind of vague empirical eclecticism if difficult choices about terminology and perspective are not confronted. This is why I find Gilpins definition of political economy disappointing. He states that he uses the term 'simply to indicate a set of questions to be examined by means of an electric mixture of analytic methods and theoretical perspectives.[3] Of course, there is no one theoretical perspective or methodological apparatus that can tackle the range of problems that arise in the study of the politics of economic or industrial policy, but some choices do have to be made, otherwise the term 'political economy' becomes so elastic as to be meaningless.

Atkinson has observed that , 'At the core of the debate on industrial policy is the question of market allocation. Can we trust or expect the market to allocate resources in a manner that will ensure economic growth and political stability?[4] Another way of putting this question is how far we can trust the state to make interventions that facilitate the process of industrial adjustment, rather than preserving products or processes that are no longer required. All too often, help has not been concentrated on workers who have suffered in the process of industrial change and who need to rebuild their lives, but on propping up firms which have no future at a considerable cost to the public purse.[5]

What political scientists can bring to the analysis of these problems is an appreciation of the nature of the modern state, an understanding that it is not a monolith, but a complex mixture of historical traditions, symbols, formal structures, informal 'rules of the game', competences, powers and constraints. In short, I would make a plea for the relevance of the new institutionalism', with its emphasis on the way in which the state shapes society, and on the centrality of process. At its simplest, the 'new institutionalism' is arguing that 'the organization of political life makes a difference'.[6]

The interpretation of the *new* institutionalism advanced here would place an emphasis on considering institutions other than those considered appropriate objects of analysis by political scientists.[7] For example, markets may be treated as institutions.[8] Such an institutional approach permits an analysis 'of the political determinants of economic policy that links those policies to the structural constraints implicit in the socioeconomic organization of each nation'.[10] It should also be possible to extend the analysis to other actors traditionally regarded as the preserve of the economist, notably the firm. At a general level, such a project involves drawing on the insights of organizational theory, as well as those of political science. More specifically, it leads to such areas as the behavioural theory of the firm; intra-organizational behaviour within the firm — where hierarchical models, informed by bureaucratic theory, may be as useful as utility-maximizing models; and the consideration of the firm as a political actor. However, such an attempt to bring the firm into the analysis of political phenomena should not be allowed to lead to the neglect of more traditional political formations. Hence, the substantive part of the chapter starts witha macro-level analysis of the failure to develop an adequate industrial policy in the United States, particular attention being paid to the ability of American political institutions to develop and implement such a policy.

The industrial policy debate in the United States

The industrial policy debate in the United States was characterized by the brevity of the period during which the concept attracted academic, journalistic and political attention; the confusion and inconclusive character of much of the debate itself; and its lack of lasting political impact. One of the proponents of the concept in the United States, Robert Reich, has observed that 'industrial policy is one of those rare ideas that has moved swiftly from obscurity to meaninglessness without any intervening period of coherence'.[10] Although the idea of industrial policy (even if not referred to by that term) is still on the agenda at state level, it was effectively buried at national level by the failure of Walter Mondale's 1984 campaign. Why, then, bother to consider a set of ideas which have had no enduring effect on policy? There are at least two reasons for doing so. First, as Norton observes, 'Although the debate has come and gone, the question of American decline remains.[11] Just how serious the problem of American decline is, and how it might be remedied, was, of course, at the heart of the industrial policy debate itself. But the problem of 'competitiveness' remains a central concern of observers of the American industrial scene. Second, the industrial policy debate in the United States underlines that what is possible in terms of a 'national political economy' approach is constrained by a nation's institutions, political processes and generally shared assumptions about the proper role of government. As Heclo comments, 'The real challenge is not to specify the contents of an industrial policy but to find a politically sustainable process for arriving at and adapting such policies.[12]

From a political perspective, the industrial policy debate was, at its most basic, a debate within the Democratic Party about how Democrats should respond to an economic onslaught on part of their traditional power base, and how they should respond to the economic policies advocated by Ronald Regan. Much of the industrial policy debate has been concerned with the economic and social consequences of the rapid deindustralization of what is variously referred to as the 'frost belt', the 'snow belt' or, most evocatively of all, the 'rust belt'. Blue-collar workers (especially blacks) in areas such as the Upper Mid-West have suffered as industry has closed or transferred to the increasingly Republican 'sunbelt'. Democrat concern about these transformations has been based on a mixture of genuine social concern about the consequences of plant closures on what have become blighted communities, narrow political interest, and a wider concern about the ability of the United States to remain a leading industrial nation. One recurrent element in all the discussion — almost to the point of obsession — is a preoccupation with the threat posed to American industry by Japanese competition.

It should not be supposed, however, that the Democratic Party has been united on the question of industrial policy. At the risk of oversimplification, three broad tendencies can be discerned. On the one hand, there was a group of academics and individuals associated with labour organizations who were concerned about the need to revitalize traditional manufacturing industries. Much was made by this tendency of the fact that government in the United States already interacted with industry in a number of significant areas. However, these interventions were uncoordinated, and their quality and impact could be improved by a new agency charged with co-ordination and implementation of federal government programmes. Rather than a Pentagon-led industrial policy, 'the Democratic alternative might feature a hierarchy of 'tripartite' boards comprised of the elites of organized labour, big business and finance.'[13] It is evident that foreign models had some influence on the thinking that emerged, although what often seemed to be advocated was a confused mixture of Britain's National Economic Development Council (NEDC) and Japan's Ministry of International Trade and Industry (MITI).

Another group within the Democratic Party was less concerned with smokestack America, and drew its political strength from parts of the country not afflicted by the decline of traditional industries. This group, somewhat derisively referred to as the 'Atari Democrats', focused on the potential of high-technology 'sunrise' industries. The leading representative of this group was Gary Hart, who opposed the Chrysler bailout and criticised the Democrats for being 'a party that responds to companies, individual companies if not whole industries, that find themselves in trouble primarily because of international competition, poor management, or poor agreements among management and labour.[14]

There was a third group of Democrats, loosely associated with the Brookings Institution (but not representing any collective viewpoint on its part), who denied the need for any kind of industrial policy. As far as they were concerned, although they were prepared to accept traditional neo-Keynesian macro-economic management, they did not see a need for more detailed interventions at the micro-economic level. The Chairman of the CEA in the Carter administration, Charles Schultze, provided a wide-ranging critique of industrial policy, arguing that MITI was much a consequence as a cause of Japan's success, that the economy of the United States had not deindustralized in the 1970s, and that, in any case, the government of the United States was not capable of picking winners and imposing its choices.[15] Lawrence identifies slow growth in the economy and a strong currency (he was writing in 1984) as the main reasons for the adjustment problems facing American manufacturing.[16]

This political debate was linked with and paralleled by an academic debate. Although there have been individual contributions of a high quality, it cannot be said that the debate was always marked by a high level of sophistication. Part of the problem was that it was not clear what was being debated. What was the United States' industrial problem? Low productivity? Overcapacity? A deficit on trade in manufactured goods in a country increasingly exposed to international competition? Failure to compete with the Japanese? A fall in the real income of the median household? A review of the debate prepared by the Congressional Budget Office notes that 'the discussion would be made easier if agreement could be reached on the goals of industrial policy. The current debate focuses too much on solutions and not enough on problems and goals.[17] However, this failing was not entirely accidental. Allen and Rishikof draw attention to the failure of the participants in the debate 'to go beyond the respective intellectual traditions from which they stem. Most emphasize policies that resonate best with the constituency groups and value systems with which they are most closely associated.[18]

As is so often the case with debates about industrial policy, the division between the different participants in the debate was based on their attitude towards the free-market system. Allen and Rishikof use this distinction to draw attention to three approaches to industrial policy. One is a private sector, self-help approach which places considerable emphasis on the ability of a rejuvenated management to cope with the problems of industrial change. Allen and Rishikof point out that such an approach fails to take account of the short-term orientation which is encouraged by the equity-market-based financial system of the United States, and underplays the role of advances in production technologies which have been encouraged in countries such as Japan. While I am also sceptical about the value of this kind of business school approach, given that the only kind of adjustment that the United States is likely to experience in the foreseeable future is going to be company-led adjustment, the quality of management, and in particular its ability to develop sufficiently wide-ranging 'appreciative systems' remains a key issue.

Allen and Rishikof next distinguish what they term a 'neoliberal' approach 'that favors a stronger role for the public sector in facilitating economic adaptation and change'.[19] In essence, this approach is seen as involving government assistance to industry to shift upmarket towards the production of more specialized products through the use of flexible systems of manufacturing. Allen and Rishikof question what evidence there is that the private sector would go along with these proposals. One mechanism for influencing the private sector which has been suggested in the literature might be some kind of national industrial development bank, loosely modelled on the former Reconstruction Finance Corporation, which could target assistance to sectors or firms to promote public policy goals that would not be achieved through the operation of the market mechanism. One might also add that the neo-liberal variant does sometimes take a corporatist path. Hudson points out that the institutional arrangements recommended by industrial policy advocates conform to a democratic corporatist model, even if they generally like to avoid the label.[20].

Allen and Rishikof distinguish a third approach which 'favors a stronger role for the labor movement in the industrial policy debate'.[21] Unfortunately, much of this literature is preoccupied with declining industries, and often tries to impose an over-rigid Marxist framework of analysis on the problems being considered. Even so, working within the notion of 'urban political economy', this approach has contributed to our understanding not only of the phenomenon of uneven regional development in the United States, but also of the hidden substratum of deprivation to be found even in areas such as Silicon Valley and Houston.[22] Wood's careful analysis of the political economy of North Carolina shows how state economic policy has kept union membership at a lower level than in any other state, favouring both existing producers and incoming 'labor-intensive, low-wage industries seeking to escape unionization, labor market competition, and higher wages in other regions.'[23] Although 9 million new jobs were created in the American economy from 1979 to 1985, 44 per cent of them pay $7,000 a year or less.[24]

As Norton observes in his review of the industrial policy literature, 'Industrial policy has turned out to be an idea with a brief career.'[25] The debate can be traced back to the summer of 1980, and came to an end as a live issue with the presidential election of November 1984, although considerable symbolic significance has been attached to the four-to-one vote in Rhode Island against a bond issue intended to fund a state industrial policy. There were special circumstances at work in Rhode Island, although the electorate's verdict there does demonstrate the difficulty of constructing an electoral coalition of support for industrial policy.[26]

The values held by the majority of Americans do not favour an interventionist industrial policy. This explains the constant references by industrial policy advocates to Hamilton's 1791 Report on Manufactures in an attempt to legitimize their ideas in the light of the work of one of the founding fathers. Fallows terms the desire for industrial policy 'a craving that dare not speak its name because it is so much at odds with other traditions in the American political and economic tradition, especially the desire for a market economy'.[27]

One also has to reckon with the institutional fragmentation of the American system of government. As Heclo points out, legislative parochialism is matched by a kind of functional localism in the executive branch.[28] One could tinker around with the executive branch, and create new co-ordinating staffs, although no doubt much of the time would be spent in fighting for organizational turf, and their effectiveness would depend in large part on the vagaries of administration politics. However, the real obstacle to an industrial policy as it is conventionally conceived is Congress. As Russell comments, 'Congress probably *is* the greatest barrier to an industrial policy or industrial strategy in the United States ... Perhaps no industrial policy structure is consistent with congressional politics'.[29] As he goes on to point out, the Congress cannot be reinvented to suit the needs of industrial policy advocates. Nor, for that matter, is it possible to redesign the judicial system to ensure that the development of policy is not impeded by legal challenges. As Chalmers Johnson observes, the federal court system is increasingly entrusted with 'coordination and reconciliation of conflicts among federal economic programs'.[30]

Does this combination of ideological antipathy and institutional obstacles mean that an industrial policy could not be implemented in the United States? Certainly, it does mean that certain kinds of highly co-ordinated and centralized policy are not feasible. Even so, the United States government is involved in a range of activities which have a considerable impact on business operations. Industry faces a more complex and, in some respects, more burdensome system of regulation than Western Europe,[31] while anti-trust policy has been portrayed as an inadvertent but successful industrial policy.[32] These complex areas of policy cannot be examined in more detail, but more needs to be said about the way in which the United States conducts a surrogate industrial policy through its trade policies and its defence budget.

In a system of government in which the lower house of the legislature is re-elected every two years on the basis of geographical constituencies, it is not surprising that protectionist measures are a frequent response to the problems posed by foreign competition. The United States has pioneered a variety of voluntary export-restraint agreements, orderly market agreements, trigger price mechanisms, and so on, and, very often, only the free-trade inclinations of presidents such as Carter and Reagan have forestalled a resort to more throughgoing forms of protectionism. Unfortunately, protectionist measures are not usually accompanied by any attempt to deal with the underlying problems of industrial competitiveness. Government confines itself to providing a framework within which, it is hoped, company-led adjustment will take place.

Defence spending has a considerable impact on a number of key American industries. 'According to Department of Defense data, in 1980 the defense share of industry output as a result of weapons purchases was 56.8 per cent of aircraft engine and parts, 53.6 per cent of shipbuilding and repairing, 32.7 per cent of radio and television communication equipment, and 25.7 per cent of engineering and scientific instruments'.[33] More generally, a national security rationale can be used to justify a variety of interventions in industry. For example, the Office of Technology Assessment has argued that 'government policies to aid the U.S. steel industry are necessary in part because steel is vital to national security'.[34] In the American Enterprise Institute discussions on industrial policy, an anonymous contributor from a machine tool company tried to claim that 'government does have a legitimate national security interest in preserving some remnant of the machine tool industry.'[35] The national security argument has even been used by the Chairman of the Senate Committee on Agriculture to justify assistance to the dairy industry.[36]

A defence-driven industrial policy may have beneficial unintended by-products (for example military spending helped to get the semiconductor industry off the ground in the United States), but it will not of itself address the problems of the American economy. However, as Hudson points out, it is clear that 'proposals for comprehensive industrial policy are seriously flawed'.[37] This does, however, leave room for a more incremental approach to industrial policy. As Schneider points out, 'What (Americans) object to about industrial policy is precisely what most academic theorists find attractive; elevating government intervention in the marketplace into a system for allocating resources'.[38] As mentioned earlier, Heclo draws attention to the need for improvement in the management of micro-economic policies. Hudson points out that there is a case for 'ad hocism' of the kind which industrial policy advocates abhor. It worked well in the Chrysler cases, and the intense public debate it provokes forces issues out into the open and permits discussion of the direction of industrial policy.

Despite claims that 'A coherent industrial policy may be politically easier for Republicans than for Democrats to attain',[39] it is probable that a future Democratic administration would be more likely to implement an incrementalist industrial policy of the type outlined above. Pending such an event, it is clear that a great deal is happening at the state level in terms of the development and implementation of industrial policy.[40] The more general lesson to emerge from this consideration of the American industrial policy debate is of the need to emphasize the 'national' element in 'national political economy'. Not only is industrial policy 'inescapably a form of economic nationalism',[41] it also requires a sophisticated appreciation of what is and what is not possible in a particular political system. Such an appreciation was missing from much of the industrial policy debate in the United States which sought quick solutions to ill-defined problems without considering what was politically feasible.

A new phase of the debate: Competitiveness

As was pointed out earlier, although the industrial policy debate as such has come to an end, the problems of the American economy remain. Or, to put it another way, as the American economy has become more exposed to international competition, its weaknesses have become more apparent.[42] By 1987, the debate had become one about 'competitiveness'. A Council on Competitiveness was formed, a new Washington-based organization of corporate chief executives, university presidents and labour leaders. In a special report on the theme of 'Can America Compete?' published in April 1987, *Business Week* linked the theme of indifferent industrial performance to that familiar standby of American television commercials, the American Dream. The journal asked: 'Is the American dream about to end? For the first time since the Depression, millions of Americans face the growing likelihood that they will not be able to live as well as their parents'.[43] Despite an increasing reliance on credit, and increased participation by women in the work-force, living standards of two-parent families had not been maintained. Does this mean that the industrial policy debate was continued under a new label? It was continued in the sense that familiar problems such as poor American productivity growth remained on the policy agenda. However, relabelling the problem 'competitiveness' in effect ruled out of the argument the kind of radical, left-orientated analysis that had been present in the industrial policy debate. Even so, it is interesting that the American Enterprise Institute held a conference in April 1987 on 'Industrial Policy Revived' (broadcast on the C-span cable network) with conference speakers more sympathetic to the idea than those at an earlier conference.[44]

The 1984 *Economic Report of the President* set out the case against industrial policy, concluding that 'Our market economy and its system of rewards for superior performance have made the American economy the most productive and innovative in the world.'[45] However, concern about the underlying performance of the American economy was reflected in the calling of the White House Conference on Productivity (which reported in 1984). This was followed in 1985 by the report of the President's Commission on Industrial Competitiveness which defined competitiveness as 'the degree to which a nation can, under free and fair market conditions, produce goods and services that meet the test of international markets while simultaneously maintaining or expanding the real incomes of its citizens'.[46] The report noted that, 'reflecting ... a dismal record in productivity, Americans' standard of living has grown more slowly than that of our trading partners ... We lead only the British in growth of standard of living — and that just barely'.[47] The report also noted that the United States had lost world market share in seven out of ten high-technology sectors.[48] Many of the report's recommendations were directed at the fragmentation of the decision-making process. It was, for example, noted that decisions on trade policy were split between 'at least twenty five executive branch agencies and nineteen congressional subcommittees'.[49] In January 1987 the white house sent members of Congress a 1,600-page document detailing dozens of proposals to improve competitiveness — 'a phrase that has come to embrace everything from revisions in antitrust laws to assistance for dislocated workers and new legislation that would protect intellectual property'.[50]

For its part, the Democratic Congress turned in the direction of protection. In April 1987, against the opposition of the President, the House of Representatives passed the Gerphardt amendment which would require countries with so-called 'excessive' trade surpluses and a record of 'unfair trade practices' to correct them or face retaliation. While this measure is unlikely to become law, it reflects Congressional concern about the size of the American trade deficit. Even President Reagan felt obliged to impose (admittedly largely symbolic) tariffs on a range of Japanese goods. Although one can sympathize with American frustration at the difficulty of selling to Japan, the protectionist mood in the Democratic Party is worrying to anyone who believes that the world economy as a whole would suffer from a major lurch in the direction of protectionism. A notion which recurs again and again in American discussions of trade policy is that of the 'level playing field'. In other words, the United States is prepared to compete, but only on fair terms. Although measures do have to be taken against really unfair trade practices (as distinct from practices labelled as such because of an inability to compete)' it should not be forgotten that protection is really about sheltering inefficiency to the disadvantage of consumers. Protection unaccompanied by any measures to tackle the underlying problems of the American economy is a particularly unattractive mixture.

One measure of the extent of the problems facing the American economy which should impress even the most devoted adherent of the superiority of an unrestrained free-market mechanism is that the profit margin before taxes of American manufacturing companies dropped from an average of 8.6 per cent in the 1972-9 period to a 5.6 per cent level in the fourth quarter of 1985; the profit margin after taxes was only 3.6 per cent.[51] The 1985 figures were below those for British manufacturing companies. The upheavals on the financial markets in the fall of 1987 were a recognition that something is seriously wrong with the American economy (other than the failure to deal with the budget deficit). Unfortunately, it is questionable whether the American political system is capable either ideologically or institutionally of facing up to the extent of the problem, and starting to tackle it. Even more unfortunately, the consequences of this failure impact on the world economy, as well as on that of the United States.

Flexible specialization

Although the industrial policy debate in the United States has not produced a consensus on the existence of a problem, let alone any agreement on feasible solutions, it has yielded some interesting new ideas about more flexible approaches to the politics of industrial adjustment which seek to avoid the state bailouts of failing industries and firms all too characteristic of the 1970s. Of particular interest is the idea of 'flexible specialization' which represents an attempt to learn from the experience of the 'Third Italy', although sceptics argue that 'a major move toward flexible manufacturing would turn the U.S. into a 'boutique economy' too fragmented to be efficient.[52]

Italy was one of the more successful Western economies in the early 1980s, particularly in terms of moving away from a policy of the massive subsidization of loss-making firms through state holding companies.[53] Although the question of whether it has achieved a *sorpasso* in relation to the United Kingdom remains controversial, there is no doubt that it has a better record of recent performance on some indicators.[54] A large part of Italy's success is due to the so-called 'Third Italy', the networks of small family-based firms to be found in towns such as Bologna and Prato manufacturing quality products with small production runs. Undoubtedly, part of the success of these firms is to be attributed to the strength of the Italian extended family; to traditions of merchanting high-quality goods, in which design is a key selling point, to foreign customers; and the existence of an ideology of artisanship supported across the political spectrum from the Christian Democrats to the Communists. Such conditions cannot be easily replicated elsewhere, although the German *Handwerk* system would seem to be a propitious base for a similar pattern of economic activity.[55]

Flexible specialization is an interesting strategy not only because, in the right circumstances, it seems to pay off, but also because it could be acceptable to politicians who see a relatively limited role for government in relation to industry. Flexible specialization does not require that governments plays more than a *facilitative* role: often, as in the Italian case, this is best done by regional or municipal governments. The essence of flexible specialization is co-operation between firms on matters of mutual interest, but not to the extent that competition is undermined. Thus, the wool textile industry of Prato sustains a number of consortia of firms pursuing common interests such as *Promotrade Internazionale* looking after foreign promotion; *Texma,* concerned with overseas sales of textile machinery; *Progetto Acqua,* which is carrying out a water-purification programme; and *Associazione Sprint* rationalizing the information and communication system among firms and encouraging data transmission services.[56] Faced with a crisis provoked by the emergence of a Japanese synthetic silk on the market, the silk industry of Como formed the *Tessile di como* bringing together firms, unions, the regional government and the local technical school. Although it is too early to assess the success of the initiatives taken by the *Tessile,* it has 'displayed a remarkable activism' and has been characterized as 'an emergent visible hand that tries to steer the district, mediating between market and community'.[57]

However, the argument about flexible specialization has a broader basis than the success of Italian artisan firms. The control of production processes by computers allows standardized products (such as motor cars) to be produced in a variety of designs without retooling whole production lines. The production of small batches tailored to particular niches in the market can take place in factories formerly confined to producing standardized products in large runs (or, at best, products with superficial variations such as cars in different colours).[58]

The argument about flexible specialization has been popularized and generalized in the work of Piore and Sabel. They claim that 'the present deterioration in economic performance results from the limits of the model of industrial development that is founded on mass production: the use of special purpose (product-specific) machines and of semiskilled workers to produce standardized goods'.[59] Methods of craft production lost out in the nineteenth century in the first industrial divide. According to Piore and Sabel, we are experiencing a second industrial divide in which new technologies make possible a restoration of craft methods. They maintain: 'The computer is ... a machine that meets Marx's definition of an artisan tool: it is an instrument that responds to and extends the productive capacities of the user'.[60] One consequence of these developments is the re-emergence of the industrial district, often centred on a university or universities (Stanford and Silicon Valley; Harvard/MIT and Route 128; the University of North Carolina, Duke University and North Carolina State University and the Research Triangle). Such localities can sustain small enterprises in a 'complex web of competition and cooperation'.[61] An important element of their analysis, which is in conformity with the emphasis placed earlier on seeing markets as social institutions, is that 'flexible specialization works by violating one of the assumptions of capital political economy: that the economy is separate from society ... in flexible specialization, it is hard to tell where society ... ends, and where economic organization begins'.[62]

Does the notion of flexible specialization have any relevance to the United Kingdom? At first sight, it might seem not. As Doran has shown in an important but neglected study, the craft enterprise in Britain has lacked the legal and institutional structure of support to be found in other countries, and has reinforced the marginalization of small businessmen. Apart from a few luxury trades in London the economic and social status of the independent artisan in Britain collapsed at the time of the industrial revolution.[63] In West Germany, the *Handwerk* sector is particularly strong in producing 'in the luxury goods field where demand has increased with rising standards of living, and a premium is placed on originality and individuality of design and high quality.[64] The *Handwerk* sector also makes an important contribution to skill formation in the West German labour force as a whole. In collaboration with Streeck, I have attempted to show how the *Handwerk* system in the construction industry allows the easier resolution of conflicts of interest which beset the British construction industry.[65] However, one should not pretend that these very different arrangements, which have grown up over the centuries, can be easily transplanted into the United Kingdom.

Some of the nearest approaches to flexible specialization in Britain are to be found in Scotland (although one hesitates to suggest that this reflects a different industrial culture north of the border). The wool textile industry of the North-East and Border region exported 75 per cent of its relatively high-value products in 1981. The manufacturing establishments in the industry generally have less than 100 workers each. However, the industry is more vertically integrated than that of Prato (where production is from non-integrated units), a feature to which attention is drawn in a report on industry.[66]

In the food processing industry in Scotland, the Speyside firm of Baxter's has concentrated on upmarket, high-quality products, produced in a plant with a high degree of automation, with a considerable proportion of staff engaged in quality-control activities. Batch-production activities include, for example, producing small pots of jam for particular airlines.[67] In Motherwell, the Scottish Development Agency (SDA) has been responsible for the construction of a Food Park. The buildings provided take account of the special needs of food production and adjacent firms are able to benefit from, for example, sharing transport to particular markets.

Bodies like the SDA are able to bring about partnerships between the public and private sectors, involving, for example, universities, local authorities and firms. The SDA has been able to play an important facilitative role in attracting new investment to Scotland, and in acting as a catalyst in the development of new industries and enterprises, although it has been argued that the Agency has had to downgrade its wider social objectives to survive in the harder political climate since 1979.[68] A joint review by the Treasury and Scottish Office reported in 1986 that it has had 'a substantial and positive impact on Scotland's economy and environment'. It was concluded that 'The private sector could not at present satisfactorily fill the gap if the agency were to withdraw completely from any of its main functions'.[69] Canada's announcement of the formation of two new regional development agencies in 1987 was influenced by what was seen as the success of the SDA model.[70]

The SDA's Chief Executive has argued that much of its success is due to factors peculiar to Scotland — 'a tightly-knit organization operating in a small country with a limited elite of business, financial and political leaders who know each other extremely well'.[71] Whether the SDA model can be transferred to England is therefore open to question. (There is also a Welsh Development Agency which is often perceived as less successful than its Scottish counterpart, although it may face more intractable problems and be sustained by a less strong regional elite). However, a Northern Development Company has been formed in the North-East and Cumbria. This is an exercise in regional self-help, backed by companies, unions and local authorities, with a limited amount of financial assistance from government.

The firm as a political actor

The example of the Scottish Development Agency shows that it is possible to give intervention an acceptable face, even under a market-orientated government. However, the SDA approach relies even more on an appropriate response by firms to its initiatives than more traditional forms of industrial policy. The SDA can, for example, try to promote the more effective dissemination of exploitable ideas from Scottish higher education institutions, or set up public-private partnerships to promote environmental development, but these and other initiatives rely on the willingness of firms to respond to the opportunities that the Agency has to offer.

Traditional forms of industrial policy — the provision of a variety of subsidies — have often been response-constrained; firms have not always come forward to take up the money available. Even when they do not take it up, they may not modify their behaviour in the desired way in response to the incentives offered by governments.[72] All too often, various government incentives have been regarded as a useful bonus, providing additional funding for an already planned investment. In the worst cases in terms of policy effectiveness, government funds have been used to sustain inefficient firms that would otherwise have gone out of business, thus slowing down the adjustment process.[73] Although steps could be taken to improve the design and monitoring of policies, there are limits to what can be achieved when government operates within a paradigm that gives priority to the firm's autonomy in making commercial judgements.

Thus, in either conventional or more flexible forms of industrial policy, the success of the policy in terms of achieving desired outcomes depends on the extent to which it influences the decision-making process within firms. There is no point in having an industrial policy which consists of giving firms public money to do things that they would have done anyway. Industrial policy, particularly in its more flexible forms, does not depend on substituting a judgement made by government for that made by the firm, but it does depend on influencing the environment in which firms make decisions, and in particular making them aware of new possibilities in terms of technologies, products and markets.

Given the importance of the firm in industrial policy, it is unfortunate that political scientists have paid so little attention to it (leaving aside the extensive but rather specialized literature on multinationals — and relatively little of that has been written by political scientists). The place of the firm as a basic unit of analysis in economics is well established, and important contributions to our understanding of how firms actually behave has been made by economic and business historians, organization theorists, industrial sociologists, and by business studies specialists (particularly those who favour the use of the 'case study'). A particularly important contribution has been made by Chandler, who has stressed the multi-divisional form of the modern firm; the slow adoption of this format in the United Kingdom may help to explain the poor performance of many British firms.[74] Rather more arcane contributions have been made by experts in company law and in accountancy. However, one has to look very hard to find a distinctive political science contribution to the study of the firm. This neglect is even less justified than it ever was, with an increasing emphasis in many Western countries on company-led strategies of industrial adjustment, and indications that firms are becoming more sophisticated in their conduct of political affairs.

The neglect is particularly suprising in the case of British political scientists. In West Germany, for example, there has been a much greater emphasis on the co-ordination of the political actions of firms through industry associations, although even major firms are developing their own internal co-ordination capabilities to deal with European Community affairs.[75] In Britain, however, firms have a long tradition of autonomous action at the expense of co-ordination. It is difficult, for example, to imagine a West German chemical firm developing its own line on a tax-policy question separate from that arrived at by the *Verband der Chemischen Industrie*. In the United Kingdom, however, faced with a tax concession which favoured Shell and Esso, 'BP and ICI did not see eye to eye about the appropriate remedial action'.[76] Consequently, one minister fought for the BP solution, and another for that of ICI.

In the British case, three factors have contributed to direct political action on their own behalf by firms. First, there is a long tradition of government dealing direct with large firms in what is a very concentrated economy by international standards. For example, when he was Secretary of State for Trade and Industry, Peter Walker instituted a procedure whereby he received a monthly letter from the ICI chairman setting out any problems or complaints which could be remedied by government. The problems were then relayed to the relevant parts of the government machine for action, and a detailed reply was sent to ICI.[77] Since the mid-1970s, there has been an even greater emphasis on direct contact between government and individual companies.[78] Second, the Confederation of British Industry (CBI) has been seen to suffer from problems of 'stifling breath', and some companies (such as Lucas) have resigned so that they can concentrate on direct political action on their own behalf. Third, since the early 1970s, very large firms in the United Kingdom have developed their own government relations divisions, usually small units high up in the firm's structure. These divisions give the firm a capability to monitor and co-ordinate the whole range of its political activities, and hence enhance its potential significance as a political actor.[79]

In the space available, it is not possible to provide an extended discussion of how the analysis of the firm as a political actor might be developed. However, in work with Paterson, I have suggested some areas which might be considered.[80] Any analysis of a particular enterprise should start with a consideration of the nature of the firm itself; in particular, is it a conglomerate with a wide spread of interest, or confined to one industrial sector, witha long-term commitment to the success of the industry in which it is engaged? It is also important to examine the internal organization of the firm, particularly in relation to whether or not it is highly centralized. The question of whether or not the firm has developed a corporate political philosophy — as many do — needs to be discussed. The interest that government takes in the firm's strategies is another important factor, as is the nature of the markets to which the firm is selling. Last but not least, if the firm is highly internationalized, it may need to develop a political capability at an international, as well as at a national, level. For internationalized industries like the chemical industry, the decisions of inter-governmental bodies such as the EC and the OECD may be potentially as important as those of national governments.

Conclusions

Industrial policy in the 1970s often seemed to take one of two equally unacceptable forms: either the payment of large and seemingly never ending subsidies to firms or industries in difficulty, or the payment of subsidies to relatively prosperous firms for activities they would have undertaken in the absence of government assistance. In the former category, the British Steel Corporation absorbed at least £12,000 million of public money between the late 1960s and the early 1980s.[81] In the latter category, large sums of regional aid were paid to oil and chemical firms to locate capital-intensive plants on sites they would have probably utilized in the absence of assistance.

Thus, in the 1980s, Western governments such as those of the United Kingdom, France and Italy (and, with rather limited success, that of West Germany) have tried to move away from interventionist industrial policies. One indication of this trend was the apparent intention of the British Secretary of State for Trade and Industry, Lord Young, to dismantle, or at least downgrade, the 'sponsorship' divisions concerned with particular sectors of industry. However, although activist industrial policies may be out of favour, any government (such as that of the United States) is going to be involved with industry in at least four areas: as a customer (particularly if there is a significant domestic defence industry); as a regulator; through its responsibility for trade policy (although, in the case of the United Kingdom, this is primarily a European Community matter); and through the conduct of competition policy. To this basic minimum, one can add special policies towards small firms which *are* very much infavour in a number of countries, regional policies (outside the United States), and policies for high-technology industries and/or the encouragement of the adoption of new technology by existing industries. One might add, although there has not been space to deal with the issue here, that there is evidence of an increasing involvement by sub-national governments in industrial policy, for example, *Land* governments in West Germany.

However, the existence of these various policies does not add up to an 'industrial policy'. Indeed, not only may these policies be formulated in isolation from one another, but they may also contradict one another. One issue which it has not been possible to tackle here is the adequacy of policy-co-ordination arrangements in different countries, whether focusing on 'lead' industrial departments, or, as in Canada, on inter-ministerial committees.[82]

Having an industrial policy does not seem to have worked as in the United Kingdom, but then not having an industrial policy (as in the United States) does not seem to have worked very well either. It may well be that the term 'industrial policy' itself may have become something of an obstacle to further progress. As Heclo has argued, 'we would do well to shift debate from industrial policy *per se* and talk more in terms of improving the management of microeconomic policies'.[83] The analysis presented here has suggested that there is much to be said for institutional innovations such as the Scottish

Development Agency which facilitate partnership relationships between the public and private sectors, and which support firms who wish to build on their competitive strengths. Whatever the quality of the institutional design, no policy is going to work if it does not make an impact at the level of the firm, and one theme of this chapter has been that firms should receive more systematic attention by political scientists interested in how industrial policy is formulated, and how it can best be implemented.

Notes and references

1. Stuart Holland uses the term 'meso' to refer to the sector of the economy dominated by large multinational firms. See S. Holland, *The Market Economy: from Micro to Meso Economics* (London Weidenfield and Nicholson, 1987) and S. Holland, *The Global Economy: from Meso to Macro Economics* (London: Wiedenfeld and Nicholson, 1987).
2. R.N. Langlois (ed), *Economics as a process: Essays in the New Institutional Economics* (London: Cambridge University Press, 1986).
3. R. Gilpin, *The Political Economy of International Realtions* (Princeton, NJ: Princeton University Press, 1987), p. 9.
4. M.M. Atkinson, 'The Bureaucracy and Industrial Policy' in A. Blais (ed.), *Industrial Policy* (Toronto: University of Toronto Press, 1986), p. 259.
5. For an extended analysis of this problem, see M. Trebilcock, *The Political Economy of Economic Adjustment* (Toronto: University of Toronto Press, 1986), especially Chapters 1 and 9.
6. J.G. March and J.P. Olsen, 'The New Institutionalism in Political Life', *American Political Science Review,* vol 78 (1984), p. 747.
7. March and Olsen are a little vague about what is *new* about the 'new institutionalism': see ibid., p. 738.
8. P.Hall, *Governing the Economy* (Cambridge: Polity Press, 1986), p. 46.
9. Ibid., p. 231
10. Quoted in R.D. Norton, 'Industrial Policy and American Renewal', *Journal of Economic Literature,* vol. 24 (1986), p. 2.
11. Ibid., p. 1.
12. H. Heclo, 'Industrial Policy and the Executive Capacities of Government' in C.E. Barfield and W.A. Schambra (eds), *The Politics of Industrial Policy* (Washington, DC: American Enterprise Institute, 1986), p. 293.
13. R.B. Reich, 'An Industrial Policy of the Right', *The Public Interest* (Autumn 1983), p. 16.
14. G. Hart, 'Gary Hart', in Barfield and W. Schambra, Politics of Industrial Policy, p. 223.
15. C.L. Schultze, 'Industrial Policy: a Dissent', *Brookings Review,* vol. 2 (1983), pp. 3-12.
16. R.Z. Lawrence, *Can America Compete?* (Washington, DC: The Brookings Institution, 1984).
17. US Congress, Congressional Budget Office, *The Industrial Policy Debate* (Washington DC: US Government Printing Office, 1983), p. 69.
18. C.S. Allen and H. Rishikof, 'Tale Thrice Told; a Review of Industrial Policy Proposals', *Journal of Policy Analysis and Management,* vol. 4 (1985), p. 234.
19. Ibid., p. 238
20. W.E. Hudson, 'The Feasibilty of a Comprehensive U.S. Industrial Policy', *Political Science Quarterly,* vol. 100 (1985), pp. 461-78.
21. Allen and Rishikof, 'Tale Thrice Told' p. 241.
22. See J.K. Larsen and E.M. Rogers, *Silicon Valley Fever* (London: Allen & Unwin, 1985), Chapter 11; Anna Lee Saxenian, 'The Urban Contradictions of Silicon Valley' in L. Sawers and W.K. Tabb (eds), *Sunbelt/Snowbelt* (Oxford: Oxford University Press, 1984), pp. 163-97.
23. P.J. Wood, *Southern Capitalism: the Political Economy of North Carolina, 1880-1980* (Durham, NC: Duke University Press, 1986), p. 165.
24. *Business week,* 20 April 1987, p. 52.
25. Norton, 'Industrial Policy and American Renewal', p. 1.
26. J. Carrol, M. Hyde and W. Hudson, 'Economic Development Policy: Why Rhode

Islanders rejected the Greenhouse Compact', *State Government,* vol. 58 (1985), pp. 110-12.
27. J. Fallows, 'Commentary', in Barfield and Schambra, *Politics of Industrial Policy,* p. 87
28. Heclo, 'Industrial Policy and the Extensive Capacities of Government', p. 303.
29. R.W. Russell, 'Congress and the Proposed Industrial Policy Structures' in Barfield and Schambra, *Politics of Industrial Policy* p. 330.
30. C. Johnson, 'Introduction: the Idea of Industrial Policy' in C. Johnson (ed.), *The Industrial Policy Debate* (San Francisco: ICS Press, 1984), p. 15.
31. See D. Vogel. *National Styles of Regulation* (Ithaca NY: Cornell University Press, 1986).
32. T.K. McCraw, 'Mercantilism and the Market: Antecedents of American Industrial Policy', in Barfield and Schambra, *Politics of Industrial Policy,* pp. 33-62.
33. US Congress Congressional Budget Office, *Industrial Policy Debate,* p.34.
34. Quoted in L. Tyson and J. Zysman, 'American Industry in International Competition' in L. Tyson and J. Zysman (eds), *American Industry in International Competition* (Ithaca, NY: Cornell University Press, 1983), p. 45.
35. 'Discussion', in Barfield and Schambra, *Politics of Industrial Policy* p. 342.
36. Interview in *Hoard's Dairyman.*
37. Hudson, 'Feasability', p. 475.
38. W. Schneider, 'Commentary', in Barfield and Schambra, *Politics of Industrial Policy* p. 278.
39. Reich, 'An Industrial Policy of the Right', p. 17.
40. For a review, See S. Hansen, *The Political Economy of the State Industrial Policy* (Washington DC: Urban Institute Press, Forthcoming).
41. McCraw, 'Mercantilism', p. 57.
42. Imports and exports represent twice as large a proportion of GNP as they did two decades ago. See the report of the President's Commission on Industrial Competitiveness, *Global Competition: the New Reality, vol. 1* (Washington DC: US Government printing Office, 1985), P. 9.
43. *Business Week,* 20 April 1987, p. 48.
44. Information from professor William Hudson, 28 April 1987.
45. 'Industrial Policy' in 'Annual Report of the Council of Economic Advisors', *Economic Report of the President 1984* (Washington, DC: Government Printing Office, 1984), p. 111.
46. President's Commision on Industrial Competitiveness, *Global Competition,* p. 6.
47. Ibid., p. 12.
48. Ibid., p. 13.
49. Ibid., p. 38.
50. D.E. Sanger, 'Trying to get America into Competitive Trim', *New York Times,* 22 March 1987, Section 12.
51. Figures from *1987 U.S. Industrial Outlook* (Washington, DC: Department of Commerce, 1987), p. 21.
52. *Business Week,* 20 April 1987, p. 47.
53. See P. Bianchi, 'The IRI in Italy: Strategic Role and Political Constraints, *West European Politics,* vol. 10 (1987), pp. 269-90.
54. A. Britton, F. Eastwood and R. Major, 'Macroeconomic Policy in Italy and Britain', *National Institute Economic Review,* November 1986, pp. 38-52.
55. See W. Streeck, 'The Organization of *Handwerk* in West Germany', paper prepared for the Conference on the Regional Organization of Business Interests and Public Policy, McMaster University, Hamilton, Ontario, May 1985.
56. See A. Mutti, N. Addario and P. Seglati, 'The Organization of Business Interests: the case of the Italian Textile and Clothing Industry', European University Institute Working Paper No. 86/205, Florence.
57. J.P. López Novo, 'Community, Market, Association and the small Firm: The Case of an Italian Industrial District', paper presented at the ECPR workshop on 'Meso-Corporatism', Amsterdam, April 1987, p. 23.
58. See W. Streeck, 'Industrial Relations and Industrial Change in the Motor Industry', public lecture, University of Warwick, 23 October 1985.
59. M.J. Piore and C.F. Sabel, *The Second Industrial Divide* (New York: Basic Books, 1984), p. 4.
60. Ibid., p. 261.

61. Ibid., p. 265.
62. Ibid., p. 275.
63. M. Doran, *Craft Enterprises in Britain and Germany* (London, Anglo-German Foundation, 1984), p. 121.
64. Ibid., p. 81.
65. W. Grant and W. Streeck, 'Large Firms and the representation of Business Interests in the UK and West German Construction Industry' in A. Cawson (ed.), *Organized Interests and the State* (London: Sage, 1985), pp. 145-73.
66. Information from D. Crichton, 'The Textile and Clothing Sectors' in N. Hood and S. Young (eds), *Industry, Policy and the Scottish Economy* (Edinburgh: Edinburgh University Press, 1984), pp. 213-48.
67. Information from factory visit.
68. M. Keating and R. Boyle, *Remaking Urban Scotland* (Edinburgh: Edinburgh University Press, 1986), p. 24.
69. Industry Department for Scotland, '1986 Review of the Scottish Development Agency', p. 7.
70. Interview information, Ottawa.
71. *Financial Times* 14 October 1986.
72. For a fuller discussion, see W. Grant, 'Large Firms and Public Policy in Britain', *Journal of Public Policy,* vol. 4 (1984), pp. 1-17.
73. See, for example, R.T. Lambert, 'Clothing Industry Scheme', Government Economic Service Working Paper no. 61, Department of Trade and Industry, 1983, typescript.
74. Hall, Governing the Economy, p. 42.
75. See W. Grant, W.E. Paterson and C. Whitston, *International Industry, National Governments and the EEC* (Oxford'; Oxford University Press, forthcoming).
76. J. Bruce-Gardyne, *Ministers and Mandarins* (London: Sidgwick and Jackson, 1986).
77. P. Walker, *The Ascent of Britain* (London: Sidgwick and Jackson, 1977), p. 87.
78. A. Mueller, 'A Civil Servant's View' in D. Englefield (ed.), *Today's Civil Service* (Harlow: Longman, 1985), p. 105.
79. See W. Grant, *Business and Politics in Britain* (London: Macmillan, 1987).
80. W. Grant and W. Paterson, 'Large Firms as Political Actors: the Case of the Chemical Industry in Britain and West Germany', paper presented to the annual conference of the Political Studies Association, Aberdeen, April 1987.
81. Figure calculated from Y. Mény and V. Wright, 'Introduction' in Y. Mény and V. Wright (eds), *The Politics of Steel: Western Europe and the Steel Industry in the Crisis Years (1974-1984)* (Berlin: de Gruyter, 1986), p. 21.
82. This problem will be discussed in W. Grant, *Government and Industry: a Transatlantic Comparison* (Aldershot: forthcoming).
83. Heclo, 'Industrial Policy and the Executive Capacities of Government' p. 302.

Chapter 5

Executive Autonomy and Economic Policy: Thatcher and Reagan Compared

David McKay

Uniquely in the post-war period, in 1979 and 1980, electorates in two of the major OECD countries voted into office chief executives intent on establishing new ideological regimes of the right. Both promised to repudiate the old order by moving the British and American economies towards a more purely market-determined production of goods and services. Taxes, inflation and the size of the public sector were to be reduced, and the marketplace given a freer reign. Although differences existed in the means towards these ends, it was broadly accepted that the two governments had very much more in common than either had with any of the governments then incumbent on the other major Western countries.

Moreover, a growing literature on state-society relations tended to place the United Kingdom and the United States at quite a different level. Governments in both countries were apparently unusually constrained by societal pressures. Both lacked intrusive national bureaucracies representing a hierarchy of values above and beyond those of society.[1] Both also lacked the sort of consensual or corporatist political arrangements that are recognized elsewhere as crucial in reconciling state-societal differences.[2] Instead, British and American politics were variously characterized as pluralistic, or conflictual or overloaded.[3] Political and economic elites were fragmented and divided ideologically or by institutional base. Organized interests were internally divided but economically powerful. Trade unions and financial capital in the United Kingdom and a myriad of interests in the United States were, apparently, able to gain access to decision-makers either directly through elected officials or indirectly through the application of coercive pressures such as strikes, or the threat of economic dislocation and decline.[4] State and local governments also displayed a high level of independence and were in turn major conduits through which societal interests were represented and advanced.[5]

Institutional arrangements were relevant to this analysis — especially in the United States where Congress was so often identified as an agent more of society than of the state. However, the implication was that executive autonomy was limited by societal pressures whether expressed through elections, legislatures or economic demands and sanctions. *A priori*, then, not much should have been expected from the Reagan and Thatcher experiments. Pluralism and overloaded political systems imply either some sort of perpetual political or economic crisis, or a capacity only for incremental, damage-limitation policies. Nine years later, however, few could dispute that both governments have wrought major changes on their respective societies. It is the major claim of this chapter that executive autonomy is much higher in both countries than was ever the case in the 1970s. As an explanation of executive power, institutional arrangements must be assigned pride of place. While this applies *tout force* to the United Kingdom, even in the United States, presidents have been able to exercise much more autonomy than is supposed by the paradigmatic political science literature.

The sheer force of executive power has precipitated a major intellectual reorientation in both countries. Two distinctive reassesments have occured. In the United States, there is an emerging consensus that the Reagan years represent an imprint not a revolution.[6] In contrast, in the United Kingdom there is talk of the emergence of a system dominated by one party, Japanese style, and the Thatcher revolution continues apace. Margaret Thatcher does, of course, enjoy the advantage of a third term and the momentum that this implies. But assessments up to 1987 or 1988 can still be made and comparisons drawn. In particular, this chapter has three main objectives. The first of these is to catalogue the performance of the two economies over the period, with a particular emphasis on those indicators invoked by both governments as evidence of success. The second is to make some general assessments on the relationship between performance and institutional structure. The third is to draw conclusions on the likely consequences of the analysis for future economic policy-making.

The British and American Economies, 1979-88

On coming to power, both chief executives declared that fighting inflation would be their number one goal.[7] At first, both governments employed a monetarist policy (control of the money supply and interest rates). In the American case, Reagan actually inherited such a policy from the Carter years, monetarism having been implemented by newly appointed Federal Reserve Chairman, Paul Volcker, in 1979. After 1982 and what were widely perceived as the potentially disastrous consequences of high interest rates on the international banking scene, the United States effectively abandoned monetarism. The United Kingdom continued with the policy for much longer, and it was not until 1984 or 1985 that references to money supply measurements were quietly dropped from official discourse.

Neither country abandoned its low-inflation goal, however, with a combination of government spending, interest-rate policy being used to combat rising prices. As can be seen from table 5.1, the United Kingdom was more successful than the United States at squeezing inflation out of the economy, having started from a much higher level. Both countries were, of course, able to benefit from the significantly lower commodity — and especially oil — prices which were generally prevalent after 1982. One undoubted result of tight money policies was deep recession in the domestic economies — although again external forces paid some part in explaining the downturns in 1981 and 1982.

In the United Kingdom, however, the recession hit earlier and deeper and was exactly contemporary with the Thatcher government's first full three years in office (Table 5.1). In the United States the worst recession years were 1981 and 1982 (Table 5.1). Both economies recovered thereafter, although by most

Table 5.1: American and British Economies, Key Indicators, 1980-87

	1980	1981	1982	1983	1984	1985	1986	1987	% changes 80-87	% changes per year
Consumer Price Rises (%)										
USA	13.5	10.4	6.1	3.2	4.3	3.5	2.0	4.4	-9.1	
UK	18.0	11.9	8.6	4.6	5.0	6.1	3.4	3.3	-14.7	
Growth in Real GDP (%)										
USA	-.2	1.9	-2.5	3.6	6.8	3.0	2.9	3.8	19.3	
UK	-2.4	-1.2	1.5	3.3	2.7	3.6	3.3	5.3	16.1	
Industrial production growth (%)										
USA	-.1	-8	-3	15.2	2.9	7.2	.3	4.9	18.5	2.3
UK	-11.5	-1	1.5	4.1	.6	2.5	.9	6.0	3.1	.38
Unemployment (%)										
USA	7.0	7.5	9.5	9.5	7.4	7.1	6.9	6.0	-1	
UK	6.4	9.8	11.3	12.5	11.7[1]	11.2	11.1	10.0		3.6
Investment growth* (%)										
USA	-7.9	1.1	-9.6	8.2	16.8	5.5	1.8	N/A	15.9	2.27
UK	-5.4	-9.6	5.2	5.2	8.2	3.1	.3	N/A	7.0	1.0

1. New series

* Growth of total Fixed Capital Formation

Sources: OECD, *Economic Outlook,* no.42, December 1987 (Paris OECD, 1987)
1987 figures from various sources.

indicators — and especially investment and unemployment — the British recovery was slow and uncertain. Not until 1987 was the British recovery transformed into a rapid expansion. For that year and 1988 (for which data are unavailable) the British economy was outperforming both the American and the OECD average on almost all indicators except industrial investment.

Thatcher and Reagan shared an antipathy to the public sector. On coming to power both declared that public spending and taxation should be reduced as rapidly as possible. In spite of these common objectives, subtle differences between the two governments existed. Reagan and his advisers were, notwithstanding public statements to the contrary, less concerned about the federal deficit than the British. It is always part of the Thatcher scheme to reduce the public sector borrowing requirement (PSBR). As David Stockman's autobiography and other sources confirm, the Reagan governments became increasingly aware that reducing the deficit was not only politically a very difficult thing to do, but might also risk another recession with all the electoral costs that this implied.[8] As a result the US deficit rose rapidly under Reagan, although it levelled out at about 3.5 per cent of GNP by 1986-7 (Table 5.2). The Thatcher governments were much less constrained. In the first few years raising taxes to reduce borrowing was considered permissible. Even so, it was not until 1985 that sizeable inroads into PSBR were made — and then only as a result of sizeable contributions to the Exchequer from the sale of council houses and publicly held assets. By 1988 a rapidly expanding economy enabled the Chancellor of the Exchequer actually to preside over a surplus.

Table 5.2: General Government Financial Balances as a percentage of GNP, UK and USA, 1980-87

	1980	1981	1982	1983	1984	1985	1986	1987*	% change 80-87
USA	-1.1	-1.0	-3.5	-3.8	-2.8	-3.3	-3.5	-3.4	-2.1
UK	-3.5	-2.8	-2.3	-3.6	-3.9	-2.9	-2.1	-2.0	+1.5

*Estimate
Source: as Table 5.1.

Taking the broader measure of the percentage of the GNP accounted for by public spending, the Thatcher governments were again able to achieve much more than the Reagan governments. Taking the whole 1975-86 period, the federal governments' share of GNP actually increased by two percentage points, although the 1981-86 increase was more modest (Table 5.3). In the United Kingdom general government expenditures declined by a full 5¼ per cent between 1975 and 1986, and although no decrease occurred between 1979 and 1986, a sharp downward trend was established after 1982. Moreover, the British projected figures for 1987 through 1989 are probably quite accurate. It is generally accepted in the United States, however, that federal government projections bear little resemblance to reality. Very often they are used as a political device to influence Congress.

Table 5.3: Government Expenditure as a percentage of GNP
Selected Years, 1975-989

Year	USA*	UK
1975 +	21.8	48.5
1979	20.9	43.25
1980	22.1	46.0
1981	22.7	46.25
1982	23.8	46.75
1983	24.3	45.75
1984	23.1	45.5
1985	24.0	44.00
1986	23.8	43.25
1987§	23.0	42.75
1988§	21.7	41.75
1989§	21.1	41.25

Notes

* US figures refer to federal government expenditures only, UK to general government expenditures.

\+ UK figures are for fiscal years 1975/76 through 89/90;

§ Estimated.

Sources: *The Government's Expenditure Plans 1987/89-1989/90*, Cm. 56-I (London: (HMSO, 1987), Table 2.22;)

The Budget in Brief, 1988 Washington, DC: Office of Management and Budget 1987), Table 7.

Not suprisingly in view of what has already been established, British tax receipts remained relatively high as a percentage of GNP under Thatcher, while the Reagan governments was able to finance public accounts by running a deficit. (Table 5.4). What is, perhaps, most notable about Table 5.4, however, is how little taxes have moved over the whole period. As with expenditure, the most significant shift has occured in the United Kingdom since 1982. The considerable drop in taxes since that year is likely to continue following the stimulus provided by the 1988 budget and the restructuring of the British tax system. It is generally agreed that the effects of the 1986-7 tax overhaul in the United States will be neutral.

Table 5.4: Government Receipts as a Percentage of GNP, 1975-87

Year	USA*	UK
1975	18.3	41.3
1979	18.9	39.3
1980	19.4	41.0
1981	20.1	43.1
1982	19.7	44.2
1983	18.1	43.2
1984	18.1	43.7
1985	18.6	43.7
1986	18.5	41.2+
1987	19.1+	40.3+

* Federal government expenditures only
\+ Estimated

Sources: Central Statistical Office, *Economic Trends*, various issues (London: HMSO, 1979-87); *The Budget in Brief, 1988*, Table 7.

Finally, how do the two countries compare in the ways in which the distribution of public expenditure has changed over the period? As can be seen from Tables 5.5 and 5.6, the problem is broadly similar for the two countries in a number of crucial respects. First, defence spending has been increased — although much more in the United States than in the United Kingdom. Second, neither government has been able to hold back social security or health expenditures. (In the United States these are generally subsumed under the heading of 'payments to individuals'). Third, housing, transport and aid to lower-level governments have borne the brunt of expenditure cuts in both countries. (These are generally included under grants in the United States). Two further points are worthy of note. In the United Kingdom, spending on industry declined sharply as the government pursued its privatization and disengagement policies. (For a discussion, see Chapter 4 of this volume). In addition, the British 'other' category includes debt interest, which has been declining since the early 1980s. The American figure has, of course, been rising steadily.

Economic Performance and Institutional Structure: an Assessment

From the above, it is clear that the Thatcher governments were able to achieve many more of their objectives than the Reagan governments. Both faltered on initial monetary and public spending targets, but from around 1984 onwards the Thatcher government has been much closer to achieving stated aims. Indeed the Reagan governments were unambiguously successful in just three areas — increasing defence spending, reducing discretionary social spending (mainly in 1981 and

1982), and reducing inflation. If we base our assessment on what was happening in the 'real economy', however, the costs of the Thatcher policy were high. Industrial production and GDP plunged in 1980 and 1981 and unemployment increased very quickly. The Reagan recession was less deep and recovery from it much more rapid. Only after 1985 did the British economy show signs of real recovery. Margaret Thatcher may have been able to reorder spending priorities, reduce inflation and eventually reduce spending, taxes and the PSBR, but only at the cost of high unemployment, the erosion of Britain's manufacturing base, and, arguably, damage to the social fabric.

Table 5.5: Distribution of Federal Budget Outlays, 1980-87 (per cent)

Item	1980	1984	1987*
Defence	23.5	26.8	28.1
Payments for Individuals	46.5	44.7	45.5
Grants +	9.8	6.2	5.3
Interest	8.9	13.0	13.4
Other	14.8	11.2	11.4
Total non-defence	76.5	73.2	71.9

* = Estimate
+ = Mainly to state and local governments.

Source: The Budget in Brief, 1982 and 1988.

Table 5.6: Distribution of British Central Government Expenditures, 1978/79-1989/90 (per cent)

Item	1978/9	1986/7	1989/90*
Employment training	1.6	2.7	2.7
Health & Personal Social Services	13.9	15.1	16.0
Law and Order	3.7	4.8	5.0
Defence	11.3	12.6	12.1
Agriculture, Food & Fisheries	1.5	1.6	1.8
Transport	4.8	4.0	3.9
Industry, Trade and Energy	5.1	2.1	.9
Housing	7.6	4.1	3.9
Education and Science	14.3	13.1	13.4
Social Security	25.0	31.1	31.6
Other	10.5	8.8	8.6

* = Estimate

Source: The Government's Expenditure Plans, 1987/88-1989/90 Chart 1-11.

Measuring the extent to which these changes are attributable to incumbent executives is, of course, very difficult. Precise quantifiable measurement is almost certainly impossible. Even general assessments of autonomy are difficult, given the problem of distinguishing between executive preferences, on the one hand, and legislative/judicial and broader societal preferences, on the other. When preferences converge the methodological problems are legion.[9] Even so, some conclusions can be drawn by utilizing what is by now a large body of research on British and American economic policy-making. Such an exercise can be expedited by breaking down the influences on policy-making into distinct categories. Hence, Table 5.7 provides nine indications of executive autonomy from other governmental institutions and from broader societal pressures. Let us analyse each of these in turn, concentrating on the relative role played by institutional, as opposed to societal, influences on policy-making.

Table 5.7: Relative executive autonomy in the United Kingdom and the United States, 1980-88.*

	USA	UK
Executive unity	Medium/High ▲	High▲
Executive societal scope	Medium ▶	High▲
Executive electoral dependency	High ▼	Medium▼
Legislative compliance	Low ▼	High▼
Implementation compliance	Medium ▶	Medium/High▲
Judicial compliance	Medium ▼	High▼
Corporate independence	High ▲	Medium▲
Trade union independence	Low ▼	Medium/High▼
International interdependence	Medium ▲	High▼

*Arrows indicate direction of change

EXECUTIVE UNITY

One of the most common criticisms of executive power in both countries during the 1960s and 1970s was the inability of chief executives to control cabinet members, executive departments and agencies and, in the American case, the White House staff. All continue to assert some independence, but this earlier image of a rudderless ship was clearly not an accurate portrayal of executive power by the late 1980s. Within the American presidency power has been progressively centralized since 1939, and this process has accelerated since 1980. In particular, the Office of Management and Budget (OMB) has been elevated to the role of central expenditure controller and rule-making gatekeeper.[10] By some measures it is now the functional equivalent of the British Treasury. Presidents have always had constitutional authority over their cabinets, of course — a power which the British Prime Minister lacks. In this sense the command structure within the American executive branch is more hierarchical than in Britain. It is also accepted that presidents have more control over executive appointments than in the past. Party political cues and past obligations are now weak, giving presidents greater scope to appoint personal favourites or ideological allies. Within the civil service, reforms introduced in 1978 increased the executive control over senior bureaucrats by encouraging merit payments, increased mobility and an increase in the number of political appointees.[11]

Within the literature on American economic policy-making it is accepted that presidents have much greater control over macro- than over micro-economic policy.[12] Even with regard to the Federal Reserve Board there is little evidence of the assertion of independent power.[13] The only clear example occurred in 1979-80 when Board Chairman, Paul Volcker, pursued a much tighter money policy than President Carter wanted. But Carter was by then politically very weak. During the Reagan years, the Chairman and the President were never seriously out of tune.[14]

Presidential control over interest-rate and money-supply policy is, therefore, considerable — at least in relation to other political institutions. Even in micro-economic policy, control of the independent agencies and commissions has increased through the exercise of the appointment and OMB rule-making power.[15] American federal governments have less *scope* in micro-economic policy, of course, of which more later.

On the face of it, British executive unity may be lower than in the United States, the Prime Minister always having to confront a potentially hostile cabinet. Certainly, cabinet disunity over the fundamentals of economic policy has occurred in the past.[16] While, under Margaret Thatcher, dissent has not been eliminated — witness the dispute with Chancellor Nigel Lawson over exchange rate policy in 1988 — it has been reduced. Moreover, once policies are decided on, the Thatcher government has been more determined than most to implement them with vigour and determination. As important, most observers agree that in spite of the increased power of the OMB and the consensual nature of relations between the Federal Reserve and the President, the British Treasury is more centrally placed to monitor spending than OMB, and the Bank of England is more subject to executive authority than is the Federal Reserve.[17]

Institutionally, therefore, the degree of executive unity is relatively high in both countries. Where they have differed is in the will and/or ability to use this institutional advantage. As suggested, the Thatcher government has utilized it to the full. Reagan, however, has exercised a much lower degree of control, not so much because of institutional barriers, but because in some areas of economic policy, notably expenditure and tax policy, divisions within the executive branch have been common. As David Stockman and others have documented, after the initial successes of 1981, the OMB clashed with a number of cabinet secretaries over the extent of the cuts.[18]

EXECUTIVE SOCIETAL SCOPE

What cannot be disputed is that British governments have very much more scope in economic policy than do American governments. American executives can affect state and local finances only indirectly.[19] British governments are able to intervene in local government finance in the most profound manner, as the recent abolition of the Greater London Council and the metropolitan councils and the introduction of a poll tax demonstrate. The scope of federal authority in micro-economic policy is also limited. The United States effectively has no nationalized sector and education, training and labour market policies are poorly developed. The Thatcher government has been active in all these areas. Even privatization does not necessarily reduce executive scope, as prior to any sell off the government has actively directed a major restructuring of the affected industries and sectors (British Airways, Rover Group, Jaguar). Restructuring has also occurred in those enterprises not sold off (British Coal, British Steel). Britain's unitary political system additionally makes available to the government a police power which under some circumstances can be used to further the ends of economic policy (the miners' strike of 1984-5, for example). Only in the general area of defence does the United States have a developed micro-economic policy. Most federally funded research and development is defence-related, and defence expenditures are used as a sort of regional employment programme. Members of Congress rather than presidents are the key actors in the distributional policies involved in this process, however.

EXECUTIVE ELECTORAL DEPENDENCY

By definition, governments in both countries are electorally dependent. However, American presidents are subject to what amounts to a plebiscite after four years.[20] During their second terms their electoral dependence is effectively zero, but their second term is their last. The state of the economy is almost certainly the key variable in determining whether presidents are re-elected. This is usually measured by voters' real income relative to four years earlier.[21] First-term presidents cannot afford a recession late in their incumbency, therefore — as Jimmy Carter found out to his cost. At one time it was common to apply a similar calculus to British governments.[22] Margaret Thatcher's incumbency more resembles one-party dominance, however. A combination of the electoral system and a split opposition guarantees a parliamentary majority for the Conservatives should they win around 40 per cent of the popular vote. Margaret Thatcher won re-election in 1983 during a deep recession, and although some evidence exists to suggest that a moderate economic recovery was beginning and helped to ensure victory,[23] most contemporary comment concluded that the economic environment was hardly conducive to electoral success.[24] Certainly, compared with first-term presidents, the Thatcher governments pursued economic objectives with little apparent deference to electoral strategy.

LEGISLATIVE COMPLIANCE

This indicator provides the sharpest contrast between the two systems. By either of two obvious measures, American presidents are at a serious disadvantage, compared with British prime ministers. At the most basic level, Congress is constitutionally separate and can block presidential initiatives with little or no cost to members. Second, even members of the president's own party display relatively low levels of solidarity with their chief executive. After 1981, Reagan's support scores among Republicans in the Senate were as low as those recorded by the embattled presidents Nixon and Ford.[25] Given the fragmented and highly personalised nature of modern American politics, presidents can never be assured of support from Congress, even when their party is nominally in control.[26] No area better demonstrates this point than budgetary and fiscal policy. Ronald Reagan achieved two famous victories in 1981, by persuading Congress to accept very substantial tax and expenditure cuts.[27] Since then, however, the Reagan government's budgetary targets have never been met. This is not necessarily indicative of Congressional fiscal irresponsibility, as the government has constantly alleged. Instead, the two branches have irreconcilable objectives which in combination have led to deficits. Congress has attempted to protect social programmes and is reluctant to raise taxes. The administration protects defence spending and is also reluctant to raise taxes.

British prime ministers face no such constraints. By definition, they must command a majority or a winning coalition in the House of Commons. What is true is that dissent among government MPs has been increasing and votes against governments which tend to be non-economic — often conscience — issues, and revolts (not always successful) on economic-related questions such as student loans and the poll tax, occur.[28] In no sense are there the equivalent of the obstacles facing American presidents, however.

IMPLEMENTATION COMPLIANCE

Generalizing on the experience of the two countries in this area is highly problematical. The easy conclusion to draw would be a low level of compliance in the United States and a higher level in the United Kingdom. Certainly the American implementaion literature assumes low compliance levels.[29] Much of this relates to the *scope* of executive authority, however, as many domestic programmes are actually implemented via state and local governments. Federal control is consequently reduced. British governments have a wide range of powers which can be invoked against local governments. American federal authorities are much more circumscribed in this area.

Beyond the inter governmental dimension the picture is much murkier. Some macro-economic policies are *ipso facto* relatively easy to implement with such indicators as interest-rate changes resulting in automatic adjustments. Budgetary and micro-economic policies are in a different league, however. Perhaps the most surprising development of the 1980s is how *easily* both British and American governments implemented budget cuts and tax-system overhauls. In the American case, the 1981 cuts resulted in much reduced welfare provision and capital spending.[30] In the United Kingdom new spending on one of the major post-war welfare programmes, public (council) housing, was almost eliminated altogether. British education spending was also reduced in real terms. Constraints on spending cuts do apply — especially in the broad areas of social security (pensions) and health (in the United Kingdom National Health Service, and in the United States Medicare and Medicaid). But the capacity of society to resist laws reducing social provision in a range of other areas has been much less than would have been expected in the 1970s. In the United Kingdom, implementation compliance has almost certainly increased since 1979. We will return to this theme when discussing corporate and trade-union independence.

JUDICIAL COMPLIANCE

Since the 1937 Court Packing Plan and the subsequent shift in court opinion, the US Supreme Court has generally deferred to the other branches in economic matters. Even so, the potential for court action is always there, and in micro-economic policy, the Court continues to assert its power of judicial review. So in the areas of social and economic de-regulation, court action remains common. In the United Kingdom, judicial statutory interpretation — but never review — is increasing but from a very low level. Moreover, there is little evidence that the British courts act as agents for societal interests. Instead they more resemble a further, and sometimes independent, institution of the state. In the United States, the courts are often used by societal interests as a weapon against executive power. This can compromise executive authority in such areas as environmental and consumer protection. More dramatically, the courts can and have reinterpreted such key economic measures as the Gramm—Rudman—Hollins Deficit Reduction Act.

CORPORATE INDEPENDENCE

Compared with the so-called corporalist political systems in countries like Austria and Sweden,[31] British and American corporations display a high degree of independence from executive authority. Along with Lindblom and others, this author agrees that the needs of corporations constitute the single greatest constraint on governments' freedom of action in economic policy.[32] This accepted, both Reagan and Thatcher helped deepen recessions between 1980 and 1983 which could hardly have been welcomed by most corporate interests. In the British case, the average tax burden on corporations was increased during the same period. British executives have much greater scope to affect corporate activity via what is a large industrial public sector. As earlier catalogued, the restructuring of individual firms and sectors was stated government policy.

Moreover, serious conflicts of interest exist on both sides of the Atlantic between industrial and financial capital and between large and small firms. It was pressure from the financial sector that led Reagan to modify his tight money policies in 1982,[33] and throughout the Thatcher years it could be argued that government policy has better served financial than industrial capital.[34] The extent to which this represents pressure from the City of London rather than a convergence of perspectives and values is difficult to say, however. Past research would suggest it was the latter.[35]

What can be concluded is that the internationalization of both finance and industry has increased their independence from executive influence in both countries. This point will be resumed below.

TRADE-UNION INDEPENDENCE

American executives have relatively little control over trade unions, most of whom operate under state law. Some federal employees are unionized and thus subject to federal authority. Thus Reagan was able to 'bust' the air traffic controllers' union, PATCO, in 1981. Apart from such actions there is little presidents can do directly to affect trade unions short of sponsoring new legislation in Congress which would have little chance of success. As it happens, trade unions have provided little of an impediment to Reagan's economic policies because they have been greatly weakened over the last few years by changes in the industrial structure and by recession. The best estimates are that only 19 per cent of the American work-force is now unionized.

In sharp contrast, the British Employment Acts of 1980 and 1982 and the 1984 Trade Union Act have substantially eroded the legal position of British trade unions. In addition, the Thatcher governments pursued a series of direct confrontations with public sector workers (railwaymen, miners, public health service workers) designed to hold down pay and/or implement industrial restructuring. As Peter Hall has noted, these attempts have been 'remarkably successful'.[36] Recession and industrial reorganization have also taken their toll on union power. Indeed, in the five years to 1984, the Trades Union Congress lost 17 per cent of its affiliated members,[37]

Few now argue that unions are a threat to the United Kingdom's governability, or to the 'fabric of society'. They remain more central to industrial organization than in the United States, of course, but an impressive exercise of executive power has greatly reduced their actual and potential influence on economic policy-making.

INTERNATIONAL INTERDEPENDENCE

Historically, the American economy has been far more insulated from international pressures than the British. However, by 1985 around 25 per cent of GDP was accounted for by imports and exports — up from 10 per cent in the early 1960s.[38] (The British figure was just over 50 per cent in 1982.[39]) The increasing interdependence characteristic of the American economy has undoubtedly reduced the autonomy of presidents and other national institutions. As a declining hegemon the United States can no longer dictate the terms of global economic relations. Even so, of the major OECD states, the United States remains the country with the largest domestic market and the greatest number of major corporations dependent on that market. Moreover, she retains the status of world economic leader — if not economic locomotive. Presidents wield corresponding political power over international economic events. What they say and do is far more relevant than what British prime ministers say and do. Indeed it is remarkable that the United States has been able to withstand a trade deficit for so many years without a total collapse of its currency.

When the International Monetary Fund was called in to rescue the British economy from collapse in 1976, the British governments were judged to have virtually no independent say in economic policy. Since then, a combination of increased oil revenues, fiscal rectitude and, since 1984, improved competitiveness (or, more accurately, a sharp slow down in the deterioration of Britain's competitiveness) have increased executive discretion over economic policy. In sum, the United Kingdom and the United States have to live in an interdependent world, and the latter remains less interdependent than the former, but since 1980 British executive autonomy, measured in international economic terms, has increased, while that of the United States has decreased.

Conclusions

As suggested, in both the United Kingdom and the United States, executive autonomy is higher than was supposed in the 1970's. As far as economic policy is concerned, this has shown itself in the ability of the Thatcher governments to pursue a range of macro and micro policies independent of societal interests and of other state factors. Even in the United States, the Reagan governments have exercised a much higher degree of control over macro-economic policy than conventional wisdom would have it. Very broadly, the British Conservatives have been more successful in achieving their economic objectives than have the Republicans, but this may in part be because the Thatcher governments have been consistent about their objectives. The British Conservatives have also enjoyed a number of institutional advantages compared with their American counterparts. Parliamentary opposition has been limited (if growing), executive societal scope is higher, and electoral and judicial dependence is lower.

Institutional arrangements are not fixed; they do change through time, as the evolution of the American presidency and British parliamentary government shows. If present trends persist, presidents will continue to try and concentrate power in the White House, even as Congress attempts to counter any such move with new executive-curbing measures. Similarly, British prime ministers and cabinets are likely to continue the extension of their powers into the rest of the polity and society. How successful presidents and prime ministers are will depend in part on the personalities and capacities of incumbents. But in economic policy — as well as in many other policy areas — any incumbent will inherit institutional arrangements which are now very different from those in operation twenty years ago. Certain constitutional laws and norms do, of course, prevail, but beyond these, British and American executives have wide powers available to them to change the style and substance of macro- and macro-economic policy.

Notes and references

1. For a comparison, see Peter T. Katzenstein, *Between Power and Plenty: The Foreign Economic Policies of Advanced Industrial States,* (Madison: University of Wisconsin Press, 1978), Chapter 9.
2. See Gary W. Marks, 'State-Economy Linkages in Advanced Industrial Societies' in Norman T. Vig & Steven E. Schier, (eds), *Political Economy in Western Democracies* (New York: Holmes and Meier, 1985), and sources cited.
3. There is a vast literature on this theme. For American examples see the collection of essays celebrating the tenth anniversary of *The Public Interest*, published as *The New American Commonwealth, 1976* (New York: Basic Books, 1976). For British perspectives, see Samuel Britton, *The Economic Consequences of Democracy,* (London: Temple Smith, 1977); A.M. Gamble and S.A. Walkland, *The British Party System and Economic Policy, 1945-1983* (Oxford: Oxford University Press, 1984).
4. See James Buchanan and Richard Wagner, *Democracy in Deficit*, (New York: Academic Press, 1977); Samuel H. Beer, *Britain Against Itself* (London and New York: Norton, 1982).
5. This is particularly true of the United States where an emerging 'topocracy' of inter-governmental lobbies, was identified as a major cause of rising federal spending; see Samuel H. Beer, 'Federalism, Nationalism and Democracy in America', *American Political Science Review*, vol. 72 (1978), pp. 9-21.

6. B.B. Kymlicka and Jean V. Matthews, *The Reagan Revolution?* (Chicago: The Dorney Press, 1988).
7. For a discussion on the United States Fred I. Greenstein (ed.), *The Reagan Presidency: An Early Assessment* (Baltimore, MD: John Hopkins University Press, 1983), especially the chapters by Heelvard Penner and Greenstein. For Britain, see Peter Hall, *Governing the Economy: The Politics of State Intervention; Britain and France* (New York: Oxford University Press, 1986), Chapter 5.
8. David Stockman, *The Triumph of Politics: Why the Reagan Revolution Failed* (New York: Harper 1986).
9. This theme is developed by Eric Nordberger, *On the Autonomy of the Democratic State* (Cambridge, MA: Harvard University Press, 1981), Chapter 1.
10. See US Senate, Committee on Governmental Affairs, *Office of Management and Budget: Evolving Roles and Future Issues*, (Washington, DC: US Government Printing Office, 1986); Terry M. Moe, 'The Politicized Presidency' in John E. Chubb and Paul E. Peterson (eds), *The New Direction in American Politics* (Washington, DC: The Brookings Institution, 1985).
11. For a discussion and sources, see David McKay, *Domestic Policy and Ideology, Presidents and the American State, 1963-1988*, (Cambridge: Cambridge University Press, 1988), Chapter 7.
12. Paul Peretz, The Politics of Fiscal and Monetary Policy in Paul Peretz (ed.), *The Politics of American Economic Policy Making,* (New York: Sharpe, 1987), pp. 139-151.
13. Nathaniel Beck, Presidential Influence on the Federal Reserve in the 1970s, *American Journal of Political Science,* vol. 26 (1982).
14. This does not in itself demonstrate executive dominance, of course, the more likely probability is a convergence of presidential and Federal Reserve views. For a counter-view claiming that the Federal Reserve has considerable autonomy, see William Greider, *Secrets of the Temple: How the Federal Reserve Runs the Country* (New York: Simon and Schuster, 1988).
15. See McKay, *Domestic Policy and Ideology,* Chapter 7.
16. For a discussion see Gamble and Walkland, *The British Party System,* Chapter 4.
17. Michael Moran, *The Politics of Banking* (London: Macmillan, 1986) shows how British Governments have extended their control over the Bank of England. Even so, the Bank retains some autonomy.
18. David Stockman, *The Triumph of Politics.*
19. Mainly via grants in aid to state and local governments and through the manipulation of the macro-economy. For a discussion of the effects of the Reagan cuts on the states, see Richard P. Nathan *et al., Reagan and the States,* (Princeton, NJ: Princeton University Press, 1987).
20. Theodore T. Lowi, *The Personal President: Power Invested, Promise Unfulfilled,* (Ithaca, NY: Cornell University Press, 1985), Chapter 5, calls the office the plebescitary presidency.
21. For a full discussion see Samuel Kernell, *Going Public: New Strategies of Presidential Leadership* (Washington, DC: Congressional Quarterly Press, 1986), Chapter 7.
22. See Britton, *The Economic Consequences of Democracy.*
23. David Sanders, Hugh Ward and David Marsh, 'Government Popularity and the Falklands War: A Reassessment', *British Journal of Political Science,* vol. 17 (1987), pp. 281—313.
24. David Butler and Dennis Kavanagh, *The British General Election of 1983* (London: Macmillan, 1984), Chapters 12 and 13.
25. Norman T. Ornstein, *et al., Vital Statistics on Congress, 1984—5* (Washington, DC, American Enterprise Institute, 1985); *Congressional Quarterly, Weekly Report,* various issues.
26. See the data presented by Morris P. Fiorina, 'The Presidency and Congress: An Electoral Correction' in Michael Nelson (ed.), *The Presidency and the Political System,* (2nd edn (Washington, DC.: Congressional Quarterly Press, 1988).
27. See the contribution by Heclo and Penner to Greenstein, *The Reagan Presidency.*
28. See Philip Norton, *Dissention in the House of Commons 1974—1979* (Oxford: Oxford University Press, 1980). See also Bruce Cain, John Ferejohn and Morris Fiorina, *The Personal Vote: Constituency Service and Electoral Independence,* Cambridge, MA: Harvard University Press, 1987), Part Three.
29. See *inter alia,* Eugene Bardach, *The Implementation Game,* 4th edn (Cambridge MA: MIT

Press, 1982); Richard E. Neustadt and Harvey V. Fineberg, *The Swine Flu Affair: Decision-Making on a Slippery Slope,* (Washington, DC: Department of Health, Education and Welfare, 1978); Martha Derthick, *New Towns in Town: Why a Federal Program Failed,* (Washington DC: The Brookings Institution, 1982); Jeffrey L. Pressman and Aaron Wildavsky, *Implementation* 3rd edn (Berkeley and Los Angeles: University of California Press, 1984). The general assumption that federal officials complicate, - and ultimately undermine, - the implementation of policy is implicit in much of the work produced by the Advisory Commission on Intergovernmental Relations (ACIR). See in particular, their bimonthly *Intergovernmental Perspective.*

30. See Nathan, *et al., Reagan and the States,* and George E. Peterson and Carol W. Lewis (eds), *Reagan and the Cities* (Washington, DC: Urban Institute Press, 1986).
31. See, 'State—Economy Linkages in Advanced Industrial Societies'.
32. Charles E. Lindblom, *Politics and Markets: The World's Political Economic Systems* (New York: Basic Books, 1977).
33. William Greider, *Secrets of the Temple: How the Federal Reserve Runs the Country* (New York: Simon and Schuster, 1988), Chapter 14.
34. Moran, *The Politics of Banking,* Chapter 7.
35. Hall, *Governing the Economy,* Chapter 5 and sources cited.
36. Hall, *Governing the Economy,* p. 109.
37. Ibid.
38. OECD, *Economic Survey, United States* (Paris: OECD, various years).
39. OECD, *Economic Outlook,* December 1987 (Paris: OECD, 1987, p. 105).

Chapter 6

Liberal International Political Economy

Roger Tooze

Any attempt to understand the nature and meaning of the contemporary world political economy will at some point involve consideration of 'liberal' international political economy. This is both because the liberal perspective has become the mainstream or conventional theoretical and policy perspective on international political economy (IPE), and as such other perspectives are obliged to respond to its claims, and because the basic framework of the post-1945 international economic order was fashioned on liberal values and assumptions (the two factors clearly being related). To the extent that this international economic order and the political structures that support it are relevant to our understanding of the late 1980s, and I would argue that they are very relevant, we need to confront and comprehend the liberal perspective. Significantly, the inclusion of the international realm was an integral part of the genesis and development of liberal political economy, particularly in the articulation of the principle of comparative advantage in trade, and we do not have a separate and separable 'international' version of liberal political economy. The analytical and organizational distinction we use here between international and 'domestic', i.e. *intranational,* liberal political economy is not one that would necessarily be recognized by liberal political economists. Indeed, the increasing difficulty of distinguishing between the 'domestic' and the 'international' is one of the factors that prompted dissatisfaction with prevailing views of international relations and the contemporary resurgence of academic interest in IPE.[1]

Given the 'non-separability' of liberal political economy we will for much of this chapter use and build on the assumptions of 'domestic' liberal political economy laid out by Barry Jones in chapter 2 of this volume. However, while we use the core assumptions of liberal political economy that he has broadly identified, this chapter will locate these in a different theoretical context and within a different structure of political economy. The central argument, derived from the attempt to understand and explain substantial outcomes in the world political economy, is that 'liberal international political economy' as a perspective needs to be understood as more than a set of assumptions which produce explanatory and prescriptive theory. That is, liberal IPE, and indeed the other perspectives, are more than intellectual devices that enable us to make sense of a complex world political economy. Because the values and concepts of liberal IPE establish a particular relationship between the material circumstances of the international political economy and a system of meaning which creates a shared understanding, the perspective itself is part of the objective 'reality' of the contemporary IPE. This argument partially reinforces the 'polylectic' view of this volume's Introduction, but it suggests that the perspective is a fundamental part of the structure of political economy and therefore needs to be understood as such.

Accordingly, this chapter lays out a framework for the analysis of liberal IPE that necessarily involves a consideration of wider theoretical concerns and procedures. Here, the consideration of underlying theoretical and philosophical issues is not undertaken to turn IPE into philosophy or to indulge in an exercise of 'grand theory', but in the belief that we need to examine the way in which our knowledge of IPE is constituted by underlying philosophical assumptions because these assumptions can (and do) have important political implications. More specifically, the chapter suggests that unless we re-evaluate the purposes of and the possibilities for the analysis of the liberal perspective as *political economy,* rather than as conventional positivist theory, we risk misunderstanding the nature of the IPE, as well as the nature of liberal political economy as a perspective. Once we have established the framework to support the central argument, we shall consider the theoretical status and political significance, as well as the assumptions, values and claims of liberal IPE (and various extensions of the liberal perspective) in the context of the world political economy of the 1980s.

Liberal International Political Economy and 'Perspectives' on Political Economy

The identification and analysis of 'perspectives' in the study of political economy is an integral part of the process of evaluation and argument. The way we analyse a perspective and what we do with this analysis is contingent upon our understanding of how we know what we know; that is, our epistemology. The field of mainstream international relations and liberal IPE itself have both been developed within an epistemology that constructs the notion of a 'perspective' in a distinct way. This positivist epistemology denotes a perspective in the following generalized form: a number of *a priori* linked assumptions and values from which can be derived theoretical statements that allow the identification and selection of 'facts', and, by establishing causation with reference to these 'facts' provide an explanation and understanding of reality which can be tested against that reality.

In this positivist conception, a perspective provides an individual with the only systematic way of approaching the 'sea of facts' that constitute reality; without the values and assumptions embodied in a perspective we could not make sense of a highly complex reality. Moreover, conceptual frameworks contained within a perspective are imposed on an *independent* data base.[2] That is, the perspective is separate from the 'facts' and constitutes an attempt to make sense of the 'facts' in an ordered and economical way.[3] For the positivist, 'The data of politics are externally perceived events brought about by the interaction of actors in a field'.[4] Here, perspectives are necessary tools for the process of description and explanation of these events.

Within positivist epistemology the test of a perspective is whether it produces explanations that correspond to reality. Any number of perspectives is possible, but progress is only achieved through the process of refining or rejecting perspectives in order to move closer to an objective account of reality. Hence, perspectives can be analysed for the assumptions they make, the methodology they employ, their internal logic and their consequent correspondence to reality. Moreover, the process of evaluating perspectives can be objective, value-free and 'scientific', without the distortion of 'ideology', because in the tradition of positivism an objective, value-free account of social reality is both desirable and possible, given the assumption that 'facts' exist in their own right and are epistemologically prior to perspective and theory. Perspectives, and individual or group belief systems related to perspectives, are differentiated from 'ideology' in that they can be objectively tested against a presumed reality. 'Ideology', on the other hand, interferes with an objective understanding and is therefore the antithesis of science. Finally, because perspectives are purely instrumental, the process that produces perspectives as knowledge is a neutral, 'scientific' one, divorced from all interests and purposes apart from that of objective understanding.

If we accept this epistemological tradition as the basis for our examination of liberal international political economy as a perspective we accept the denomination of liberal IPE as a specific instance of the generalised form of a perspective as outlined above. As such we can identify, define and discuss the assumptions and values that collectively make up the liberal perspective on IPE, consider them for their relationship to the 'real' IPE and their internal logic and consistency, and come to some evaluation of the adequacy of the liberal view. This may in itself always be worth doing because it could generate new insights and/or draw interesting conclusions on a range of important questions, as Robert Gilpin demonstrates in his recent evaluation of the liberal perspective.[5] New insights and conclusions then become part of the 'polylectical' process. But, however interesting and useful such evaluations are, they are still dependent for their *significance* upon a predefined mode of knowledge: a mode of knowledge that is based on the assumed separation of subject and object.

The positivist separation of subject and object has additional and important implications for our analysis of the liberal perspective on IPE. First, positivist thought denotes a particular view of science and social science in its claim to produce 'law'-like generalizations that are consequently universal in their validity.[6] The claim to universality of the generalizations means that 'The universality of the basic attributes of the social system comes to be perceived as standing outside of and prior to history'.[7] Yet, the historical emergence of liberal political economy, in opposition to a strong mercantilism which appropriated economic power to the state, *itself* demonstrates the problems and limitations of 'universal' social attributes. As Karl Polanyi so clearly argues, the primacy of the economic motive in Western liberal societies is based on the (liberal political economy) view of the 'institutional separation of society into an economic and political sphere'.[8] Such a separation reproduces what Polanyi calls the 'economistic fallacy' where this separation of the political and the economic sphere is assumed to be common to all societies at all times. In addition, it leads to the assumed dominance of economic (as opposed to social) motivation in all societies at all times. But the market, and hence the distinct separation of the economic from the other aspects of society in which it is normally embedded (which results in the primacy of the economic motive), is a historically specific political creation.[9]

The weaknesses of positivist thought in this context clearly limits, but does not invalidate, any analysis of liberal IPE as an abstract body of concepts or assumptions separated from the social and political conditions within which it is articulated. Moreover, as we might expect, the process of definition of core liberal IPE concepts is similarly conditioned by this aspect of the dominant epistemological tradition.[10] The content of the definition is not, at this stage, the problem. It is rather that we have 'a definitional concern with obtaining a basis for consistent, non-contradictory usage that is abstract in so far as it does not refer *directly* either to *a particular location or to a particular time*'.[11] Such a definition would be considered 'objective' and disputes would centre on consistency, rigour, economy and (in the case of liberal IPE) problems of interpretation from the original texts. Yet, the concepts of liberal IPE are not easily understandable separated from a specific historical context, as Polanyi shows for 'market'[12] and MacLean shows for 'interdependence'.[13]

Second, and related, the separation of subject and object makes it difficult to consider the liberal perspective on IPE as anything *more* than an analytical framework, dependent for its 'power' on its intellectual coherence and its ability both to explain reality and to convince individuals and groups of its veracity and its desirability in terms of its prescriptive content. Here, the separation of subject and object serves to define our analysis of liberal IPE as a consideration of abstract concepts, propositions and values, and it serves to confine our analysis to empirically testable events and behaviour. But what happens when individuals and groups in power consciously or unconsciously hold a particular perspective in terms of a belief system? And what if they then incorporate the values and assumptions of the perspective in policy, and translate the values into elements of the international political economy; that is, the beliefs become internationalized? Clearly, the perspective is then more than an analytical construct; it can be, in some sense, part of the reality of the system that confronts many in a subordinate position within the system. When we examine the actual outcomes of IPE it becomes increasingly difficult to understand and explain these outcomes without reference to a broad set of beliefs about the IPE, particularly those of liberal political economy, that have become universalized. Moreover, it is not sufficient or appropriate to see these beliefs, in the traditional international relations sense, as 'ideology' interfering with objective understanding, or as individual psychological characteristics.[14] As John MacLean so cogently argues:

> A more likely hypothesis is that individual belief systems are actually a part of the *material* conditions of international relations — that is, they are causal to them to the extent that large scale relations of power require extended adoption of some beliefs rather than others ... And, at the same time, those belief systems are themselves caused by the material conditions in the world.[15]

If this is the case, and I argue that it is, to the extent that liberal values and assumptions become internationalized, liberal IPE becomes translated from an individual or group intellectual perspective (testable against the reality of the IPE) to part of the structure of the IPE itself (to become part of the assumed reality of IPE).[16]

This conclusion serves as the starting point of the analysis of liberal IPE that follows, but it also brings us squarely into a different epistemological tradition. And we come to this different tradition not through an intellectual process of evaluating alternative epistemologies, but through necessity, given the inability of positivism to facilitate acceptable explanations of IPE. Without going too far into further discussion, it is worthwhile identifying certain key aspects for our purposes in this chapter.

In this critical or historicist tradition there is an identity of subject and object: 'The objective realities that this approach encompasses — the state, social classes ... and their practices — are constituted by intersubjective ideas ... none of the realities exist in the same way as individuals exist, but individuals act *as though* these other realities exist, and by so acting they reproduce them'.[17] Hence, in this approach, as distinct from positivism, systems of meaning, practices and material conditions are 'reciprocally confirming'. An understanding of concepts cannot be divorced from the practices and material constructions associated with them.[18] Inter-subjective meaning — its creation and maintenance — is itself an aspect of power. Andrew Sayer crystallizes the implications of this interpretive tradition for the analysis of international political economy when he discusses the relationship between the construction of the material world and the construction of meaning in the context of systems of domination. Systems of domination are maintained not only through the appropriation, control and allocation of essential material requirements by the dominant class, race or gender, but also through the reproduction of particular systems of meanings which support them.[19] Hence, in the IPE analysis, say, of American hegemony, it is not sufficient to consider only material factors,[20] particularly if the 'myth' of hegemonic decline itself becomes significant in understanding American policy action (or inaction) and associated legimating beliefs.

We shall now turn to an examination of liberal IPE on the basis of the framework set out in this discussion. This examination will be indicative rather than comprehensive, because although we shall consider the wide range of values and assumptions that are part of liberal political economy, the methodological demands of the interpretive framework are different and greater than those of positivism. Consequently, much of the original research remains to be done.

Language and Context

One of the problems of offering an analysis of liberal IPE is that its meaning and content changes over time and context. The epithet of 'liberalism' was not attatched to the work of Adam Smith and his followers until the early 1850s, nearly eighty years after *Wealth of Nations* appeared. Then the term was largely used by the opponents of commercial freedom concerned to identify the dangers of free trade and liberalism in a political economy in which the state had certain social responsibilities and in which the idea of unfettered individual economic freedom was disruptive. The free traders themselves preferred the term 'free traders' or 'Manchester men' rather than 'liberal'.[21] The denotion of the set of ideas originating from Adam Smith as liberalism, dominated by the idea of and the political movement for free trade, and the systematic association of this economic doctrine with political liberalism, which is taken as given in the contemporary context, is thus a late nineteenth-century fusion. Moreover, it is a fusion peculiarly Anglo-Saxon in origin and application: in 1927 von Mises could assert that 'The world today wishes no longer to know about Liberalism. Outside of England the description 'Liberalism' meets with scorn'.[22] The incorporation of liberal values into the emerging positivist 'science' of economics in the late nineteenth century established the formal basis for the translation of 'liberal' economic values and assumptions from prescriptive claims (and political movement) to academic orthodoxy and analytical legitimacy. Through an extended process of identification with particular interests and more broadly-based concrete developments, 'liberalism' evolved from a political critique of then existing practices to become part of the definition of the reality it purported to explain.

In Robert Cox's helpful terms, liberalism becomes a perspective which generates 'problem-solving' theory. The essence of such theory is that it

> takes the world as it finds its, with the prevailing social and power relationships and the institutions into which they are organized, as the given framework for action. The general aim of problem-solving is to make these relationships and institutions work smoothly by dealing effectively with particular sources of trouble.[23]

As Cox makes clear, the assumptions that problem-solving theory makes enable statements to be made which 'appear to have general validity', and therefore claim status as (objective) laws, but which are dependent upon the holding of the initial perspective for their validity.

Instrumental in the process of translating the claims of liberal international political economy into statements claiming general validity were the twin processes of the dominance of the United States in the world political economy and the dominance of economics in the social sciences. The dominance of the United States enabled the internationalization of a specific mode of liberal IPE, supportive of a particular conception of the wider interests of the United States. This is not to say that the version of liberal IPE internationalized through American power and interests was not also supportive of other interests in the international system, state or otherwise. Nor is it to say that the eventual realization of a structure of political economy at the international level which was characterized by liberal norms and practices was *only* (and always) to the benefit of the United States. But it is to say that in order to understand the nature of the liberal IPE as a perspective we need to understand the conjunction of material interests and inter-subjective meaning which translated liberal political economy from a diversely constituted but widely held individual/group perspective into the basis of the post-1945 world political economy.

The dominance of economics, particularly but not only in the United States reinforced the claims of liberal IPE to a general validity. Two aspects of economics are of interest here: the attempt by economists to construct economics as a positivist science; and the apparent success of neo-classical, mainstream economics in providing 'explanation' and policy advice.[24] The decoupling of politics and economics inherent in liberal political economy itself encouraged the process of the 'technicalization' of economic analysis (typical of problem solving theory in general). But it was the attempt to model economics on science that provided the methodological underpinning of the claim to general validity. Positivist science claims to produce objective knowledge and, as such, a positivist economics similarly claims objectivity in the attempt to transcend its original problematic, rooted in a particular time and place. Economics as scientific knowledge is a different form of knowledge, with different social and political implications, than economic knowledge as 'doctrine', clearly associated with particular values and goals: 'Economics is not only a branch of theology. All along it has been striving to escape from sentiment and to win for itself the status of a science'.[25] The claim to the objectivity of economic analysis is part of a process of legitimizing a particular perspective and defending that perspective against criticism. In addition, the apparent success of the liberal prescription for the international political economy in the 1950s and early 1960s reinforced the claims of general validity with regard to the direction and content of economic policy. Moreover, the explosion in popularity of economics as an academic discipline propogated the liberal view 'as the given framework for action' for mainstream economic analysis.

Before we come to locate liberal IPE within the specific historical framework of the post-1945 world order it is appropriate to consider the range of claims that the liberal perspective makes about world order. Because of the social and political nature of knowledge and its production we are not confronted by a necessarily coherent body of thought and principals, neatly labelled as 'liberal IPE'. As Barry Jones points out in Chapter 2 of this volume, liberal political economy is a widely diverse disposition. The difficulty of identifying a coherent, unifying view of liberal thought is emphasized by McKinlay and Little in their identification of 'pure' and 'compensatory' liberalism.[26] However, we can identify a number of core claims which have an important bearing on our discussion and it is to those we now turn.

Claims and Assumptions

Much that is distinctive about liberal IPE comes from the initial assumption that 'politics and markets exist, at least ideally, in separate spheres'.[27] Moreover, the structure and role of the political *should* be shaped by the needs of the economic structure. Economic activity is essentially rational, a liberal economy is directed towards the maximization of wealth through economic efficiency, whereas politics is irrational and perverse and tends to interfere with the rational workings of a market economy. In this conception of political economy the separation of economics and politics enables the development of the market economy, but only within the context of a 'political structure of a definite kind with specific but limited functions'[28] A number of aspects of this hierarchical separation are important here. First, given the core notions of individualism and man as both self-centred and rational, ever seeking to 'optimize' his position, the natural size for an economic community is a world market. McKinley and Little see this as liberalism's 'universalizing tendency' in that, 'other things being equal, liberalism considers that the larger a liberal community can become the better'.[29] This position clearly brings the liberal market economy into tension with the state whenever the boundaries of the market transcend those of the territorial state. When this occurs, the rationality of the market may be frustrated by the more parochial concerns of the state (in territorial terms) and the 'pure' liberal would argue that the state was now anachronistic, necessary for the initial development of the liberal economy but at this stage preventing the realization of the gains of economic organization based on a world (that is, not an *international*) economy. The problem for liberalism is how to achieve this transition given that the state is not going to wither away, as liberalism in some versions assumes.

Second, the nature of the economic-political relationship is not as straightforward as some liberals might like to think. That the state should interfere as little as possible in markets and in trade is a logical extension of the superior rationality of the liberal economy over politics, but there is a clear minimum political framework necessary for the successful working out of the long-term harmony of interests presupposed by the liberal view. Within the state this minimum was the maintenance of the framework necessary for the operation of the 'natural law' of liberal economic freedom. On the level of the international system the efficiency of the liberal economy depended on the maintenance of peace among nations. In this context it is important to note that, as Robert Gilpin points out, there is in liberal theory 'no *necessary* connection between the process of economic growth and political developments such as war and imperialism', although a liberal international economy is viewed as exerting a 'moderating influence' on international politics because it reinforces both the harmony of interests and, significantly, a commitment to the status quo.[30] The nation-state is then viewed as an enabling framework for the liberal economy, and if that framework is threatened liberal efficiency comes to nought. Consequently, given that defence was preferable to opulence, as Adam Smith argued, defence industries should be maintained, often in defiance of the principle of comparative advantage. On this point James Mayall rightly argues that 'at the source of liberal theory ... there is this major concession to realism',[31] although, as Mayall also emphasizes, no such concession is found at the international level where economic rationality reigns throughout.[32]

The theoretical preference of liberalism for economic rationality over political decision-making processes produces a third category of consequences for its application to IPE. The economic voluntarism explicit in liberalism's view of the individual is implicitly held in liberal IPE, particularly in its trade theory, giving rise to the important notion in liberalism that explains (or assumes) the expansion of the international economy: 'To the extent that liberal trade theory appeared to imply that societies had freely determined how (and whether) they would take part in international commerce, it almost seemed to embody an international version of the social contract'.[33] Hence, the expansion of the liberal international economy and the incorporation of new economic actors is a matter of rational calculus, free from any actor-related or structural imperatives. This form of international voluntarism is, however, far from convincing in historical terms, as even a brief consideration of imperial and hegemonic relationships will indicate.

The preference for market solutions to 'distributional' problems is revealed in policy terms as well as more theoretical systemic notions. As we have seen above, since liberal theory treats national economic systems as if they were the firms and individuals which constitute the actors of 'domestic' liberal economy, the primacy of the market is thus extended to governments and international economic policy. This, as Susan Strange demonstrates, results in a position where 'each individual government can then be blamed — since it is never the system's fault — for the excesses of inflation or recession. Since market operators act on equal terms and with equal power ... the decision of the market must be fair and just and must not be interfered with'[34] Of course this theoretical construction has immediate and important political implications in that in a world economy structured on liberal lines (that is, in contemporary terms to reproduce and maintain an 'internationally oriented capitalism') the primacy of the market thesis favours those groups and states that are supportive of the status quo.[35] In the sense illustrated above, the notion that the market 'must be fair and just and must not be interfered with' is an essential component in the translation of liberal values into a structure of action, within which this value becomes the implicit starting point for analysis, prescription and policy.[36]

A fourth consideration stemming from the hierarchical separation of economics and politics is that liberalism almost totally neglects power in its view of the world. Neither the basic assumptions of liberal political economy nor the analytical concepts and methods designed to elicit 'understanding' of matters economic take power into account. A partial explanation for the neglect of power is in the dominance in liberal theory of 'perfect competition' as the basic model for theorizing: 'perfect competition was both an abstract analysis of a decisive economic force, and the Utopian formulation of a society in which power is so widely and thinly distributed that its influence can be neglected'.[37] In addition, the claim of liberal political economy to produce determinate knowledge of economic life focused on models and concepts that could produce such knowledge. The result is an international political economy that is an undifferentiated system, with no significance given to power in any shape or form. It is not difficult to show that the omission of power, even in the example used by Ricardo originally to demonstrate the validity of comparative advantage, fundamentally weakens the liberal argument. And where liberal IPE does take account of power, for example in the neo-classical analysis of protectionism, it, not unexpectedly, naively 'incorporates the political theory of pluralism', that is, protectionism is seen as the outcome of a number of competing interest groups pressurizing the state into action, with no consideration given to the structure of politics or to the state.[38]

Finally, the nature of the international economy itself is derived from the factors we have considered. Given the separation of politics and economics, the liberal international economy is self-sustaining in both theoretical and policy terms. The core assumption is of a long-term harmony between all groups and interests; trade is mutually beneficial and free trade achieves the harmony of firms and individuals with national *and* international interests. Once established, 'liberalism can be regarded as a self-reinforcing system, in which declines in trade barriers both foster prosperity and weaken the inefficient sectors pressing for protection'[39] thus further reinforcing the political support for the liberal system. Within liberal IPE the overwhelming theoretical concern is with explaining trade and the justification for free trade as the key ingredient of a liberal international economic order. As Barry Jones has shown, the concept of comparative advantage aims to explain the content and direction of trade, and we will not repeat his discussion here. It is sufficient to say that for many the principle of comparative advantage does not explain trade and trade problems in the contemporary system, nor has it ever explained trade in more than a simplistic sense because of its inability to come to terms with power and political configurations. Moreover the theoretical tunnel vision of liberalism which produces a concentration on international trade tends to obscure developments in other sectors of the IPE, such as monetary and financial affairs, and prevents any systematic consideration of these sectors in any causal or explanatory sense.[40]

The assumptions and claims of liberal IPE that we have identified and discussed here are general and reflect the comprehensive nature of the liberal problematic. However, in the context of the post-war international political economy they have acquired a specific meaning and significance. We shall briefly consider the nature of this meaning in the next section.

The Contemporary Context of Liberal International Political Economy.

Liberal international political economy as a perspective undergoes a change of emphasis as it becomes the basis of the post-1945 international economic order. The international mechanisms set up in the earlier phase of liberal dominance, under the hegemony of the United Kingdom, were in effect the embodiment of 'pure' liberalism. A system of free trade and payments was institutionalized in the mechanism of the international gold standard. The international gold standard required for its effective working national subservience to the very existence of an international mechanism. The national economy was manipulated to fulfil the needs of the country's external balances: a trade deficit meant domestic deflation to reduce costs and to realign the external value of the currency. However, the gold standard became more than just a mechanism to achieve the liberal goal of equilibrium, it became the keystone of the international economic system. In his analysis of the 1930s Karl Polanyi argues that 'Belief in the gold standard was the faith of the age', but that effort to re-establish the gold standard, in the face of widely differing domestic needs and a very different international structure, ultimately led to the complete breakdown of the international economy and with it the growth of fascism.[41] The automaticity of the gold standard carried all before it in its primacy of economic rationality over other values and, in this sense, it was the logical international extension of liberal political economy

The experience of the 1930s demonstrated the problems in the practice and theory of a liberal *international* political economy in the context of the twentieth century. The major tension was produced by the requirement that the state should manipulate the domestic economy in order to achieve liberal goals regardless of the consequences of this manipulation for the individual members of the national political economy. The social, economic and political changes that had taken place in the capitalist states and in the role of those states within the economy, however, made this theoretical imperative almost impossible to fulfil without destabilizing the national political economy itself. Consequently, however 'liberal' the view held by those who constructed the post-war order, it was clear that the practices of a liberal IPE and the assumptions that legitimized that IPE would necessarily be different from the earlier internationalization of liberal thought.

Building upon Polanyi's analysis, John Ruggie has developed an exceptional framework for the understanding of liberal IPE after 1945. He denotes the 'restored' international liberalism as 'embedded liberalism', signifying the compromise between the extremes of 'orthodox' liberal IPE and economic nationalism: 'unlike the economic nationalism of the thirties, it would be multilateral in character; unlike the liberalism of the gold standard and free trade, its multilateralism would be predicated upon domestic interventionism'.[42] 'Embedded liberal' IPE produces an interesting response to the hierarchical separation of economics and politics that we have discussed, whereby liberalism in foreign economic relations is coupled with 'activist, welfare oriented policies at home'.[43] Because the practices of the liberal IPE had to be consistent with the development of the welfare state they were far less demanding in their international obligations, but they still constituted those obligations within the framework of a liberal (rather than mercantilist or Marxist system.

To those familiar with the seeming paradox of embedded liberalism the duality of thought and policies necessary to sustain this form of liberal IPE is indeed a compromise. The elements of the liberal perspective that are either international or do not deny a totally negative role for the state are incorporated into a 'new' liberal IPE, much like the notion of 'compensatory liberalism' developed by McKinlay and Little.[44] In this way the perspective is changed to reflect and legitimize the purpose of the structure.

How this partcular structure of liberalism is constituted is related to American power and purpose. Ruggie's central point is that the fact 'that a multilateral order gained acceptance reflected the extraordinary power a perseverance of the United States'.[45] The initial thinking behind the multilateral order clearly reflects the dominance of liberal assumptions: the proposed separation of economics from politics in the institutions of Bretton Woods, and the basic acceptance of the principles and values of liberal international economics, moderated by a pragmatic realism that recognized the near-impossibility of reaching 'free' as opposed to non-discriminatory trade.[46] Further, the construction of a liberal order was tied into the definition of American security; 'the idea that American interests would be best served by an open and integrated economic system, as opposed to a large peacetime military establishment was firmly established during the wartime period',[47] and was directly based on the belief that it was the breakdown of the international economy that was largely responsible for the outbreak of war.

The way in which this initial definition of the post-war order changes is interesting, but will have to be considered elsewhere. What is important here is that the historical material development of the post-war order is at first seen to reinforce the validity of the liberal perspective, at least to those who benefited from the economic growth that liberal analysis attributed to the 'free' system. At the same time, liberal values become the orthodox intellectual position and become more and more directed towards solving the problem of the liberal system. Two observations are pertinent. The first is that at the very time liberalism was being developed into an elaborate theoretical structure the system to which it referred embodied a basic contradiction in liberal values — the necessary coexistence of interventionist states seeking domestic stability with the construction of a basically liberal international economy *made possible* by American power and serving American and other interests. The second is that, whatever the particular interests served by the liberal theory, it was articulated as the only possible scientific explanation of the nature of the international economy — 'the way it is'.

The internationalization of liberal values through the construction of the post-war international economy meant that these values became part of the framework of action for participants, both voluntary and involuntary, in the system. Not only did it provide specific explanations for particular developments and the policies for particular agencies, such as the IMF, but it also provided *the* definition of international economic reality against which all other views and all actions were to be evaluated. Hence, for example, 'the increasing economic interdependence between advanced countries and the newly industrializing countries is seen as a triumph of liberalism, only somewhat tarnished by economically irrational, politically inspired protectionism'.[48] And, with reference to North-South relationships, James Mayall comes to the conclusion that 'the Western objective remains to make only those concessions which are consistent with the spirit of the liberal order and which will enable Third World countries to stay within it'.[49] Here, it is important to reinforce the earlier methodological point that the liberal belief system does not just enter international political economy as individual or group 'filters' and preference systems, it is part of an objective power structure.

The material changes that have ocurred in the IPE have brought about interesting responses in liberal theory which are essentially attempts to maintain the balance among a constellation of international, national and private interests, while preserving the liberal nature of the international economic order. The development of 'regime' analysis can be seen as a response to the failure of the 'managed liberalism' of the immediate post-war years though I would see it more as an American response to the changed structure of the world political economy and the perception of the loss of American hegemony in the world economy.[50] Despite a large number of problems, the liberal perspective still provides the dominant view. This is best illustrated through the way that a contemporary issue, such as the 'new protectionism', is analysed. Protectionism is defined as a threat to the prevailing system and a political intrusion into the rational working of the liberal order. Liberal theorists 'still continue to have difficulty appreciating that the new protectionism is not an aberration from the norm of postwar liberalization, but an integral feature of it'.[51] More importantly, as Susan Strange has long argued, the liberal perspective defines protectionism as important because it continues to give international trade, and its explanation, far too high a priority, leading to a neglect of the key structures of the world economy.[52]

Conclusions

The liberal perspective still defines the nature of the IPE, although it is undergoing a series of fundamental challenges to its meaning and its practices. It is also being reinforced materially by the development of a world political economy of integrated production and service structures, and the emergence of a new group of countries commited to the maintenance of the present multilateral economic order. However, liberal theory of IPE does seem to be very much on the defensive. The perspective has not yet been successfully modified to take account of 'embedded liberalism', and the resulting disjunctions clearly create major problems for the ability of the perspective to explain contemporary developments. What is particularly noticeable is that internationally there appears to be two versions of the liberal view, defining two different realities. One, that used among the industrialised countries, acknowledges the reality of state intervention, and in some cases encourages this through international policy co-ordination involving the domestic economic policies of the co-ordinating states. The second, presented to the non-industrialized countries by those who define the structure, is the reality of pure liberalism and the sanctity of liberal principles in trade, investment and domestic policy. However, the two versions are not used consistently or coherently, with particular inconsistencies being noticeable over the question of trade.

Having said that liberalism is facing major challenges to its claimed general validity. Liberal IPE still possesses great power as a perspective and there is little doubt that the perspective can be adapted. Whether it will be adapted or not depends on its relationship to material developments in the world political economy and whether it continues to serve a legitimate purpose, particularly in terms of policy. Some doubt on this has already been provided by Robert Keohane in his analysis of 'the crisis of embedded liberalism'. He concludes that 'unless its effects are cushioned by deliberate policy, the success of liberalism, even embedded liberalism, tends to destroy the conditions for its existence'.[53] This paradox is, I suggest, the fundamental problem facing liberalism as a perspective on international economy.

Notes and References

1. For example, see Susan Strange, 'International Economics and International Relations', *International Affairs,* vol. 46, (1971), pp. 304-15.
2. Among the mass of literature on this topic I have found the work of John Gunnell both accessible and useful. See J.G. Gunnell *Philosophy, Science and Political Inquiry* (Morristown, NJ: General Learning Press, 1975).
3. J.G. Gunnell, 'Philosophy and political theory', *Government & Opposition,* vol. 14, no. 2 (1979).
4. Robert W. Cox, 'Social Forces, States and World Orders: Beyond I.R. Theory' in Robert O. Keohane (ed.), *Neorealism and its Critics* (New York: Columbia University Press, 1986), p. 242.
5. Robert Gilpin, *The Political Economy of International Relations* (Princeton, NJ: Princeton University Press, 1987), particularly pp. 43-6.
6. See, for example, Kenneth N. Waltz, *Theory of International Politics* (London: Addison-Wesley, 1979), particularly Chapter 1.
7. Cox, 'Social Forces', p.243.
8. Karl Polanyi, *The Great Transformation* (Boston: Beacon Press, 1957) p.71.
9. Ibid., pp. 71-2.
10. For this argument, see John MacLean, 'Interdependence — an Ideological Intervention in I.R.' in R.J. Barry Jones and Peter Willetts (eds), *Interdependence on Trial* (London: Frances Pinter, 1984).
11. Ibid., p. 135 (emphasis added).
12. Polanyi, *The Great Transformation*
13. MacLean, 'Interdependence'.
14. John MacLean, 'Belief Systems and Ideology in I.R. — A Critical Approach' in R. Little and S. Smith (eds), *Belief Systems and International Politics* (Oxford: Blackwell, 1988), has cogently and convincingly set out this case.
15. Ibid.
16. This point is argued at length in Roger Tooze, 'Economic Belief Systems and Understanding I.R. 'in Little and Smith, *Belief Systems.*
17. Cox, 'Social Forces', p. 242.
18. For an excellent guide to this argument, see Andrew Sayer, *Method in Social Science* (London: Hutchinson, 1984), particularly pp. 31-46.

19. Ibid., p. 37
20. For such an argument, see Robert W. Cox 'Gramsci, Hegemony and I.R.: An Essay in Method', *Millenium Journal of International Studies,* vol 12, no 2 (1983).
21. See Rudolph Walther, 'Economic Liberalism', *Economy and Society,* vol. 13, no. 2 (1984).
22. L. von Mises, cited in ibid., p. 198.
23. Cox, 'Social Forces', p. 208
24. For a critical view from within economics, and which does not take 'liberalism' as an appropriate label, see Ken Cole *et al., Why Economists Disagree: The Political Economy of Economics* (Harlow: Longman, 1983).
25. Joan Robinson, *Economic Philosophy* (Harmondsworth: Penguin, 1962), p. 25.
26. R.D. McKinlay and R. Little, *Global Problems and World Order* (London): Frances Pinter, 1986).
27. Gilpin, *Political Economy,* p. 26.
28. James Mayall, 'The Liberal Economy' in James Mayall (ed.) *The Community of States* (London: Allen & Unwin, 1982).
29. McKinlay and Little, *Global Problems,* p. 44
30. Gilpin, *Political Economy,* p. 30
31. Mayall, *'Liberal Economy',* p. 99
32. Barry Buzan, *People, States and Fear* (Brighton: Wheatsheaf, 1983), presents an interesting discussion of liberal IPE and security.
33. Martin Staniland, *What is Political Economy?* (London: Yale University Press, 1985), p. 103.
34. See Susan Strange, 'Interpretations of a Decade' in Loukas Tsoukalis (ed.) *The Political Economy of International Money* (London: Sage for the RIIA, 1985).
35. See the interesting discussion by Robert Keohane, 'The World Political Economy and the Crisis of Embedded Liberalism' in John H. Goldthorpe (ed.), *Order and Conflict in Contemporary Capitalism* (Oxford: Clarendon Press, 1984).
36. As well as Susan Strange, 'Interpretations', see John Odell, *US International Monetary Policy* (Princeton, NJ: Princeton University Press, 1982).
37. See K.W. Rothschild, 'Introduction' in K.W. Rothschild (ed.), *Power in Economics* Harmondsworth: Penguin, 1971), p. 9.
38. See R.O. Keohane, After Hegemony: Cooperation and Discord in the World Political Economy (Princeton, NJ: Princeton University Press, 1984), p. 27.
39. Ibid., p. 17.
40. See, in particular, Susan Strange, *States and Markets* (London: Pinter, 1988).
41. See Polanyi, *The Great Transformation.*
42. John Gerard Ruggie, 'International Regimes, Transactions and Change: Embedded Liberalism in the Postwar Economic Order' in Stephen D. Krasner (ed), *International Regimes* (London: Cornell University Press, 1983).
43. Keohane, *After Hegemony* p. 19.
44. McKinlay and Little, *Global Problems.*
45. Ruggie, 'International Regimes', p. 213.
46. See, among many others, Richard N. Gardner, *Sterling-Dollar Diplomacy in Current Perspective* (New York: Columbia University Press, 1980).
47. Robert A. Pollard, *Economic Security and the Origins of the Cold War, 1945-1950* (New York: Columbia University Press, 1985), p. 13.
48. Keohane, *After Hegemony,* p.33
49. Mayall, 'The Liberal Economy', p.109
50. See, in particular Krasner, *International Regimes* and Susan Strange, 'The Persistent Myth of Lost Hegemony', *International Organization,* vol. 41, no. 4 (1987).
51. Ruggie, 'International Regimes', p. 226.
52. See, most recently, Strange, *States and Markets.*
53. Keohane, *After Hegemony,* p. 350.

Chapter 7

Marxist Approaches to International Political Economy

Chris Brown

Up to a generation or so ago, Marxism was seen by both adherents and critics as the quintessential form of political economy - a mode of thought characterized by the rejection of sectoral boundaries between 'economics' and 'politics' and whose seminal text, *Capital,* was an exemplar of what political economy could offer. This now seems terribly outmoded; late twentieth-century Marxism, or 'post-Marxism', or 'critical' thought, is now distinguished above all by its rejection of this characterization. The proposition that Marx was the greatest of all political economists is tantamount to a charge of 'economism' if not of vulgarity'; modern critical studies focus on the Frankfurt School, Gramsci, Habermas and Foucault — Those elements of twentieth-century Marxism least concerned with, indeed most hostile to, Marxist economics. Modern attempts to relate Marxism to international relations rarely put much stress on the issues of international political economy (IPE), prefering instead the more seductive pleasures of grand theory.

In this light, this chapter is unashamedly old-fashioned and unreconstructed. Although the work of the modern critical school will be discussed briefly in the final section, the main emphasis will be on Marxist political economy as that term would have been understood by its greatest practitioners over the last century. The first section will examine the legacy of Marx and Engels with respect to IPE; the second section will focus on the classical Marxists of the Second International, and in particular on Luxemburg, Hilferding and Lenin; the third section will examine 'dependency' theory and, more generally, the shift of emphasis in much modern Marxism towards problems of development and underdevelopment; and the final section will look at the 'critical' school of international theorists and at the small number of independent-minded Marxists, largely unconnected with any school or faction, who continue to work within the older traditions.[1]

Marx, Engels and international political economy

Marx without doubt saw capitalism as a phenomenon unconstrained by national boundaries and ungraspable within the confines of conventional intellectual disciplines.[2] None the less, there are serious obstacles to the discovery of the basis for a Marxist IPE within the volumes of *Capital* or Marx's other major works of theory. These obstacles are created by Marx's method which was to begin with abstractions which would then be made concrete as the work progressed. Volume 1 of *Capital* starts with the most abstract level possible, the commodity and generalized commodity production, and is situated in a two-class self-contained mode of production — in a world in which the characteristic problems of IPE by definition cannot exist. His intention was to move out of this world over a series of volumes which would have dealt with the state and foreign trade and thus with the subject matter of IPE.[3] Of course, this prospectus was never fulfilled and the existing three or four volumes of *Capital* only briefly and inconclusively touch on these issues. By contrast, Marx wrote a great volume of journalism and occasional pieces — with or without Engels — on international affairs but largely on the *Grosspolitik* of the mid-nineteenth century and only marginally on specifically economic international issues.[4] In part, this silence is a product of the age; while tariff policy was a live issue — and one on which Marx held conventional liberal views — the era of competitive capitalism simply did not generate many of the characteristic problems that have concerned mainstream and marxist IPE over the last hundred years. The giant international firm, inter-governmental economic institutions and government attempts to manage in detail the national economy all postdate Marx, as does the later association of capitalism with militarism and imperialism. More to the point, perhaps, Marx wrote at a time when there was in effect only one advanced industrial capitalist country; the spread of the capitalist mode of production was a more pressing concern than inter-capitalist relations.

On the latter subject, 'imperialism' within the usual meaning of the term, Marx has much to say, little of it to the taste of twentieth-century Marxists. His work on India and China[5] clearly supports the extension of capitalism to these parts of the world as a pre-condition of their eventual liberation; while condemning the brutality of imperialism, he defends its historic mission as the unwitting agent of progress, breaking down the barriers of timeless Asiatic despotism. This is, of course, highly controversial in the context of twentieth-century writings on imperialism. Neither Marx's cavalier disregard for indigenous culture ('this undignified, stagnatory, and vegetative life'[6]) nor his optimistic belief that capitalism would develop at speed in India have stood the test of time, and modern Marxist theorists of development have generally declined to build on this aspect of his work — although, as will be argued below, some of the failings of modern dependency theory would have been avoided had they taken more notice of the underlying argument and less of the ethnocentric manner of presentation.

While Marx has much to say on the expansion of capitalism, on the more central areas of IPE his contribution is less easy to identify, and, where it can be discerned, surprises by its conventionality. Marx's understanding of the international system and of domestic sources of foreign policy seems to have been largely disassociated from his understanding of the nature of the capitalist mode of production, and more akin to what would today be characterized as 'realist' thought on these subjects. This is a large claim — too large to be justified within the confines of this chapter — and one body of work will be examined briefly in its support, namely, Marx's account of the Eastern Question and the Crimean War. This war was, of course, highly controversial at the time; it produced one of the first large-scale and popular 'peace movements' and intense debate within the political elite. The Manchester Liberals — Bright, Cobden and others, the representatives of industrial capitalism — were the leaders of this peace movement; in so far as there was a 'war movement' it consisted of Whig and Peelite Grandees and political freebooters such as Disraeli. The majority of the 'great and good' of mid-Victorian England were probably pro-Russian, while genuine pro-Turks were hard to find.

Marx's contribution to this controversy was made in his journalism for the *New York Daily Tribune* and for a variety of English radical papers, as well as in pamphlets, broadsheets and even a short book.[7] It was consistently pro-Turk, anti-Russian and bellicist. At a time when most liberal-minded people saw Palmerston as a warmonger, Marx gave some credence to the view — promoted by a pro-Turk fanatic, Urquart — that he was a Russian agent. Marx lambasts the government for its failure to prosecute the war with vigour and expresses deep contempt for the pacifism of the Manchester School.[8] The reason for this surprising — and, to modern Marxists, embarassing — attitude is clear. Essentially Marx regarded Russia as the most dangerous enemy of the Revolution, a semi-Asiatic country, possibly immune itself to revolutionary change, and thus the natural enemy of all progressives to be opposed in all circumstances and by all means — even at the expense of alliance with Louis Bonaparte, the Sultan of Turkey and domestic British reactionaries. This revolutionary opportunism ought not to pose problems; what is more disturbing is Marx's approach to the formation of foreign policy and the nature of inter-state relations. Although he makes some attempt to demonstrate that war with Russia would be in the economic interests of Britain, this is clearly not the basis on which he believes British policy is made; indeed in a passage which should be placed at the head of much subsequent Marxist writing he makes the point that governments often *invent* economic rationales for policies adopted for non-economic reasons.[9] The capitalist class in Britain does *not* control British foreign policy, greatly to Marx's relief, and those who do have no clear class base on which to draw. Nor can it be said that the international crisis is to be understood in terms of the dynamics of capitalism. The problem as identified by Marx is far simpler; it is a matter of Russian expansionism pure and simple. The Czars' desire to extend their Empire - 'from Dantzic or perhaps Stettin to Trieste' and, albeit for different reasons, both Britain and the Revolution have an interest in resistance.[10] International class forces *do* come into the discussion but not as determinants of either the threat or the response; the fate of both the bourgeoisie and the proletariat in Britain and elsewhere may be determined by the outcome of the crisis but neither class has any degree of control over the course of events, nor indeed a coherent attitude to them.

To expect a simple correlation of class forces and the determinants of foreign policy, or between the needs of international capitalism and the functioning of the international system, would be to put one's faith in a very simple-minded version of Marxism. When Marx examined political issues in detail he was always obliged to produce complex and subtle accounts of the operation of class forces — as in, for example, his accounts of the struggles over the working day in England, or the rise of Bonapartist dictatorship in France.[11] But there is, none the less, a striking contrast between his approach to these 'domestic' issues and his account of the Eastern crisis. In the former cases the end result *is* a class-based account of the course of events with anomalies — such as the apparently independent role of the state bureaucracy in France — accounted for in class terms. The international writings have no such satisfactory outcome; the external policy of the British state and the causes of the crisis in the East seem simply to lie outside the possibilities of class analysis or political economy. What is at issue here is not the 'relative autonomy' of international relations, it is autonomy without qualification.

It would be wrong to leave the impression that all of the international writings of Marx and Engels are similarly devoid of 'Marxism'. Engels in the *Anti-Dühring* and its less well known supplement *The Role of Force in History* offers a much more conventionally 'Marxist' analysis, demonstrating the ways in which what seem to be international political phenomena actually reflect socio-economic forces, and the latter work in particular deserves to be better known for its analysis of Bismarck's 'blood and iron' policy in the light of the increasingly disruptive effect of Germany's industrial development on its internal political structure.[12] However, it must be said that the main message of the founders of Marxism to their successors is the negative point that not everything that happens in the world can be found a suitably materialist explanation. In matters of substance Marx and Engels provided fewer guidelines, and what we nowadays think of as the classical Marxist approach to IPE originates not with Marx and Engels but with the writers who in different circumstances, facing different political problems, were forced to invent solutions to issues of which their illustrious forebears had little conception. It is to these writers we now turn.

The Second International

In the years between 1890 and 1914 Marxist writers were obliged to face a number of problems that had not confronted Marx or Engels, and in meeting this challenge they produced what is still the most impressive body of work in Marxist IPE, the starting point for virtually all later Marxist thought on the subject. Much had changed since the mid-nineteenth century; the nature of capitalism, the nature of the international system and the nature of the relationship between Marxist theory and Marxist practice. While the degree of concentration of industry was minimal by comparison to what was to come, the emergence of 'giant' firms in place of capitalist competition — the rise of 'monopoly capitalism' — was already an issue. Britain's pre-eminence as the 'workshop of the world' had by the late nineteenth century disappeared (though not her financial dominance) and inter-state relations were now unmistakably relations between advanced capitalist societies — and highly competitive and tense at that, with the rise of militarism and imperialism. Perhaps most of important of all in terms of the work produced, Marxist thinkers were now part of an active and successful political movement with, in many countries, mass support and corresponding responsibilities: whereas Marx and Engels could approach the problems of the mid-century with a degree of detatchment, judging events in terms of opportunistic calculations of their revolutionary import, the theorists of the Second International were obliged to be conscious of the direct political consequences of their words and deeds. Marx could see imperialism as a progressive force; Marxists at the turn of the century were obliged to consider the impact of imperialism not simply on abstractions such as 'world history' but on their own supporters and potential supporters at home. And national economic success or failure has an ambiguous quality for the would-be revolutionary who is also a practising politician in a mass party.[13]

For all these reasons the international dimension of capitalism impinged on most of the deliberations of Marxists in this period. Imperialism - which to all Marxists then meant inter-capitalist rivalry in general and not simply the drive for colonies; militarism, the harnessing of the resources of capitalist society, both physical and human, to the expansionist policies of capitalist states; and monopoly, the growth of giant firms, the interlock between financial and industrial power and its consequent influence on state policy, formed a complex of problems that were both political and economic, national and international, theoretical and practical. And this complex equally intersected with the general problems of political strategy raised by the failure of capitalism to develop along the lines envisaged by Marx and crystallized by the debate on 'revisionism' launched by Bernstein in the German Social-Democratic Party in the 1890s. All the theorists of this period responded to these factors, albeit in different ways and with different emphases. Most attention here will be given to the two writers, Luxemburg and Hilferding, representing the best that Marxists had to offer then (or since) and to Lenin, who is less interesting but unavoidable.

Rosa Luxemburg was a Polish Jewess, Reichstag Deputy for the German SPD, leading 'left' theorist of the period and arch opponent of Bernstein's revisionism.[14] Her most important theoretical work is *The Accumulation of Capital,* first published in 1913.[15] This work addresses what was then and is now a serious technical problem arising in Marxist economics out of the 'schemas of reproduction' employed by Marx in volume 2 of *Capital* to demonstrate how a self-contained capitalist economy could produce capital accumulation without interacting with a non-capitalist world. The first two sections of Luxemburg's work demonstrate that this is not possible and dismiss at considerable length those of her predecessors and contemporaries who have attempted to show that it is. Essentially Luxemberg shows that for extended reproduction to be possible in a closed economy capitalists would have to accumulate simply for the purpose of accumulation; she considers this to be irrational — which indeed it may be but is not necessarily relevant since capitalism may indeed be driven by desires which at a macro level make no sense but which are perfectly explicable at the micro level.[16] For the modern reader what is important in Luxemberg's analysis is not so much the detail of her probably mistaken theoretical argument but the resonances of the more empirical third section of her work where the historical conditions of accumulation are examined.

Luxemberg believes that the capitalist mode of production needs to interact with pre-capitalist economic forms if it is to avoid crisis. Whether capitalism actually *needs* a non-capitalist environment may be doubtful but that it *has* actually developed in such an environment cannot be denied and this actuality is the subject matter of the final section of her work. Capitalism has always been obliged to expand and in the process destroy 'natural' and 'peasant' economies by introducing commodity production and forcing the non-capitalist world into a trading system dominated by capitalism. Luxemburg's account of the destruction of pre-capitalist economic forms, the elimination of rural industries, the penetration of the hinterland by railway construction and loans for 'development' is brilliantly realised. As capitalism develops, new capitalist centres emerge; the capitalist frontier with the pre-capitalist world is pushed further back and increasingly becomes the location of fierce inter-capitalist rivalry; imperialism and militarism are the product of this intensified competition. They are phenomena associated with capitalism throughout its history but take on a new significance as the frontier era gradually comes to a close. Since for Luxemburg the expansion of capitalism is a precondition of its survival, capitalist countries are not simply competing for commercial advantage but for life itself. Luxemburg believes, in any event, that their struggles are doomed to failure; eventually the possibility of further expansion will disappear and the contradictions of capitalism will finally bring about its collapse — the choice is 'socialism or barbarism', the rational reconstruction of society or a collapse into war and savagery.[17] Inter-imperialist co-operation is, by definition, impossible: this is a zero-sum game with the reward for success slowly disappearing. Reformism is as hopeless a cause as capitalism itself; only revolution can 'solve' the problem and the conditions for revolution are being created by the very policies designed to avert the final crisis — however much appearances may suggest the contrary.

The Accumulation of Capital was not well received by Luxemburg's contemporaries. In part this reflected her controversial political persona; too serious about the revolution for the majority of her increasingly respectable SPD colleagues, too serious about democracy for the eventually successful Bolshevik revolutionaries. Also her work downplayed some of the most popular current themes such as the rise of monopoly and the importance of the banks. Even later, although her ideas on democracy have proved important to non-Soviet Marxists and her personality retains its attractiveness, her economic ideas have struck chords only with a few radical Keynesian economists.[18] None the less, Luxemburg has had influence, albeit indirect and often unacknowledged; her insistence that capitalism has always and necessarly expanded and imposed itself on the non-capitalist world, destroying pre-capitalist economic forms and creating a capitalist world-economy, finds obvious echoes in the work of the later 'dependency' school. Her lack of intellectual contact with the majority of her contemporaries has done her no damage as their concerns have passed into history, and as the first major Marxist theorist to focus specifically on the impact of 'cores' on 'peripheries' she must be granted an important place in the history of Marxist political economy.

In contrast to Luxemburg, Rudolph Hilferding was a more orthodox and mainstream Austrian social democrat, later to become a leader of the German SDP and Finance Minister in the Weimar Republic. His *Finance Capital: A Study of the Latest Phase of Capitalist Development* became on publication in 1910 the most influential contemporary work of Marxist political economy and, via Lenin's popularization of its major themes, its influence continues to the present day.[19] While Luxemburg accepted the essential framework of *Capital,* Hilferding engaged in a wholesale revision of Marx's formulations to take account of the changes that had taken place since the 1860s. These he saw as the concentration of industry ('monopoly' — although not as defined by 'bourgeois' writers), changes in the pattern of ownership with the rise of the joint-stock company, and a changing role for the banks, creating together a new form of capitalism, a fusion of industrial and financial capital, that is, finance capital. Quite possibly Hilferding over-estimated the importance of these changes and over-generalized on the basis of specifically German experience, but his insistence that a new understanding of the laws of motion of capitalism was called for, and the categories he created for this task, remains relevant. Of particular importance to IPE is his realization that changes in the nature of capitalism require a new understanding of the relationship between capital and state. Whereas under competitive capitalism the 'national' economy is difficult to conceptualize, it now becomes the crucial notion of political economy.

The key difference between competitive capital and finance capital is that finance capital has an economic policy in a sense that competitive capital does not. Under competitive conditions capitalism opposes state intervention; finance capital — 'the unification of capital' — requires the state to perform a positive role on its behalf if the advantages of concentration are to be realised.[20] Cartellization and the formation of monopolies take place on a national basis; it is assumed that no monopoly could be strong enough to dominate the world market and thus capitalism as an international phenomenon consists of a series of national capitals. Each national concentration of capital requires a 'national economic territory' within which it can gain the benefits of monopoly pricing. This requirement generates two policy imperatives; first, the national economic territory must be defended from other outside concentrations of capital, and thus protective tariffs are the basis of commercial policy. Second, the national economic territory must be expanded to keep pace with the rate of capital accumulation, and thus imperialism is the 'foreign policy of finance capital'.[21] The international system reflects these imperatives and is the stage for confrontation between national capitals; international competition follows from the national basis of economic organization.

A central feature of Hilferding's analysis is the importance he places on the export of capital. Protective tariffs lessen competition and thereby restrict the growth of productivity which in turn leads to falling rates of profit — or so Hilferding believed — and the export of capital to take advantage of higher rates of profit elsewhere is thus a prime feature of finance capital. It is worth noting that this is not simply a matter of transfers of capital between developed and less developed areas within the national economic territory. Capital export takes place in the form of both interest-bearing loans and profit-yielding capital and can be the means to penetrate the national economic territory of other capitals.[22] Hilferding is not simply envisaging the export of capital as a weapon of imperialist foreign policy; he anticipates the eventual internationalization of capital, even if for the time being capital export is best seen as a means of expanding the national territory. Hilferding's stress on capital export is not at the expense of the importance of trade — indeed the need to export capital is partly created by trade policy — and this aspect of the foreign policy of finance capital is less prominent in his work than in Lenin's popularization, but in assigning to the phenomenon the importance he does, he radically shifts the emphasis of Marxist IPE and, indirectly, prepares the way for the later debate on the internationalization of capital.

It would be difficult to exaggerate the importance of *Finance Capital,* even though most of its central ideas have survived largely through the medium of the Russian Bolshevik writers, Bukharin and Lenin. Hilferding's work became almost immediately the orthodox economics text of Marxist parties before the First World War and has been the starting point for most subsequent Marxist

IPE. The contribution of Lenin and Bukharin can only be judged in the light of Hilferding's work, and the best way to approach these texts is by highlighting the differences between them and *Finance Capital*.[23]

The most important difference, of course, concerns the changes in the world that took place between 1910 and 1916-17, the date of composition of the Bolshevik works. The outbreak of the First World War and the collapse of the putative unity of the international working-class movement largely account for the shift from theory to polemic; Lenin's pamphlet is a direct political intervention designed to attack the 'renegades' of 1914 (including Hilferding) and to exploit the opportunities for revolution created by the imperialist war. Much of the intellectual content of this intervention is devoted to demonstrating the inevitability of war under monopoly capitalism. This is a question on which Hilferding is somewhat ambiguous: he seems to have felt that inter-imperialist conflict was for the time being inevitable but there is nothing in *Finance Capital* to suggest that war — actual armed conflict — is inevitable. If Hilferding is unclear on this issue, Karl Kautsky, the leading theoretician of German social democracy, in a series of articles entitled 'Ultra-Imperialism' published just before the outbreak of war, argues that a combination of imperial powers is a possibility if not a probability. His point is that while there is clearly a contradiction between the interests of the imperial powers there is equally an even more fundamental contradiction between capitalist and non-capitalist classes on a world scale, and there is no reason to assume that the former and lesser contradiction will always prevent different finance capitals from realising their common interest in the preservation of the system. On this basis the First World War — though the product of imperialist rivalries — was the product of contingent forces rather than historical inevitability. It is this argument that Lenin is most concerned to undermine.[24]

In so doing, he introduces a formulation that is still of great relevance, the notion of 'uneven development'. Although competing national finance capitals (monopoly capitals in Lenin's terms) may attempt to reach agreements on spheres of influence, such agreements can never be more than temporary expedients. Capitalism develops at different rates in different countries; agreements on spheres of interest reflect the balance of forces of the moment and since this balance is subject to continual change such agreements can never last. Those advantaged by a particular balance of forces will defend their advantage and refuse to surrender without a fight, and thus imperialism means inevitable war. Although the suggestion that changes in the balance of forces can only be ratified by war seems to owe more to a Clausewitzian conception of the international system than to a class/economic structure starting point, and although the subsequent history of inter-capitalist relations, certainly since the Second World War, seems to give more support to Kautsky than to Lenin, the latter's 'law' is firmly established in the vocabulary of much subsequent Marxist writing.[25]

If the law of uneven development does constitute a genuine, if not unproblematic, theoretical advance, much of the rest of Lenin's pamphlet represents a coarsening of Hilferding's original theory, a source of confusion and of dogmatism. The title of *Imperialism: Highest Stage of Capitalism* is itself a source of confusion and dogmatism. On the one hand, the identification of imperialism with a *stage* of capitalism is confusing; confusion already existed between the 'bourgeois' notion of imperialism as the drive to acquire colonies, and the orthodox Marxist notion of imperialism as a general description of the foreign policy of finance capitalism; to this is added the conflation of a policy and the source of that policy. More damaging has been Lenin's dogmatism, symbolically reflected in his choice of adjective — *highest* stage rather than Hilferding's *latest* phase — and in his brutal abuse of political opponents, especially, but not exclusively, the 'arch-renegade' Kautsky. These qualities would be of little significance had it not been for Lenin's undoubted talents as a revolutionary. The success of the October Revolution in Russia and the talismanic status attributed to Lenin as a consequence have given his work an intellectual standing far beyond its merits and done great harm to Soviet IPE.[26]

Before turning to modern Marxist IPE, it may be helpful to come to some sort of brief assessment of the emerging pre-1914 orthodoxy. First, as indicated above, it has to be said that the theorists of finance capital were running some way ahead of the actual state of capitalism at the time. Concentration of industry was in most countries still at an early stage and the role of banks was nowhere near as important as advertised. Even in Imperial Germany the degree of control of finance capital was greatly exaggerated. In the most important financial centre of the time, Britain, the link between financial and industrial capital was tenuous to non-existent. Second, the Marxist attempt to explain both colonial expansion and great power politics in terms of the driving force of finance capital cannot be accepted as it stands. The events leading up to the First World War require a multi-faceted explanation with at least some reference to security needs of the great powers, the autonomous dynamic of the international system and the quality of diplomacy and individual decision-making. The importance of socio-economic forces would be widely acknowledged by non-Marxist historians, and of contemporary work Marxist analysis has stood the test of time better than its rivals, but even in the hands of as sophisticated a writer as Hilferding Marxist theory is being asked to bear too great a burden. Third, and irrespective of the quality of the work, the desire of some (most) subsequent Marxists to draw on the theories of this period pays too little attention to the great changes that have taken place in the course of the last seventy years — some of them at least attributable to the political success of Lenin and the Bolsheviks.

Development and underdevelopment

For a generation after the Russian Revolution Marxist IPE meant Marxism-Leninism as purveyed by the propogandists of the Communist International, and consisted largely of restatements of the essential ideas of Lenin, adapted to political realities defined by Stalin. Original Marxist work was produced in this period but largely in the realms of political theory, philosophy and historiography. Even those Marxists most hostile to Stalinism accepted the broad lines of Lenin's work on imperialism, the inevitability of capitalist rivalry and the dominance of monopoly capitalism.[27]

When the straitjacket of orthodox Marxism-Leninism finally came apart it was in a new, and rather surprising, context — the problems of development and underdevelopment. For Marx and Engels and for their immediate successors the issue of development was not of prime importance. The focus of their work was 'metropolitan'; although the work of Hilferding, Lenin and Luxemburg is often summarized as the 'Marxist theory of imperialism' their understanding of that term was only marginally concerned with the problems of the 'less developed countries' (LDCs). What made the new emphasis on development even more surprising was the assumption of the new school of thought that capitalism constituted a positive block to the development of LDCs. This was a genuinely new perspective; all Marxist theorists up to the 1940s assumed more or less as a matter of course that capitalism would perform its historic role of developing the means of production in the non-industrial world. It was on this basis that Marx could regard British rule in India as the agent of progress and Lenin and Luxemburg could see capitalist domination of the periphery as simply a temporary respite in the inexorable movement towards capitalist crisis. Of course, as a matter of *fact,* it was clear that the colonies were *not* developing rapidly into advanced capitalist societies, but it would not have occurred to the classical theorists that this might be the result of in-built deficiences in the capitalist mode of production such that it becomes, in the periphery, a stumbling block on the path to development. On the contrary, in so far as this problem was addressed, it was seen as a sign of the incomplete penetration of pre-capitalist economic forms by capitalism, or as a distortion created by *political* forces such as colonialism — an attitude not far removed from the mainstream 'bourgeois' approach to 'modernization', and, perhaps, with a common intellectual origin in the Victorian notion of progress.[28]

The break with this attitude begins with Paul Baran's *Political Economy of Growth,* published in 1957.[29] This introduced a number of notions that would be the backbone of later 'dependency' theory, and which directly contradict classical Marxist formulations. First, Baran introduced the idea that developed *countries* exploit underdeveloped *countries,* whereas in classical accounts exploitation is something capitalists do, for Baran the working class of developed countries can benefit from imperialism, in the form of, for example, increased employment opportunities.[30] Second, he offers an account of the origins of underdevelopment that is highly unorthodox; he stresses the role of trade between developed and underdeveloped countries as a mechanism for transferring 'surplus' — a term of art for Baran not quite corresponding with surplus product — from the latter to the former. Third, and less controversially in Marxist terms, he stresses the role of class structure in LDC's as a hinderance to growth, in particular the failure of an industrial capitalist class to displace in importance the mercantile interests which grow out of trade with the capitalist centre along with the continuation of agricultural class interests inimical to growth.[31]

These ideas had only a limited impact on Marxist thought in the developed world but created more resonances in the 'South'. Already in the 1950s a distinctive school of development economics had emerged in Latin America around Raul Presbisch and his colleagues in the UN's Economic Commission for Latin America (ECLA); their approach to development — often summarized as 'import-substitution industrialization' (ISI) — was quasi-Marxist in origin and shared Baran's conception of the damage done to LDC's by unregulated trade with the developed capitalist world. Their remedy, ISI, involved no break with the capitalist mode of production, but, on the contrary, a policy designed to create a 'national' capitalist economy on the basis of government support for local industry and the exclusion of foreign competition. However, when in the early 1960s it became clear that ISI was not a conspicuous success, its successor as the prevailing development orthodoxy in Latin America was more radical in its approach to links between the developing and developed world and towards the efficacy of capitalism, whether 'nation' or global. This approach can be encapsulated by the generic term 'dependency theory'.[32]

Of the many variants of 'dependency' the two most influential have been Andre Gunder Frank's analysis of the 'Development of Underdevelopment' and Immanuel Wallerstein's studies of the 'Modern World System'. Frank is heavily influenced by Baran; much of his originality lies in his capacity to produce detailed case studies of the ways in which close contact between centre and periphery has worked to the disadvantage of the latter. Contrary to both Marxist and mainstream orthodoxy, he argues that the periphery is capitalist and has been since first integrated into a trading relationship with the centre; the solution to the problems of the periphery is not to develop a national capitalist economy but to break the 'chain of exploitation' that links the metropolitan centre with its periphery satellites. The centre exploits the periphery through 'unequal exchange' in the trading system — on which see below — and it confirms its exploitation by its support for indigenous social class collaborators representing those sections of the local bourgeoisie whose interests are tied to links with the centre. Thus, capitalism has 'underdeveloped' the periphery; Frank uses this term as a verb and contrasts the underdevelopment created by capitalism with the original 'undeveloped' state of the 'Third World'.[33]

Wallerstein accepts many of the Frankian notions of dependency, but situates them on a wider canvas; when completed, his *magnum opus,* the *Modern World System,* will constitute nothing less than a history of capitalism in all its manifestations.[34] The first two volumes are an impressive achievement in which he demonstrates the emergence of a three-tiered structure to the capitalist world economy in the sixteenth century — core, periphery and sem-periphery. These three tiers correspond to different positions in the international division of labour, are characterized by different forms of political authority and social relations of production, and have persisted — with different countries occupying the roles — since the sixteenth century. The structure is preserved by a two-faceted mode of domination by the core, economically via unequal exchange, politically via imperialism. Within the core, states compete for hegemony, control of the system generated by a central position within the structure; such hegemonic positions are only rarely and briefly achieved and are characterized by financial and industrial supremacy and a commitment to the idealogy of free trade - since the sixteenth century only the Netherlands, Britain and the United States have achieved this dominance in the seventeenth, nineteenth and mid-twentieth centuries respectively. Wallerstein is unusual among Marxist scholars in that he is prepared to attribute a high level of 'relative autonomy' to the international political system: although the real contest is based on financial and productive capacity, and although underlying all conflicts is the world-wide struggle of 'systemic' and 'anti-systemic' forces, in practice much of international politics is based on power politics as conventionally understood in the discipline of international relations.[35]

There are many other writers who form part of the dependency school broadly defined, and in particular the Egyptian scholar Samir Amin has made an important and distinctive contribution, but within the scope of this chapter, Frank and Wallerstein can be taken as the most influential.[36] However, before proceeding to a brief critique of their ideas one further writer should be considered — Arghiri Emmanuel. All dependency theorists rest much of their case on the notion of 'unequal exchange' and yet few define precisely what they mean by this elusive concept. While it is easy to see that exchange between developed and underdeveloped countries has sometimes been characterized by fraud and deceit and palpably unfair bargains, it is more difficult to see how inequality can be a *structural* feature of trading relations — and Marxist notions of exchange relations have usually assumed that commodities exchange at their average value and that profit for capitalists (surplus value) is achieved elsewhere, in the production process.[37] All dependency theorists reject this but only Emmanuel, in *Unequal Exchange,* gives a theoretically sophisticated reason for so doing. His argument is based on wages as the key independent variable. Wages are determined by the *historically determined* minimum subsistence level of the country in question, and thus are higher in some countries than in others. Since, he argues, the price at which products enter the market is largely determined by wage levels, exchanges between high-wage countries and low-wage countries work to the benefit of the former. Even under free trade, unequal exchange is the norm between developed and less-developed countries.[38]

How is the dependency school to be assessed? From a Marxist perspective it is, of course, so unorthodox as to be only tenuously connected to the work of the classics. As, among others, Brenner and Laclau have pointed out, the very definition of capitalism employed by Frank and Wallerstein — with its emphasis on relations of exchange rather than of production — is un-Marxist and Warren correctly highlights the gap between Marx's conception of the progressive nature of capitalism and the 'romantic' anti-capitalism of the dependency school.[39] However, Marxism is not, or should not be, a static mode of thought and modern scholars inspired by Marx are entitled to branch off in new directions. The key question is whether the new direction constitutes a through road or a cul-de-sac, and the drift away from dependency formulations in the late 1970s and 1980s suggests the latter. The essential point is that dependency theorists underestimate the extent to which capitalist development actually has taken place in the LDCs, devaluing such trends by the formula 'dependent development'[40] and thereby setting up a goal that is unattainable in the modern world, a truly independent national political economy. *All* capitalist economies in the contemporary system are interdependent, and although the capacity to control ones destiny does vary, the variation is a function of factors that are unsurprising and require little in the way of sophisticated theory to understand. Thus, large rich economies are more likely to be able to exercise a degree of autonomy than small poor economies. From a classical Marxist perspective the term 'economies' is, of course, unsatisfactory in so far as it implies a unity of interests of competing classes, but this is precisely the problem with much dependency literature — its assumption that exploitation takes place on a national basis.

In the 1960s there were good reasons to believe the structural blocks to development existed in much of the South, and it was not unreasonable to argue that integration in the capitalist world economy was disadvantageous. From the perspective of the late 1980's the picture is much less clear. A number of LDCs — the newly industrializing countries (NICs) — have made great strides over the last two decades and the shift of manufacturing industry to the South seems likely to continue and intensify. No one would argue that this has been a pleasant, trouble-free process; many of the NICs are authoritarian, repressive regimes, and real living standards remain low; equally a large part of the cost of this development has been carried by the unemployed of the North. Moreover, many Southern countries remain untouched by the growth that has taken place and these 'least-developed countries' seem unlikely to attract the interest of capital in the foreseeable future, while others have indeed suffered from declining raw material prices. The point is not to argue that this is a satisfactory or desirable state of affairs but to stress that the real-world problems of the South seem somewhat removed from those identified by dependency theory. The impact of the capitalist world economy varies from case to case and seems to be determined less by global trends than by the specific situation of individual economies.[41]

Whatever the weaknesses of dependency as an overall perspective, the value of many of the case studies generated by the theory cannot be denied, and equally the political success of this unorthodox brand of Marxism should not be underestimated. Demands for a New International Economic Order in the 1970s owed much to the thinking of dependency theory — although, admittedly, it was the non-Marxist *dependendistas* who had the most influence — and Southern views on international relations remain conditioned by some aspects of the approach. At the same time, this political success is itself an indication of some of the weaknesses of the approach; the readiness with which some ruling groups in the South have adopted its perspectives gives credence to Warren's description of dependency theory as a species of nationalist mythology.[42] Of course, this is most unfair to the majority of dependency writers who intended their work to undermine the hold of such groups, but it indicates the political dangers inherent in an approach that can all too easily be distorted into a justification for blaming foreigners for everything that goes wrong. The strength of a more conventional class-based approach to the problems of the LDCs is that this 'get-out' is not available to Southern ruling classes — which is not to deny that sometimes the problems of Southern countries *are* attributable to foreign interests. Unfortunately, by overstating the case and confusing the argument dependency theorists have made it more difficult to identify when the world economy as opposed to local policy decisions is the crucial factor in poor economic performance.

Contemporary Marxist International Political Economy

For all its failings, the dependency approach has generated a coherent school of Marxist analysis; other recent Marxist work in IPE is less easy to categorize, more diffuse in style and approach. In part this is a function of the virtual collapse of official Marxism-Leninism in the West after the traumas of the 1950s, and its replacement in Marxist thought by a number of approaches linked to small splinter groups, often of Trotskyist leanings, where they exist, have little direct impact on their work. Thus it is that some of the most successful attempts to apply Marxist categories to IPE have come from more or less isolated individual scholars; examples which come to mind are Fred Block's *The Origins of International Economic Disorder* on post-war American monetary policy, and Bill Warren's *Imperialism: Pioneer of Capitalism,* a defence of orthodox Marxist approaches to development.[43] However, a degree of coherence can be found in recent Marxist writing, not so much in terms of schools of thought but in so far as particular sets of common problems can be identified. The most important cluster of problems concerns the issue of the internationalization of capital and its putative consequences and most of this section will be devoted to the debate this issue has generated.

To understand the nature of the controversy it is necessary to revisit briefly the Leninist position on imperialism. It will be recalled that at the heart of Lenin's theory of imperialism lies the absolute impossibility of inter-imperialist unity. A major objective of his pamphlet is to assault Kautsky's belief that 'ultra-imperialism' is a possibility; the central 'contradiction' of monopoly capitalism is created by the law of uneven development and entails the certainty of inter-imperialist rivalry. Clearly this *a priori* position is not easy to sustain in the face of the economic history of the world since the Second World War; apparently the major capitalist countries have been able so to order their relations that co-operation is not just a theoretical possibility but a working reality. For all the stresses and strains that have occured, especially in the recessions of the 1970s and 1980s, the fact remains that the central institutional framework within which co-operation occurs — the OECD, the IMF, the GATT — has survived, while political co-operation in a system of alliances centred on the United States has resisted the centrifugal forces that might have been expected to pull it apart. How is this to be explained?

One possibility is that we are dealing here with a temporary state of affairs produced, on the one hand, by fear of the Soviet Union, and, on the other, by the peculiar set of circumstances that produced American dominance in the immediate post-war years. Because of the destruction of the European and Japanese economies in the war the United States had the unparalleled opportunity to reconstruct the world in its own interests, with the co-operation, *faute de mieux,* of its natural competitors; an Atlantic ruling class emerged, dominated by American capital.[44] As the European and Japanese economies recovered, partly with the assistance of American capital — a nice illustration of the contradictions of capitalism — so inter-capitalist rivalries re-emerge, damped down perhaps by a common fear of the socialist countries and the conservative influence of the institutional framework created during the brief period of American dominance but eventually destined to become once again the central feature of monopoly capitalism. In *Europe versus America,* and *Late Capitalism,* the leading Trotskyite writer, Ernest Mandel adopts basically this approach, while the main lines of the story — if not the potentially apocalyptic ending — are, of course, commonplace in most studies of the post-war political economy, whether Marxist or not.[45]

Although some elements of this approach are common to most commentators, a second, related but distinct, possibility exists, namely that something rather more fundamental has happened to capitalism in the last forty years, and the assumption of national capitals as inherently in competition must be abandoned. This is the putative 'internationalization of capital'. The clearest statement of the issues involved can be found in two seminal papers published in the early 1970s but still constituting the best point of entry to the debate. Stephen Hymer's 'The Multinational Corporation and the Law of Uneven Development' is an excellent account of the rise and future significance of multinationals from a Marxist standpoint, while Robin Murray's 'The Internationalisation of Capital and the Nation State' examines the failure of the modern state to fulfil the political needs of international firms.[46]

Hymer sees the development of the system in terms of two 'laws', of increasing firm size and of uneven development, the latter of which he takes to be the tendency of the system to create poverty as well as wealth. The former law has produced the multinational corporation; initially this was an American phenomenon but Europe and Japan are catching up and after a period of competition a state of oligopolistic equilibrium will be reached. Uneven development ensures that the resultant international division of labour will produce a hierarchical distribution of skills, technology wealth and power, with geographical regions corresponding to the internal divisions of the firms: 'it would tend to centralise high-level decision making occupations in a few key cities in the advanced countries, surrounded by a number of regional sub-capitals and confine the rest of the world to lower levels of activity and income i.e. to the status of towns and villages in a new imperial system'.[47] This has some resemblance to the dependency argument, but for Hymer this new system is based on material relations of exchange, classes rather than countries, and constitutes 'progress' in so far as it provides the eventual basis for the emergence of a truly cosmopolitan production system capable of completing the destiny of capitalism - the 'conquest of the material world'.[48]

One of the issues addressed by Hymer is the emerging gap between the desire of national governments to manage their economy and the internationalization of key economic decisions. Murray takes this point further, outlining the 'state functions' historically performed for capital and stressing the extent to which they rely on the territorial coincidence of capital and the state. Capital is no longer national in this sense, and the extension of capital beyond the bounds of its geographical origin is producing a mismatch between the needs of capital and the ability of any state to meet these needs. Economic interdependence is breaking the link between capital and the state and in general weakening the state as an institution — an unstable situation in the interests of neither 'national' nor international capital.

It is possible to argue that both Hymer and Murray overstate their cases, and in some respect the passage of time has gone against details of their argument — for example, Hymer's belief that the West would not allow the development of manufacturing capacity in the periphery discounts the emergence of the NICs.[49] However, the prediction, common to both writers, that economic management would prove more difficult in the future because of internationalization seems justified by the facts, even if the strength of Warren's riposte to Murray to the effect that current trends have increased the power of the state alongside the internationalization of capital is acknowledged.[50] In terms of the unity of capital versus inter-capitalist rivalry Hymer's belief in the emergence of 'oligopolistic equilibrium' seems a helpful formulation, and the recognition that when Marxists talk of monopoly they usually mean oligopoly is to be applauded. Of course, neither writer assumed that relations between capitals with different national bases would be trouble free and easily co-operative; in any particular situation conflict might be intense and in any event problems will always exist. The theoretical advance made by the debate is that the assumption that there is a built-in structural imperative towards rivalry, conflict, even war, has been abandoned.

One effect of this movement has been to blur the hitherto clear distinction between Marxist and non-Marxist writings on IPE. Those scholars who retain Leninist formulations — such as Mandel and the American 'Monthly Review' School — can clearly be distinguished from 'bourgeois' scholars, but much other Marxist writing over the last ten years has entered the mainstream of IPE — to mutual profit. Differences clearly remain between Marxists and non-Marxists but these differences are more likely to be apparent in terms of the values writers bring to the subject — and the distinctive terminology employed — than in terms of a set of ideas peculiar to Marxists. The work of, say, Brett on international monetary relations and the history of the post-war world economy, or of Harris on the political economy of the Third World, is clearly Marxist in terms of the values espoused, but many of the theoretical categories employed are simply part of the common currency of international political economists.[51]

In part this may reflect a lessening of the distinctiveness of Marxist writings, but it also reflects changes in the mainstream, a willingness on the part of conventional political economists to give more weight to some of the traditional concerns of Marxists. The failure of the monetary arrangements of Bretton Woods after 1971, the impact of successive oil crises, the ending of the post-war boom and the re-emergence of deep recessions have undermined some of the more optimistic assumptions about the world economy current in the 1960s; scholars in the mainstream are now more willing to give an ear to perspectives previously associated with Marxists. IPE examines the political structure of the world economy and combats those who insist on a purely economic analysis of international trade and money, a failing of which only the most 'vulgar' of Marxists can be accused. Scholars as diverse in approach as Keohane and Strange have acknowledged the strength of Marxist analysis and incorporated some of its insights into their work.[52]

Another aspect of the increasing openness to Marxist ideas has been the emergence of the so-called 'critical' school of international theory. The work of Cox, Alker and Biersteker, Ashley, MacLean and others is designed to constitute an ideological challenge to dominant realist, neo-realist and behavioural modes of international theory, and to restate the importance of class and economic forces in the make-up of the international order.[53] The first three authors cited above seem somewhat reluctant to place much stress on the Marxist roots of their work, preferring to use terms such as 'dialectics' and to cite authorities such as Vico or Gramsci — an unorthodox Marxist — rather than Marx or Lenin, but in practice much of what they have to say derives from Leninist and dependency approaches to the international system. Interestingly, this school of thought seems more concerned to engage in debate with non-Marxist international theorists than with the current literature of Marxist IPE. Thus the Alker and Biersteker's article refered to above examines IR reading lists of major American scholars, finding that 'Radical/Marxist

Dialectical Approaches' are underrepresented, but their account of what would be representative of such an approach is highly conventional and limited to the standard Leninist and dependency texts. Although critical theorists engage with the mainstream on such issues as the nature of 'hegemony' — employing Gramscian notions — their interest in the more down-to-earth issues of political economy is limited. In so far as it gives the impression that what Marxism has to offer is new variants of Grand Theory this is regrettable; it gives a misleading sense of what Marxist analysts actually do well, which is to use theory in a much less elevated manner, staying in touch with real-world problems while identifying their material and class roots.

Conclusion

This survey of Marxist writings on IPE makes no claim to be exhaustive or to do anything more than identify some particular schools of thought and areas of common concern. This being so, no startling conclusions are to be expected. However, one or two generalizations can be made about the body of Marxist theorizing on this subject.

In the first place it must be said that in the late 1980s it is less easy to identify a distinctively Marxist approach to IPE than it would have been thirty, twenty or even ten years ago. The distinctiveness of Marxist work has lessened under the pressure of two factors — the increasingly irrelevant nature of orthodox Leninist theorizing, on the one hand, and the increasing willingness of mainstream writers to acknowledge the importance of class and the mode of production, on the other. It is now part of the received wisdom of IPE that economic arrangements reflect political forces and vice versa; virtually no modern writers would approach the international economic system as though it were comprehensible in purely technical economic terms and few would wish to deny the role of class forces in determining national economic goals or the distribution of welfare gains created by the system. In a sense we are all Marxists now.

In another sense, of course, this is quite wrong. The second point to be made about modern Marxist IPE is that what does distinguish it from conventional work is its normative base. Marxism has a different and distinctive set of values to offer from the mainstream and the application of these values to concrete situations may be the most constructive contribution Marxists can make to IPE. The point here is not so much that Marxism is on 'the left', radical, critical, progressive or whatever, but that the radicalism of Marxism is distintively different from what generally passes for radicalism in IPE. Too often the latter takes the form either of a guilt-ridden utopianism on the part of Western elite members, or of an anti-capitalist but essentially conservative rhetoric on the part of Southern elite members. In each case industrial society and international economic interdependence are rejected in the name of 'liberation' but in the process all the hard choices faced by national societies attempting to assert autonomy are swept aside. Marxism at its best destroys such illusions. Marxists from Marx and Hilferding to Hymer and Warren have approached the world in a spirit that denies the existence of easy options; even if this sometimes involves a tone of voice that is not attractive, as in Marx's writings on India, or Warren's apparent dismissal of many of the real problems faced by developing countries. Marxist writers informed by the classical Marxist sensibility affirm capitalism as an ultimately liberating force and look to the emergence of a truly cosmopolitan production system, all the while remaining conscious of the inequities and injustice characteristic of the modern world economy.[54] This complex of values is refreshingly different from much conventional writing on the IPE — and indeed from much quasi-Marxist writing — and it may be the most important and lasting contribution that Marxism has to make to the subject.

Notes and references

1. What is missing here, of course, is extensive consideration of Soviet IPE. Most such work seems of poor quality, but this may simply reflect the ignorance of the present author. V. Kulbalkova and A.A. Cruickshank, *Marxism-Leninism and the Theory of International Relations* (London: Routledge and Kegan Paul, 1980) is the best Western overview of Soviet work. S. Brucan, *The Dialectics of World Politics* (New York: Free Press, 1978) is a Romanian synthesis of Leninist and some Western motions of world politics.
2. Studies of Marx are legion. Some works the author has found particularly valuable are: D.T. McLellan, *Karl Marx: His Life and Thought* (London: Macmillan, 1973); G. Cohen, *Karl Marx's Theory of History: A Defence* Oxford: Oxford University Press, 1978); and M.C. Howard and J.E. King, *The Political Economy of Marx* (Harlow: Longman, 1975).
3. For Marx's plan see McLellan, *Marx: His Life and Thought,* p. 293.
4. The only full scale study of this work is M. Molnar, *Marx, Engels et la politique internationale,* (Paris: Gallimard, 1975)
5. A wide selection of these writings is collected in S. Avineri (ed.), *Karl Marx on Colonialism and Modernisation*. New York: Anchor Books, 1969). The most important articles are conveniently included in D. Fernback (ed.) *Surveys from Exile* (Harmondsworth: Penguin Books, 1973).
6. 'The British Rule in India', cited in Fernback, *Surveys,* p. 306.
7. See *Marx/Engels Collected Works (MECW),* Vols 12 and 13 (Moscow: Progress Publishers, Moscow,1979 and 1980). A comprehensive selection of this journalism collected by Marx's daughter and son-in-law is Karl Marx, *The Eastern Question* 1897 ed. E. Marx Aveling and E. Aveling. (London: Cass Reprint of Economic Classics, 1969), and the longer pieces are to be found in Karl Marx, *The Secret Diplomatic History of the Eighteenth Century* and *The Story of the Life of Lord Palmeston,* ed. L. Hutchinson, (London: Lawrence and Wishart, 1969).
8. 'the hypocritical, phrase mongering, squint-eyed set of Manchester humbugs'; *MECW* Vol. 12, p. 437.
9. 'there devolved on the cabinet ... the *onus* of inventing mercantilist *pretexts,* however futile, for their measures of foreign policy'; Marx *Secret Diplomatic History,* pp. 91 ff.
10. Marx's 'Iron Curtain' article, 'The Real Issue in Turkey', *MECW,* Vol 12, pp. 13-17 was actually written by Engels for Marx to submit to the *New York Daily Tribune.*
11. See Karl Marx, *Capital,* Vol. 1 (Harmondsworth: Penguin, 1976), Ch. 10; and 'The Eighteenth Brumaire of Louis Bonaparte' in Fernbach *Surveys,* pp. 143-250.
12. F. Engels *Anti-Dühring* (Moscow: Progress Publishers, 1975); *idem, The Role of Force in History,* ed. E. Wangerman (London: Lawrence and Wishart, 1968).
13. For general studies for the period of the Second International, see L. Kolakowski, *Main Currents of Marxism, Vol. 2: The Golden Age* (Oxford: Oxford University Press, 1978); and D.T. McLellan, *Marxism After Marx,* (London: Macmillan, 1979). There are a great many studies of Marxist theories of imperialism which give accounts of the work of Hilferding, Luxemburg, Kautsky and Lenin, for example: C.A. Barone, *Marxist Thought on Imperialism* (London: Macmillan, 1985); M. Barratt Brown, *The Economics of Imperialism* (Harmondsworth: Penguin 1974); B.J. Cohen, *The Question of Imperialism* (London: Macmillan, 1974); W.J. Mommsen, *Theories of Imperialism* (New York: Random House, 1980); T. Kempt, *Theories of Imperialism* (London: Dobson, 1967); and, most useful in terms both of his scope and the quality of analysis, A. Brewer, *Marxist Theories of Imperialism* (London: Routledge and Kegan Paul, 1980).
14. See N. Geras, *The Legacy of Rosa Luxemburg* (London: New Left Books, 1976), and R. Luxemburg, *Selected Political Writings,* (ed.) D. Howard (New York: Monthly Review Press, 1971).
15. R. Luxemburg, *The Accumulation of Capital,* ed. J. Robinson London: Routledge and

Kegan Paul, 1963.)

16. For a survey of the problem of capital accumulation, see Howard and King, *Political Economy of Marx,* Chapters 6 and 7; Brewer, *Marxist Theories of Imperialism,* Chapter 3 exposes the weakness of Luxemburg's version of 'underconsumptionism'.
17. See 'The Crisis in German Social Democracy' *op. cit.* p. 334.
18. Luxemburg's answer to her critics was *The Accumulation of Capital: An Anti Critique* published with Bukharin's critique *Imperialism and the Accumulation of Capital* (New York: Monthly Review Press, 1972). Robinson's introduction to the *Accumulation of Capital* traces the link with Keynesianism.
19. R. Hilferding, *Finance Capital: A Study of the Latest Phase of Capitalist Developments,* ed. Tom Bottomore, (London: RKP, 1981). The best source for the context of Hilferding's work is T. Bottomore and P. Goode (eds), *Austro-Marxism* (Oxford: Oxford University Press, 1978).
20. Part V of Hilferding, *Finance Capital* is titled 'The Economic Policy of Finance Capital'. Of course competitive capitalism was never consistently laissez-faire, as Hilferding acknowledges (pp. 301).
21. As Brewer, *Marxist Theories of Imperialism,* remarks, Hilferding uses the term 'Imperialism' only on occasion and generally as a reflection of current political debate rather than as a scientific term.
22. See the discussion in Hilferding, *Finance Capital,* Chapter 22.
23. N. Bukharin, *Imperialism and World Economy* London: Merlin, 1972); V.I. Lenin, 'Imperialism, The Highest Stage of Capitalism' in *Selected Works* (Moscow: Progress Publishers, 1968). Bukharin's work was written first, and is, in many respects a more substantial achievement, but the influence of Lenin's work has been far greater.
24. Karl Kautsky, 'Ultra-Imperialism', *New Left Review,* no 59 (1970). In their introduction the editors of *NLR* assume rather too readily that Kautsky's argument was disproved by the outbreak of the war.
25. The theme of uneven development runs throughout Lenin's work, but see particularly *Selected Works* Section VII.
26. The naming of eras of capitalism is fraught with danger. Hilferding's adjective 'latest' is fairly neutral, but E. Mandel in characterising the present era as *Late Capitalism* (London: New Left Books, 1975) gives a hostage to fortune. Who knows in two or three hundred years' time the late twentieth century may be described as 'early' capitalism. (I am indebted to David McLellan for this point.)
27. Under Stalin tendencies towards the capture of the state by monopoly capital identified by Lenin and Bukharin were converted into the formalistic description of 'state monopoly capitalism', brutalised into 'Stamocap' (see Kulbalkova and Cruikshank, Marxism-Leninism). The work of the Trotskyists did not challenge the essential Leninist categories.
28. For example, Lenin, *Selected Works,* Section IV, p. 214): 'The export of capital influences and greatly accelerates the development of capitalism in those countries to which it is exported'.
29. Paul Baran, *Politics & Economy of Growth*, Harmondsworth: (Penguin 1973).
30. Lenin, *Selected Works*, Section VIII develops the ideal of the 'labour aristocracy' but this is a section of the proletariat that becomes bourgeois or is led by the tools of the bourgeoisie. Baran's point is of wider application.
31. This interesting line of argument is given too little attention by later writers, but see G. Kay, *Development and Underdevelopment* (London: Macmillan, 1975)
32 The term 'dependency theory' covers a wide range of material — non-Marxist, quasi-Marxist — and it would be possible to make a case for dropping the term altogether; however, it is sufficiently embedded in the literature for this to be impractical. For surveys of the field see C.J. Brown, 'Development and Dependency' in M. Light and A.J.R. Groom (eds) *International Relations: A Handbook of Current Theory,* (London: Frances Pinter, 1985) and M. Blomstrom and B. Hettne, *Development Theory in Transition,* (London: Zed Books, 1984).
33. Frank's most famous text remains *Capitalism and Underdevelopment in Latin America* (Harmondsworth: Penguin, 1971). A good recent collection is *Critique and Anti-Critique: Essays of Dependence and Reformism* (London: Macmillan, 1984)
34. I. Wallerstein, *The Modern World System: Capitalist Agriculture and the Origins of the European World-Economy in the Sixteenth Century* (London: Academic Press, 1974); *Idem, The Modern World System II: Mercantilism and the Consolidation of the European World-Economy 1600-1750* London: Academic Press, 1980).

35. See Part I of I. Wallerstein, *The Politics of the World-Economy* (Cambridge: Cambridge University Press, 1984)
36. The most important of Amin's extensive writings is *Accumulation on a World Scale*, (2 vols), (Hassocks: Harvester Press, 1978). Some idea of the differences and similarities between the different dependency writers can be gathered from S. Amin, G. Arrighi, A.G. Frank and I. Wallerstein, *Dynamics of Global Crisis* (London: Macmillan, 1982).
37. See Howard and King, *Political Economy of Marx*.
38. A. Emmanuel, *Unequal Exchange: A Study in the Imperialism of Trade*, (London: New Left Books, 1982), including 'Theoretical Comments' by C. Bettelheim. See also D. Evans, 'Emmanuel's Theory of Unequal Exchange: Critique, Counter-critique and Theoretical Contribution', Discussion Paper 149 (Brighton: Institute of Development Studies, 1980); and 'A critical assessment of some Neo-Marxist Trade Theories', *Journal of Development Studies*, vol 20, no 2, January 1984.
39. R. Brenner, 'The Origins of Capitalist Development: A Critique of Neo-Smithian Marxism', *New Left Review*, no 104 (1977); E. Laclau 'Fendalism and Capitalism in Latin America' in *Politics and Ideology in Marxist Theory,* (London: New Left Books, 1977); B. Warren, *Imperialism: Pioneer of Capitalism* (London: Verso, 1980).
40. See, for example, P. Evans, *Dependent Development* (Princeton, NJ: Princeton University Press, 1979).
41. For an interesting recent study of the NICs see N. Harris, *The End of the Third World* Harmondsworth: Penguin, 1987).
42. Warren, *Imperialism*, Chapter 7.
43. Ibid; Fred Block, *The Origins of International Economic Disorder* (London: University of California Press, 1977). Warren was a member of the Communist Party but fits into no identifiable intellectual school.
44. See K. Van der Pijl, *The Makings of an Atlantic Ruling Class* (London: Verso, 1984).
45. Ernest Mandel *Europe versus America* (London: New Left Books, 1970), *Idem, Late Capitalism*.
46. Hymer, 'The Multinational Corporation and the Law of Uneven Development' in J. Bhagwati (ed.), *Economics and World Order from the 1970s to the 1990s,* (New York: Collier-Macmillan, 1972). Robin Murray, 'The Internationalisation of Capital and the Nation State', *New Left Review*, no. 67 (1971). Both texts are to be found in the very useful, if now somewhat dated, H. Radice (ed.), *International Firms and Modern Imperialism* (Harmondsworth: Penguin, 1975).
47. Hymer, 'The MNC' in Radice, *International Firms*, p. 38.
48. Ibid, p. 39.
49. Ibid. Part III.
50. B. Warren, 'The Internationalisation of Capital and the Nation State: A Comment', *New Left Review*, no. 68 (1971), also reprinted in Radice, *International Firms*.
51. E.A. Brett *International Money and Capitalist Crisis* (London: Heinemann, 1983); and *idem, The World Economy since the War* (London: Macmillan, 1985); N. Harris, *Of Bread and Guns: The World Economy in Crisis* (Harmondsworth: Penguin, 1983). See also chapters by Harrison and Bavar, and Hoogevelt and Szeftel in R. Bush, G. Johnston and D. Coates (ed.), *The World Order: Socialist Perspectives*, (Oxford: Polity Press/Blackwell, 1987).
52. R.O. Keohane, *After Hegemony*, (Princeton, NJ: Princeton University Press, 1984), S. Strange, *Casino Capitalism* (Oxford: Blackwell, 1986).
53. See R.W. Cox, 'Social Forces, States and World Orders', *Millenium: Journal of International Studies*, vol. 10, no. 2 (1981), H.R. Alker and T.J. Biersteker, 'The Dialectics of World Order', *International Studies Quarterly*, vol 28 (1984). R.K. Ashley, *The Political Economy of War and Peace*, (London: Frances Pinter, 1980); J. MacLean 'Interdependence — and Ideological Intervention in International Relations' in R.J. Barry Jones and P. Willetts (eds), *Interdependence on Trial*, (London: Frances Pinter, 1984).
54. This sensibility is admirably summarized in a quotation from Goethe *(West-Eastern Divan)* much favoured by Marx — see, for example, the concluding section of 'The British Rule in India' (Fernbach, *Surveys*, p. 307)

    Should this torture then torment us
    Since it brings us greater pleasure?
    Were not through the rule of Timur
    Souls devoured without measure?

Chapter 8

Economic Realism, Neo-Ricardian Structuralism and the Political Economy of Contemporary Neo-Mercantilism

R.J. Barry Jones

Introduction

One of the most influential dispositions in international political economy is both little elaborated and difficult to name. Today's intellectual world is characterized by the titanic clash of a liberalism and a socialism that both advocate the diminution, if not dissolution, of the nation-state. An approach to political economy that emphasizes the collective action of societies, and their governments, in an environment characterized by constant international economic competition is largely neglected and even illegitimized. Moreover, the approach forgoes much of the psychological appeal of those forms of liberal, and Marxist, political economy that rest upon universal generalizations and which offer a determinate form of analysis that demonstrates the necessary consequences of given initial assumptions.

This approach to political economy acknowledges, and turns upon, economic competition amongst societies, and far pre-dates both liberalism and socialism. Moreover, its practical expression may often be identified in the behaviour even of societies that publicly proclaim liberal or socialist (or even Marxist) principles. Despite the intellectual popularity of liberal and socialist internationalism, and their vigorous rejection of its presumptions and prescriptions, this approach to practical political economy remains a far more durable approach than might otherwise be supposed. As a general approach it is, moreover, well equipped to accommodate concepts and insights gleaned from diverse sources.

Terms and titles

Entitling the approach to political economy to be considered in this chapter is a somewhat problematical matter. The approach is primarily a disposition that reflects and draws upon notions and insights derived from numerous sources and intellectual traditions. It marks the contemporary continuation of the mercantilism of the medieval and early modern period of European history.[1] The Keynesian 'revolution' in modern liberal economics also established the basis for a modern revival of 'mercantilist' impulses in the form, in Harry Johnson's term, of 'neo-mercantilism'.[2] Latterly, the revival of the American 'institutionalist' school of economics,[3] the emergence of a post-Keynesian 'school' of economics,[4] the growing popularity of 'neo-Ricardian' interpretations[5] and the confluence of a broad 'structuralist' critique of relations between the developed and less-developed economies,[6] have all contributed further brush-strokes to a discernible, but yet diffuse, picture of the global political economy.

The appropriate name for the perspective here under examination is contentious. National political economy and neo-mercantilism are two clear candidates. However, the term 'economic realism' links the approach with the clear, and influential, 'realist' view of general international relations, without necessarily sharing the statism with which such 'realism' has often been associated and, indeed, with which its proponents have often sought to associate themselves.

To the leading theorist of realism, Hans J. Morgenthau, states were the ultimate and sole guarantors of the well-being of their citizens in a politically fragmented world. States that overlooked their ultimate solitude, relied unduly upon others and neglected to provide for their own protection and preservation, were likely to come to grief, at some time and under some circumstances. Ensuring self-protection, creating extensive capabilities and pursuing advantageous external conditions, conflated into Morgenthau's imperative to seek and sustain 'power'.[7] There is much that is ambiguous, insecure and excessively statist in the work of Morgenthau and like-minded theorists. However, the approach to political economy that emphasized the importance of collective action does so because it acknowledges realism's identification of the self-help imperative with which all communities, and not only states, are ultimately confronted. It therefore warrants the title of *economic realism*.[8]

The origins of economic realism

TRADITIONAL MERCANTILISM

Modern economic realism has its roots deep in the past of medieval, and even pre-medieval, Europe. Historians disagree about the extent to which the principles and practices of any medieval or early-modern European state conformed to the apparent dictates of mercantilism.[9] Indeed, there are some who maintain that mercantilism, as such, was a straw-man invented by early liberal economics, like Adam Smith,[10] to justify their criticisms and prescriptions. An underlying disposition of sufficient practical influence and persistence may, however, be identified in the policies of a sufficient number of medieval rulers to warrant the view that something rather like mercantilism held sway for much of the time.

Mercantilism was not, however, a static phenomenon. Its essence lay in the primacy of the 'political' needs and purposes of the state and/or its ruler(s). These purposes ranged from territorial acquisition through to dynastic disputes. The purpose of the domestic economy was to support the rulers in the pursuit of their objectives. Food, supplies, weaponry, horses and manpower might all be required from the domestic economy. Indeed, the political system of feudalism was, essentially, a system for military supply in which feudal lords secured their lands and rights from the monarch in return for a continuing obligation to provide manpower, and other necessary resources, in time of conflict with other states or rules.[11]

If the domestic economy was a resource base for medieval rulers, the external economy was also an arena for politically and strategically directed activity. Medieval warfare was quite dissimilar to the mass 'popular' warfare that engulfed Europe periodically from the French Revolution onwards. Late medieval and early modern European warfare was often fought by troops which, if not actually outright mercenaries, required regular payment to maintain their loyalty.[12] Rulers were wise, therefore, to ensure adequate resources of money and other valuable materials for continued payments. The early phases of European mercantilism were thus bullionist in character, indicating the manner in which trade was viewed primarily as a means by which to stock the exchequers of states and their rulers.[13]

Bullionism 'prescribed' a positive balance of external trade as a means of ensuring a steady inflow of precious metals and other valued specie. Exports were promoted, while measures were adopted to minimize the volume of imports. Moreover, there was a continuing concern to identify, and if necessary control, new sources of precious metals. Indeed, the seizure of other states' supplies of precious metals was sometimes encouraged, where the dangers of exposure or unpleasant repercussions could be minimized.

The value of substantial hoards of bullion could be considerable, as witnessed in Spain's ability to hire the army of the Austrian duke and military entrepreneur, Albert von Wallenstein, to fight on its behalf during the Thirty Years War. However, states like medieval Spain still had to face the problem of what to do once their accumulated financial resources were exhausted by protracted periods of fighting. The health of the domestic economy and its population now became critical; if they had been neglected the state had little to fall back upon when foreign mercenaries could no longer be retained.

The health of the domestic base thus became a central issue for European states and wrought a profound change in the nature of mercantilism. The range of economic conditions that were now deemed pertinent to the political concerns and ambitions of states and their rulers was now considerably extended.[13] This later manifestation of European mercantilism went beyond a desire for monetary resources to embrace a concern with the stimulation of the greatest possible level of stability, vigour and general capability within the domestic economy. Agricultural self-sufficiency was much pursued, skills fostered, the means of transport developed, and new manufacturing facilities encouraged. A wide range of institutions, including medieval guilds, were reinforced or established to promote and sustain these purposes, which could, potentially, intrude into virtually every aspect of economic and social life.

The external dispositions of later mercantilism were also many and varied. A positive balance of trade was still favoured as a means of acquiring financial resources. Of equal, if not greater, significance, however, was the strategic management of international trade. It was believed to be desirable to make other states, with whom conflict was at least a possibility, dependent upon one's own society for important resources and, especially, warmaking material. It was also held to be important to avoid dependence for important supplies on external sources which might be cut off in time of war. Such imperatives encourage the steady encroachment of government regulation into many, if not most, areas of external trade. New regulative and enforcement agencies proliferated, while the state granted trade monopolies and lent official support to a variety of trading companies, corporations and associations.

Preparation for and the conduct of war lent considerable encouragement to, and often necessitated, a substantial expansion of governmental involvement with domestic economic developments. The beleaguered French Revolutionary regime introduced a range of institutional reforms that reinforced, while also modernizing, the dirigiste and interventionist inclinations of the *ancien régime*.[14] The successful defeat of Napoleonic France then left Britain with an economic and technological leadership that was to persist until the late nineteenth century.[15] Much of the industrialization of unified Germany[16] and Tzarist Russia,[17] during the late nineteenth and early twentieth centuries, was also largely motivated by political, strategic and military concerns.[18] Such strategic purposes thus sustained mercantilist impulses into the twentieth century and ensured the survival of a disposition that would revive and reassert itself whenever political or economic conditions deteriorated and threatened the well-being of nation-states and their populations.

TWENTIETH-CENTURY NEO-MERCANTILISM

Mercantilist disposition fell into some disrepute in the Britain of the later nineteenth century. The strident criticisms of Adam Smith, and many of his successors, lent intellectual weight to liberal international economic policies which could well be afforded by an economically and industrially dominant Britain. Indeed, in the view of such cynical critics as Germany's Count Otto von Bismarck,[19] such policies actually enhanced the position of a 'top economy', like that of nineteenth-century Britain. Elsewhere, many societies were practising or preparing for strongly interventionist and dirigiste policies towards their domestic economies and external trade. However, the main currents of thought within the English-speaking world ran with the liberal wind until the trauma of the Great Depression of the 1930s redirected the ideas of more responsive minds and encouraged the crystallization and widening dissemination of the ideas of John Maynard Keynes.[20]

The primary effect of Keynes's profound revision of liberal economics was to dispel the view that the economy would, if left to its own devices, eventually stabilize itself at a level at which all productive resources would be more or less fully employed. Keynes argued that the prevailing depression could continue indefinitely unless entrepreneurial confidence could be restored and investment restimulated. Moreover, it was most unlikely that entrepreneurial confidence could be revived without significant governmental action to stimulate demand within the domestic economy. The government could implement stimulating monetary or fiscal policies or participate directly in the creation of work and, hence, gainful employment. Either course should stimulate demand, increase output, improve employment prospects and, ultimately, regenerate demand for new capital equipment.[21] Both sets of measures, however, involved the assumption by government of far greater responsibility for the vitality of the domestic economy than had been envisaged by the purer forms of economic liberalism. The possible effectiveness of such governmental activity also challenged the revolutionary fatalism of the more extreme socialist doctrines, including orthodox Marxism.

The palpable enormity of the Great Depression of the 1930s did not, however, ensure the immediate acceptance of Keynes's analysis and prescriptions. Nor, moreover, did Keynes's own work resolve all issues of economic policy in the present or the future. There was considerable intellectual resistance to the new Keynsian teachings during their early years, with many notable economists fighting determined rearguard actions.[22] In the United States the largely unconscious 'Keynesianism' of the New Deal met with substantial resistance within the Supreme Court and significant sections of the Congress and the public. Moreover, the practical impact of the New Deal was, itself, beginning to wane by 1936 and 1937.

The approach of the Second World War proved to be the midwife of practical Keynesianism. The intending aggressors, and then their potential victims, initiated major, and expanding, rearmament programmes. Significantly, too, rearmament programmes, by remaining firmly under governmental direction, avoided the potentially serious problem of the leakage of Keynesian economic stimulants into increased demand for imports. Wartime economies also allowed governments to moderate inflation, and limit official deficits, by requiring compulsory 'savings' from their populations. The massive control given to governments by the pressures of modern war thus permitted a marked measure of Keynesianism, while suppressing many of the potential problems associated with protracted, and possibly incautious, Keynesian economic management.

THE TIDES OF POST-WAR 'ECONOMIC REALISM'

The ending of the Second World War ushered in a novel era of practical political economy. Governments accepted a responsibility to develop and implement policies designed to ensure the vitality of their national economies and the economic well-being of their populations. The intellectual climate had been transformed by the writings of Keynes, the dramatic achievements of war-time economic management, and national mobilization, and popular demands for relief from long-endured privations and economic reward for recent efforts. Moreover, many governments in the Western world recognized an urgent need to orchestrate economic recovery and stability, if the perceived menace of encroaching communism were to be held at bay.

A peculiar amalgam of economic doctrine and practice thus characterized the early post-war years, within the advanced industrial (or reindustrializing) countries. The aspirational rhetoric of a liberal economic order was accompanied by a profusion of interventionist activities and the elaboration of ever more sophisticated techniques of macro-economic management. With economic recovery, and the return of affluence, the 'advanced' world gradually began to believe that the economic problems of the past had finally been laid to rest.

The macro-economic management of the domestic economy could, moreover, be complemented by the American-led management of the international economic system. That management, through the International Monetary Fund (IMF), the General Agreement on Tariffs and Trade (GATT), and assorted high-level consultative arrangements, was founded on liberal aspirations, and rhetoric, but tolerated many non-liberal, and even illiberal, policies and arrangements in practice. Such evasions of liberalism ranged from the proliferation of Japanese non-tariff barriers against imports to the emergence of the European Economic Community (EEC), with its externally protectionist principles. Moreover, the central necessity for some measure of international economic management was widely appreciated; whether that management be undertaken by the United States unilaterally, or by some consortium of the leading industrial economies.

The very success of post-war economic recovery, within the more affluent nations, and an apparent ability to preserve economic well-being through fiscal and monetary management, encouraged a rather complacent acceptance of a loose version of Keynesian economic theory as the prevailing orthodoxy. This encouraged the further evolution of liberal economic analysis and the development of even more refined macro-economic models with which to enhance economic management. It also encouraged a neglect of a number of critical dimensions of political economy: the institutional analysis of actual economic systems; and the significance of a variety of supportive, and even directive, official policies in those countries that were achieving the most impressive levels and patterns of industrial growth, or that were actively seeking success in these directions. The debate about industrial policy was thus muted within many of the industrialized countries, being deflected, rather, into the esoteric realms of 'development' policy, wherein difficulties and controversies could be addressed at a 'safe' distance.

The easy 'liberal consensus' of the post-war era was, however, to be undermined by the very 'success' of the post-war 'order' and its manifestations within the international economic system. Post-war industrial recovery warranted an ending of the United States' hugely generous Marshall Aid programme and confronted each advanced industrial country with the need to 'pay its way' in the world. Recovery also brought the proliferation of centres of industrial competitiveness within the international trading system. By the mid-1960s some countries that had previously enjoyed considerable overseas markets, and reasonably secure domestic markets for manufactured goods, began to experience the increasingly cold winds of international competition. In the United Kingdom, and in a number of the more 'mature' economies, concern began to be expressed about the preservation, if not restoration, of industrial competitiveness and the role that government might, and should, play in this process.

The activities of the British Labour government of 1964-70 exemplified the growing concern with industrial policy in the Western world. A systematic assault upon the United Kingdom's declining industrial position was envisaged in a National Economic Plan, and a Department of Economic Affairs established to oversee its implementation. The experiment soon faltered in the face of a combination of apparently insurmountable institutional obstacles and short-term economic difficulties.[23] However, the notion of industrial policy was now firmly on the political agenda of those faltering national economies that were experiencing repeated and growing balance-of-payments crises, whilst also suffering a progressive decline in their international market position. Indeed, when countries like the United States also began to fear an irreversible loss of economic strength and competitiveness in the 1970s, the *explicit* concern with industrial policy became widespread within the English-speaking world and its political and academic circles.[24]

Growing international competitiveness was not, however, the only source of damage to the comfortable semi-Keynesianism of the post-war era. Much of the now independent 'Third World' continued to experience serious obstacles to substantial economic development and, with expanding populations, often appeared to be regressing economically. Growing, and seemingly irresistible, inflationary pressures were also unleashed within many advanced industrial countries. Orthodox forms of Keynesian economic policy did not appear to provide an automatic answer to the developmental problems of one part of the world and seemed, if anything, to contribute to the inflationary problems of another.[25]

The 'crisis' of 'Keynesian' economics during the later 1960s and 1970s spawned a number of significant developments.[26] It underlay the 'structuralist' critique of the prevailing international economic order and the programme of reforms contained within the call for a New International Economic Order.[27] The persisting problems of industrial competitiveness of a number of advanced industrial countries, and their serious inflationary difficulties in the later 1970s, also stimulated diverse reactions. On one side, there was a major revival of interest in the institutional analysis of real-world economies, forms of analysis directed more towards the empirical than the hypothetical world and focused industrial policies aimed at ensuring the continued international competitiveness of specific national economies.[28] On the other side, determined proponents of neo-classical economic theory and ultra-liberal political principles ushered forth their doctrines of 'monetarism', conservative 'supply-side' economics, 'rational expectations', 'balanced budgets', and constitutionally constrained economic policy, with reinvigorated and often impassioned enthusiasm.[29]

Contemporary Economic Realism

BASIC IDEAS

Contemporary Economic Realism is a diverse and loose constellation of ideas, concerns and analytical approaches. There are, however a number of elements which are common to most of those who fall within this general category. The central ideas of post-Keynsianism are, in the view of Alfred S. Eichner:

1. that economic growth and income distribution, within any economy, are directly related to one another and essentially determined by the rate of investment;
2. that the modern world is characterized by the continuous, but uneven, expansion of national economies over time and that, therefore, it is essential to distinguish between those factors that generate secular growth of output from those that produce fluctuations around the trend line;
3. That the dynamic processes of modern economies turn, centrally, around their advanced credit and other monetary institutions;
4. that multinational corporations and trades unions exist, and play a role, of varying significance, in modern economies and underlie the prevalence of *administered prices* rather than truly competitive prices;
5. that analysis is therefore concerned, centrally, with the dynamic behaviour of actual economic systems rather than the

hypothetical 'worlds' of neo-classical theorists.[30]

Richard Langlois, in his distinct, though related, exploration of the parameters of a *new institutional economics* identifies the following fundamentals of the approach:

1. Although definitely rational in a true sense, the agent of economic theory is not best conceived as rational in the narrow sense of maximizing within a framework of known alternatives.
2. Economic phenomena are in large measure the result of learning over time by economic agents; economic explanation should thus be a dynamic exercise — dynamic not merely in the sense of dynamic neoclassical models, but in a sense best rendered as evolutionary.
3. The coordination of economic activity is not merely a matter of price-mediated transactions in markets, but is supported by a wide-range of economic and social institutions that are themselves an important topic of theoretical economic enquiry.[31]

In his discussion of the revived school of *American institutionalist economics*, Warren J. Samuels identifies its central proposition, and fundamental difference from mainstream liberal economics, in the assertion that: 'The economy is both a structure, and a process of power', power being 'participation in decision-making and the bases thereof, such as property rights, income position, influence, and other rights of economic significance'.[32]

The post-Keynesian/neo-institutionalist disposition furnishes a most effective basis for the exploration and critical analysis of contemporary economies. It also provides, however, a powerful perspective upon the economic relations of modern nation-states and other transnational actors. Two elements of the approach are particularly fruitful in this respect: the central emphasis upon *power* in the conduct, and shaping, of relationships among all manner of economic actors; and the related notion that it is the peculiar socio-economic configurations obtaining within specific societies that determine the local distribution of profits and wages and, thence, much of the cost structures of local production.

Robert Gilpin's attempt to construct a *neo-mercantilist* interpretation of the essential principles of the contemporary international political economy thus emphasizes the role of power. His vision of a neo-mercantilist world identifies the nature of the economic relations among societies as fundamentally 'conflictual'; nation-states as the basic actors; the maximization of national interest as the primary goal of economic activity; 'politics' as dominating 'economics'; and change as a function of shifts in the distribution of power, particularly among nation-states.[33]

Differences in contemporary endowments and conditions are also central to the perspective dubbed the 'cost of production theory' by Chris Edwards. Here, a *neo-Ricardian* emphasis upon the prevailing technologies of production, and the struggle over the distribution of the 'surplus' arising from production, is central to the analysis of economic conditions existing within economies and the relationships that have arisen amongst national economies.[34] It is an approach which, in contrast to the liberal faith in the ability of the international 'free market' to stimulate development, and equality of economic experience, asserts the need for control of economic developments by appropriate institutions at both the national and the international levels.[35]

THE DISTINCTIVE CONTRIBUTION OF ECONOMIC REALISM

The ideas that have been identified with the approach of economic realism may not, initially, appear that distinct from some forms of liberal and Marxist analysis. The range and diversity of such studies is considerable and many may well embrace notions that are more central to economic realism. The boundary between academic and intellectual schools of thought is never as sharp as suggested in many scholarly surveys. However, it may be that many nominally liberal or Marxist studies have actually strayed so far from their self-proclaimed analytical foundations as to have crossed, albeit unwittingly, into the domain of economic realism!

The most fruitful initial approach to the distinctiveness of economic realism is, perhaps, to identify those fundamental concepts of liberal and Marxist political economy that it rejects. A distinctively *liberal* political economy rests, as has been argued elsewhere in this volume,[36] on the acceptance of methodological individualism; faith in the power and efficacy of the free market; in the desirability of minimalist government; and, in many forms, the virtues of private enterprise and the private ownership of property. Economic realism is sceptical, rather than doctrinally dismissive, of methodological individualism; it is convinced that perfectly competitive free markets are rare in reality and that the highly imperfect free markets, domestic and international, that do exist often operate to the serious disadvantage of some of their participants; and it believes that forceful governmental action, individual and collaborative, is one of the few effective means with which people are endowed in their efforts to overcome such economic disadvantages. Economic realism is also agnostic with regard to the particular value of private enterprise and the general contribution of the private ownership of property.

Neo-classical economics is one extreme form of liberal political economy. It has developed and enshrined an additional set of basic concepts and analytical techniques which are also rejected by economic realism. Central to the neo-classical paradigm are the methodology of comparative statistics, the techniques of marginal analysis, and the overall notion of general equilibrium. Comparative statics consists in the formal analysis of situations in which 'imperfections' of one kind or another are shown to exist. It then develops similar formal models of situations in which these imperfections have been corrected and 'equilibrium' achieved. Such comparative analysis demonstrates both the directions in which necessary 'adjustments' to the initial condition must be made and the level of benefit thus obtained. Comparative statics is, in turn, methodologically intertwined with marginal analysis. When adjustment follows a dynamic path, that path may be analysed as a series of marginal adjustments. Marginal analysis, moreover, provides one form of value theory, in which value is deemed to be revealed by the co-ordination of marginal choices by consumers and marginal production by suppliers, in a market that achieves long-term equilibrium.[37] Moreover, marginal analysis charts the course towards particular equilibria and, thence, general equilibrium.

Economic realists reject comparative statics for its excessive formalism, analytical limitations and consequential neglect of the dynamic processes that characterize the real world. The nature and direction of economic developments are, it is argued, primarily a function of the real conditions of concrete economic systems, and actual *processes* manifest within them. Models that merely compare some arbitrarily selected pre-adjustment with post-adjustment 'equilibrium' situations can never apprehend the essential features of changes within real, constantly dynamic systems and are, at best, no more than heuristic devices for answering purely 'theoretical' questions or at worst, major distortions of reality.[38] Related notions of general equilibrium are equally suspect as theoretical fantasies; untestable, immanent forces and tendencies,[39] and, whatever their supposed existential status, a major diversion from real progress in economic understanding and analysis.[40]

Beyond the specific methodological and theoretical quarrels with liberal political economy, and with neo-classicism in particular, economic realism rejects the determinate thrust of mainstream liberal economic analysis. This determinacy is inherent in the basic analytical procedures of comparative statics and marginalist analysis but is also encouraged by the restricted purview of modern liberal economic theory. Formalistic and determinate analysis is sustained by an approach that limits concern primarily, if not exclusively, to market interactions. Such analytical procedures are less suited to an approach that seeks to accommodate all potentially relevant features of reality, however complex and messy their character and consequences.

Marxist political economy also rests upon fundamental concepts, and analytical principles, which economic realism rejects, or accepts only with major qualifications. Many recent debates have cast doubt upon the centrality of a number of ideas that would once have been thought fundamental to 'Marxist' theory.[41] With self-proclaimed 'Marxists' arguing against the theoretical significance of one or other core notion, it requires considerable temerity to assert their continuing importance to a distinctly 'Marxist' approach. However, it is difficult to establish the distinction between radical forms of economic realism and various contemporary manifestations of 'Marxism' unless some such assertions are made.

The nature and extent of *determinism* in Marx's own theories, and in subsequent varieties of 'Marxism', has long been debated. The problematical role of human action in securing the ultimate socialist revolution exemplifies this central ambiguity. However, in this discussion it will be held that Marxism is distinguished by a significant measure of philosophical and methodological determinism, for without this it is difficult to discern the real significance of propositions about the long-run tendency of the rate of profit to fall; of intensifying crises of capitalism; or the ultimate probability (inevitability?) of a proletarian revolution and socialist transformation.[42]

A number of recent students of Marx's own work have emphasized the central importance of *non-observable* forces, factors and processes to his methodology.[43] Such non-observables may enjoy a far wider role in many approaches to the analysis of human affairs, including neo-classical economics, than is commonly appreciated. However, their possible centrality in any form of political economy creates significant difficulties regarding the possibility of falsification and the establishment of limits upon the legitimate 'stretching' of a theory or approach to accommodate 'facts' or developments that might otherwise pose a potential challenge to its veracity.

On more specific issues, 'neo-Ricardian Marxists' have argued that Marx's *labour theory of value* is erroneous and, along with the neo-classicists' marginal utility theory of value, should be replaced by Piero Sraffa's analysis of value.[44] However, many devotees contend that the labour theory of value remains essential to a distinctively Marxist approach.[45] A major emphasis upon the analysis of *class conflict* and its dynamic consequences is certainly definitive of Marxist analysis.[46] Finally, there has been a heated argument within 'Marxist' circles over the nature of the *state* within advanced capitalist society: whether the state is to be viewed as a mere instrument of the dominant (capitalist) class, or whether it operates with a degree of autonomy, and therefore as an independent influence upon developments.[47] The view here, however, is that the notion that the state in modern capitalist society is endowed with a significant level of autonomy seriously dilutes much that has been traditionally distinctive of Marxism and undermines much of the apparent clarity of its analysis of contemporary conditions and developments.

Economic realism is unable to accept either determinate analysis or deterministic philosophies. While developments are not random and are much conditioned by prevailing and preceeding conditions, these conditions are too varied and complex to support either the determinate analytical models of liberal political economy or the deterministic tendencies within Marxist theory. Moreover, the human condition is held to be intrinsically malleable. The modification of beliefs, behaviour and circumstances may not always be easy but does remain a matter, ultimately, of human volition, rather than of pure contextual determination. A measure of philosophical and methodological voluntarism thus permeates the general perspective of economic realism.

The role of 'non-observables' in economic realism is a rather more complex issue. Much of economic realism appears, at first sight, to be overwhelmingly empiricist — often looking rather like a structured series of descriptive generalizations. However, a number of the fundamental premises of economic realism, such as the constant pursuit of national well-being, share an immanent quality with other general notions of human behaviour, including, as one example, the assertion within realist international political theory of the ubiquity of the pursuit of power.[48] The disagreement between economic realism and Marxist political economy rests, therefore, upon the number, nature and analytical importance of such non-observables in the overall theoretical system, Marxism being adjudged overly reliant on too many non-observable fundamentals[49] for analytical comfort.

Economic realists of a neo-Ricardian persuasion share, as has been suggested, a wider rejection the Marxian labour theory of value as analytically ill-conceived and practically misleading. An alternative view of value is based upon Piero Sraffa's argument that the attempt to define value in terms of marginal utility (and marginal productivity) founders upon an indeterminate circularity among wages, production costs, profits and prices. The economic realist view of value, and the distribution between profits and wages, emphasizes, in contrast, the central role of the historically and institutionally based relationship established between capital and labour, or the owners and operators of the means of production, within any actual economy.[50] This distribution will be intimately connected with the technologies of production characteristically adopted, and the general costs of producing various goods and services, within that economy.

Finally, economic realism, while recognizing the important role of class conflict within many economies, also acknowledges the potentially decisive influence of other factors, forces and institutions, including the state. In this respect it shares the views of some the heterodox 'Marxists' who have latterly sought to challenge the relatively simple view of the class-dominated state, advanced by many earlier Marxists. If anything, this heterodox view is extended by the work of economic realists, with the influence of states and inter-state arrangements being seen to play a potentially critical role in economic and industrial developments.

Analytical economic realism

Many of the central features of economic realism have now been considered. It has been suggested that, in some respects, economic realism is easier to define negatively, in terms of how it differs from other major perspectives upon political economy. It does possess however, a number of distinctive characteristics as an analytical approach and as a disposition in national economic policy, domestically and internationally. A final review of the distinctive features of economic realist analysis might thus be fruitful, before proceeding to a brief survey of some of its more obvious manifestations in practical policy.

Economic realism views the human condition as complex, dynamic and marked by pervasive uncertainty. Given the malleability of human 'nature', behaviour, society and institutions, universal propositions must always be advanced with modesty and handled with considerable caution. Human beings have, however, continuously created a variety of institutions with which to confront and manage their more significant problems and pursue their more pressing goals. Many such institutions reflect a persisting wish to reduce, if not suppress, the uncertainty with which human beings are all too often faced.[51] While novelty and danger may prove stimulating to some people some of the time, many manifest a marked preference for an orderly life: few expressing a positive preference for the opaque and threatening worlds of Franz Kafka's *The Trial* or *The Castle*.

The pursuit of a degree of control over, and order within, an inherently turbulent environment indicates one compelling direction in which the concept of rationality has to be extended within a realistic approach to political economy. The broader 'rationality' of societies and their governments may be more directed towards maximizing security than material production; more concerned with the maintenance of humane values than the maximization of market efficiency; and more devoted to the preservation of community than the promotion of economic cosmopolitanism.[52] Such wider concerns may bear intimately upon their views of economic policy and management and must therefore be readmitted to a central and legitimate role within political economy.

The term 'institutions' is broadly conceived within economic realism. It encompasses all those formally instituted systems, structures and associations that people have established to deal with matters of economic moment. However, it extends beyond formal arrangements to embrace all those regularized patterns of behaviour exhibited within and between societies and those distributions of resources and capabilities that may have a potential influence upon developments within the political economy. Such institutional features, moreover, reflect and condition the *processes* through which economic developments take place.[53]

The salient features of contemporary political economies thus include the nature and role of their governmental institutions. The development of these institutions, in turn, reflects the historical coalescence of interests, aspirations, and the creation of resources for persuasion or compulsion, sufficient to meet demands for change. Government does not, however, act alone on the contemporary stage for it is accompanied by a range of competing wielders of potential power and influence. Economic realism focuses upon the central significance of trade unions, interest groups, pressure groups and, perhaps of greatest contemporary significance, the existence of firms and enterprises that occupy positions of considerable power within the domestic or international economy. Indeed, the associated notions of monopoly and oligopoly are elevated to a central role, and are a continuing expectation, within economic realist analysis.

The analysis of modern political economies has generated a number of fruitful and illuminating interpretations. The concept of *corporatism* has been widely employed to describe the peculiar configurations of influence and collaboration between governments, industries and organized labour in many modern industrial, and some developing, societies.[54] Such corporatist arrangements are not, however, merely a matter of descriptive interest for they are held to bear upon the dynamism, development and general effectiveness of the economies within which they exist. If governments are organized effectively, and are disposed to act propitiously, then they may significantly enhance the economic and industrial prospects of their societies, as many have seen in the recent record of Japan.[55]

The nature, prevalence and prescriptions of economic realism are germane to debates about the domestic economic role of governments. Such issues as the desirability of explicit policies for industrial development, regional growth or reinvigoration, the support of ailing industries and the creation of 'enterprise cultures' all involve arguments about the efficiency and veracity of practical economic realism. It is, however, in the realms of external economic policy, international economic relations and transnational economic activity that economic realism assumes critical significance. In the 'international' arena it proves a powerful guide, albeit highly contentious, to national action; an analytical perspective upon the character of contemporary North-South economic relations; and a source of novel insights into the behaviour of transnational corporations in their relations with one another and with nation-states.

As a guide to effective national or social action, economic realism emphasizes the inherently problematical character of international economic relations. While economic realism acknowledges that international trade is often highly beneficial to its participants, it is nevertheless highly critical of the unqualified welcome given to all forms and patterns of international economic exchange by the purer form of liberal economics, for two reasons. First, it indicates that even where all parties to an exchange benefit, the distribution of relative benefit may be seriously unequal and, in consequence, a source of considerable resentment, contention and instability.[56] Second, it acknowledges the possibility that a society may experience positive harm from some prevailing or potential trade relationship. Some imports might be physically harmful, culturally or destructive of emergent local industries. Exports might be 'undervalued' within the contemporary international economic system, and therefore traded on terms that, by some views, are 'exploitative';[57] absorb productive resources that might be better employed in other directions; or even be produced under conditions that are positively damaging to the environment and/or the health or well-being of local workers and populations. Where production and trade is orchestrated by transnational corporations, this activity might be undertaken in a manner that further subordinates the interests and autonomy of the local society and its government.

The message of economic realism is that societies should be attuned to the possibilities of inequitable or harmful trade relations. Actions to correct such 'distortions' are thus quite legitimate; doubly so if the distortions result, as they sometimes do, from the intentional activities of others. The only test of such measures is that they be effective within prevailing conditions: that, for instance, use be made of direct subsidies for desired developments, where feasible, rather than blanket protective measures;[58] or that actions be taken only when their potential repercussions elsewhere are fully appreciated.

The range of possible actions available to societies, and their governments in the pursuit of an improved domestic and international economic position, is vast and will be surveyed briefly in the next section. In the view of some economic realists, however, the 'structural disadvantage' of countries within the 'less-developed world' creates a particularly strong need for such measures, whether unilateral or taken in co-operation with others.

The argument of such 'structuralists', and others of related views, including some dependency theorists, identifies the roots of difficulties faced by the economies of much of the 'south' within the historical conditions within which they have 'developed' and the distorted global structure with which they are still confronted.

The structuralist analysis identifies a fundamental asymmetry and imbalance in the economic relations between the 'North' (or more properly the prosperous 'North-West) and the 'South'. In this imbalanced world the North produces high-value goods for a stable, and steadily growing, global market while the South overwhelmingly produces low-value goods for an unstable, unreliable, or even declining, international market. The result of this asymmetry is that the North continues to prosper while much of the South languishes in a seemingly irreversible condition of 'underdevelopment'. The diagnosis of the roots of this situation lie at the heart of the prescriptions offered by the structuralists: prescriptions which are essentially economic realist.

Historical developments within, and in the relations between, Northern and Southern economies have been such as to endow both with quite different internal conditions. The advantages of the North reflect a history which has left them with extensive and intensive technical knowledge and capabilities; diversified economies with a wide range of industries; well-educated and often well-organized labour forces; a highly developed economic infrastructure; well-established positions in the international trade in high-value goods and services, and even some primary commodities; well-organized work-forces;

and, the home bases of the world's most dominant firms and transnational corporations. Moreover, the firms that operate in the markets for the most typically Northern goods are often, in the view of some analysts, able to function in an oligopolistic manner.[59]

The situation of many Southern countries stands in marked contrast to that of the typical Northern economy. At the start of their modern development programmes they were faced with low levels of technical competence; an unsatisfactory mix of a few, generally low-value, export industries, with traditional artisan manufacture and relatively primitive agriculture; a weak educational and economic infrastructure; a disorganised and largely underemployed work-force; and, the presence of foreign-owned and foreign-managed businesses in many critical areas of the economy.

The implications of these contrasting sets of circumstances are seen to lie in the differing trading opportunities and conditions experienced by the two types of economies. Advanced industrial countries of the North are able to identify and move into new, technically advanced, areas of production and service, with relative ease and speed. The market for such goods and services is expanding and will continue to expand with the continued growth of income globally. Those who are employed in the production of such goods and services are, moreover, either well unionized or possessed of skills that remain in short supply. Either condition ensures that wages continue to rise steadily with international economic growth and are certainly highly resistant to reductions, at least in nominal terms, at times of faltering demand or growing productivity. For the enterprises that produce under such conditions, and especially for those that find themselves operating in oligopolistic or quasi-oligopolistic situations, *cost-plus* or *administered* pricing is both possible and desirable.[60]

Within the South, in contrast, great difficulty is experienced in entering new and technologically demanding areas of production. Activity is confined, rather, to the production of traditional, largely primary, commodities and diversification limited to the manufacture of new goods that are relatively unsophisticated, and labour-intensive, in their production technologies. A work-force that is over-abundant and generally lacking in scarce skills is unable to extract substantial wage rises from its employers and, indeed, may be unable to resist wage reductions at times of falling or fluctuating demand for its products. The prices of many Southern products are also subject to fluctuation, or secular decline, because of the existence of widespread competition from other low-cost producing nations, fluctuating demand conditions, or even progressive reductions in general demand for the product. Wages in Southern countries, therefore, remain low by comparison with those in the North and actually do fall in times of reduced demand, and hence prices, for the commodities and goods being produced.

The general conditions affecting Southern countries' production, employment and external trade are those that establish the parameters for the Sraffian distribution between profit and labour within such economies and, hence, the overall production-costs structure. These, then, are the foundations of the 'exploitation' and 'unequal exchange' that analysts like Arghiri Emmanuel discern at the heart of trade relations between the North and the South and any adverse movements in the terms of trade of the latter.[61] The policy prescriptions of the structuralists are directed at the transformation of such conditions by Southern governments acting individually and in concert with others. The range of domestic policies directed at a structural transformation of less developed economies is extremely wide, ranging from the establishment of universal education to the creation of ambitious 'parastatal' industries, major capital investments, the nationalization of foreign-owned assets and sometimes, on a contrary tack, co-operative arrangements with foreign transnational corporations.[62] However, the many setbacks and disappointments experienced by such schemes reflects a combination of over-ambition, neglect of constraining conditions and, most significantly, the persistence of the very structural weakness that development plans seek to overcome.[63]

Economic realism, of a post-Sraffian variety, also raises a number of particularly interesting questions about the prospects of the so-called newly industrialized countries (NICs) and hence development prospects generally. Many NICs have based their industrial expansion, at least in its initial phases, on exports to established markets within the advanced industrial countries. A major source of their competitiveness has rested upon an ability to combine very low labour costs with quite advanced production technologies. Three developments, in particular, could therefore weaken, if not halt, the pace of their economic advance. Externally, the advent of global recession and/or renewed protectionism within the industrialized world, would severely reduce their export markets, profits and, hence, prospects for future growth. Moreover, the very cheap labour that contributes to the competitiveness of their exports might well be used as an excuse for protectionist measures in the North. Internally, the existing 'Sraffian' distribution between labour and capital, and the contribution that makes to international competitiveness, could be disrupted by an increasingly self-assertive work-force or political pressures for significant domestic changes.

Within the advanced industrial countries recent years have also seen a sharpened struggle over the 'Sraffian' distribution between capital and labour. Indeed, the competitiveness of many industries within the advanced industrial countries will turn, critically, on the relations between the two sides of industry and the investment that enterprises are willing or encouraged to undertake. Concern with the fundamental conditions under which production takes place within the domestic economy has thus become acute within many advanced industrial countries. Supply-side economics has become increasingly fashionable within a number of those advanced industrial economies that have experienced a recent loss of competitiveness in international markets. Such problems have stimulated a wide-ranging scholarship[64] and encouraged the emergence of both liberal/conservative and radical/interventionist forms of 'supply-side' economics during the late 1970s and 1980s.[65]

LDCs have also sought to overcome structural weaknesses through major external initiatives during recent decades. Many collaborative arrangements have been mooted, and attempted, at various co-operative fora within the South. Most spectacular of all were the sweeping demands for a New International Economic Order (NIEO) made, most vigorously, during the late 1970s. The enthusiasm for this project was, paradoxically, encouraged by a novel version of Southern economic strength: a widespread illusion fostered by the short-lived, but dramatic, effectiveness of OPEC in the world oil market and the belief that this heralded an era of 'commodity-producer power' in the global political economy.[66]

In its call for regulated commodity markets; substantially improved quantities and quality of economic aid; enhanced access to developed economy markets; control over local resources and assets; a reversal of the growing South to North brain drain and a more favourable pattern of technology flow; and demands for a major reform of the international monetary system, the NIEO was intended to reverse many of the chronic sources of structural weakness among the developing countries.[67] However, the very structural weakness from which the LDCs were seeking to escape soon reasserted themselves and dissipated the hopes of a NIEO within a maelstrom of collapsing commodity prices, escalating interest rates, renewed Northern protectionism, and a looming Third World debt crisis.[68] The persistence of such profound constraints has merely encouraged those, including many dependency[69] and world capitalist systems theorists[70] who call for Southern disengagement from further economic interaction with the North or for a Southern-led global socialist revolution.

The nature and functioning of transnational corporations (TNCs) has been of particular concern to many LDCs; who often see them as a source and reflection of many of their underlying structural weaknesses. However, the operations and policies of these world-bestriding juggernauts are now also seen to be problematical for many advanced industrial countries. Whatever their supposed effects, TNCs are certainly recognized to be a phenomenon of central importance for economic realist analysis.[71]

Liberal political economy views TNCs as super-efficient enterprises that are able to transcend limitations imposed by the frontiers of nation-states and thereby compensate for any oligopolistic tendencies that they manifest. Marxists generally view TNCs as either agents of continued neo-colonial domination of the South by the capitalist metropoles or as the source of a new, self-serving form of ultra-imperialist global economic domination. Economic realism, in contrast, views TNCs as major actors that are endowed with considerable, and often special, resources of power and influence in their dealings with nation-states, many of these opportunities deriving from their ability to act as transnationally integrated actors against politically separated nation-states. Moreover, much of the behavior of TNCs is interpreted in terms of the accumulation or exploitation of 'power'. As a complex and often changing kaleidoscope of power relationships, the interactions among TNCs, and those between them and nation-states, are perceived to be predetermined neither in their outcome nor in their impact. The key to effective analysis, here, is held to lie in the careful analysis of the motives of the interacting actors, their actual resources and the skill and effectiveness with which they exploit their advantages in a variety of strategically directed actions and interactions.[72]

One major dimension of TNCs' behaviour within the contemporary international political economy is that of collaboration with other like actors. Indeed, the extent, direction and general implication of collaboration among TNCs, whether explicit or tacit, is a major issue for economic realism, as it is for contemporary Marxist analyses. It is, in particular, possible that the relative dissolution of 'organization' at the level of national capitalism is being superseded or even promoted by emergent 'organization' at the global level.[73]

Collaboration is, however, a possibility that remains open to all major international actors, but one which generates considerable complexities and indeterminacies. Economic realism encourages no prior expectations about the occurrence or efficacy of co-operative behaviour; it is not deemed analytically sufficient to establish that it would be 'rational' by some theoretical criteria, or in the interests of any given set of actors. It has to be established that the actual actors, under the real conditions in which they operate, are able to identify the desirability of collaboration; create appropriate arrangements; and then, in the face of disruptive efforts from outside and temptations to defect from within, secure the objectives towards which collaboration is directed.[74]

Analytically then, economic realism rejects *a priori* judgements about the outcome that any development *will* have or, by the tenets of some determinate theory, *must* have. Rather, it is an analytical disposition that emphasizes the historically generated institutional and structural conditions existing within and among economies. The political and economic institutions, structures and 'cultures' that have actually been established are seen to be critical to current developments and future possibilities. The implications, acceptability and potential efficacy of any proposed economic or industrial policy cannot be judged sensibly without full consideration of such conditions. They must therefore occupy a central place in any realistic analysis and take priority over the kinds of universalistic generalization proffered by both liberal political economy and some of the more ambitious variants of Marxism.

Power and influence, their many foundations and wide-ranging effects, are particularly important features of the institutional/structural analysis of any politico-economic system and its dynamics. Indeed, for some neo-institutionalists the central proposition is that the economy is a 'system of power'. However, many strands of institutionalism, structuralism and post-Keynesianism also acknowledge the important, and often critical, role of varying patterns of power and influence within economic systems and the implications of unequal endowments of potential power and influence for different actors.

Economic realism, moreover, makes no *a priori* judgements about the probable or desirable balance between private initiative and governmental or other collective forms of action within any economy. The actual balance is to be established by empirical analysis and the desirable balance to be determined in the light of prevailing conditions and requirements.

Economic realism in practice

Economic realism is concerned, among many things, with the identification of the conditions that encourage the effectiveness of domestic economies, and international economic arrangements, within an increasingly competitive and turbulent world. For the advanced industrial economies, the objective has often been the maintenance of a position of industrial competitiveness. For the LDCs, the concern has been to transform major features of the domestic economy, enter new areas of commercial production and establish more favourable long-term terms of trade.

The specification of the conditions relevant to the maintenance or acquisitiveness of competitiveness will have clear implications for policy, if not actually promising trouble-free solutions to persistent difficulties. The formal economic and industrial policies of governments form one significant set of pertinent conditions. However, many relevant conditions will have arisen from sources external to the policy process, or be the side-effects of policies adopted in the pursuit of other objectives. It is the entire range of such conditions that is of concern to economic realism.

The formal economic and industrial policies of governments are a major influence, for good or ill, upon the performance of an economy. Interventionist dispositions were quite widespread prior to the Second World War. However, the combined influences of wartime experience, Keynesian macro-economic policy prescriptions and a heightened sense of responsibility for the economic well-being of their populations, encouraged widespread governmental concern with the functioning of national economic and industrial system during the post-war era. With growing experience, governments were able to develop sophisticated macro-economic tools of demand management and selective stimuli, designed to supplement such traditional instruments as exchange controls in the overall direction of economic developments.[75] Both fiscal and monetary policies were available for such manipulative efforts, with fiscal policy finding growing favour until the 'monetarist' counter-revolution of the late 1970s and early 1980s.

Policies to influence, or even control, the value and availability of a state's currency internationally have also assumed a prominent, and often decisive, role. The management of the value of a currency may be directed towards the stimulation of exports, discouragement of imports, and/or the maintenance of a favourable balance of payments between the country and its trading partners. Moreover, formal exchange controls have provided governments with a powerful *de facto* means of influence over trade, particularly imports. When governments and their official agencies can select those who may acquire foreign currency, and the purposes for which currency may be obtained, then the government is able to exert considerable control over what is imported and by whom. The continuing prevalence of exchange controls, of varying severity, is thus evidence of widespread official influence over external trade.

Advanced industrial countries and developing countries have also initiated a range of explicit experiments with industrial planning and other forms of influence over their industrial systems. The results of these ventures has been varied. The massive industrial advances of the Soviet Union during the inter-war period demonstrate the potential effectiveness of determined industrial policy but also the awesome costs and possible misdirections attendant upon an industrialization programme that is excessively centralized and hasty in its implementation.

Elsewhere, the speed and central direction of policies for industrial development, or preservation, have often been less ambitious but no less impressive in their achievements. Japan's modernization since the late nineteenth century was both intentional and the product of high levels of co-ordination among government, industry and society. Whether a conscious conspiracy aimed at global economic dominance,[76] or the by-product of a highly suitable culture and institutional structure,[77] the consequences have been dramatic for Japan and the world. Certainly, the ability of the Ministry of International Trade and Industry to orchestrate many successful areas of industrial expansion, and the existence of large industrial-financial conglomerations, able to guarantee sustained investment and a measure of industrial co-ordination, have had much to do with the impressive performance of Japan during the post-war years.

Whilst industrial development is never unproblematical, its ease or difficulty seems to be related to the institutional and structural conditions obtaining within an economy at the outset, and subsequent germination, of its development programme. For advanced industrial countries that are experiencing a loss of international competitiveness, difficulties are often compounded by the existence of institutions, and associated attitudes, that seemed to serve well during previous periods of economic effectiveness. Indeed, such institutions and attitudes often constitute serious obstacles in the changed conditions of the present. Bland generalizations about appropriate economic and industrial policies are likely to be unhelpful if such fundamental conditions of real-world economies are neglected.

Many examples of industrial policy demonstrate the need for sensitivity towards the conditions that actually prevail within economies. The United Kingdom's flirtations with systematic industrial and economic policy have been far from happy experiences. The half-hearted, and often ill-conceived, nature of such policies reflects the institutional obstacles that confront industrial policy, *per se,* within the United Kingdom of today. The disappointing record of these policies in practice further illustrates the depth and breadth of the prevailing constraints, as the collapse of the 1964-70 Labour government's National Plan and Department of Economic Affairs in the face of bureaucratic resistance and balance-of-payments difficulties dramatically demonstrated.[78]

Ambitious national industrial plans are not, however, the only means by which governments may seek to influence the vigour and effectiveness of domestic industry. Suitable means range from highly intentional policies through to the benign effects of policies initially developed for quite other purposes. Direct intentional policies include those aimed at influencing the cost structures of domestic industry. Here formal prices and incomes policies have sometimes been introduced, but with varying success. The fitful record of prices and incomes policies in the United Kingdom contrasts markedly with the formerly highly effective 'solidaristic' wage policy in Sweden, where the requirement of equal pay across a wide range of industries encouraged the movement of labour from the relatively inefficient to the more inefficient enterprises.[79]

More specific forms of support and intervention may also be pursued through a variety of selective and sectoral industrial policies. Most countries have adopted such discriminating policies at one time or another; sometimes ill-fated; often markedly successful. In the United Kingdom, these have sometimes been *ad hoc* responses to sudden emergencies within a given industry or firm, as with the vain attempt to preserve Laker Airways.[80] They have sometimes been more systematic, as in the case, until the late 1980s, of British governmental support for the micro-electronics and computing industries, and various areas of advanced technology.[81] Japan, too, has been able to sustain systematic selective industrial intervention policies through the good offices of the Ministry of International Trade and Industry.[82]

Special forms of selective intervention are also available in programmes to support the rationalization of industries that are believed to have excess capacity and in policies directed towards the revitalization of areas and regions that are economically disadvantaged. Most advanced industrial countries, and institutions like the European Economic Community, have adopted industrial rationalization and regional development policies at one time or another. Indeed, in the case of the EEC they have been at the core of its being. Moreover, policy may be directed, on occasion, towards support for the small businesses that are believed to be the seed-corn of the major enterprises of tomorrow, particularly when those businesses operate in 'sunrise' sectors of the economy.[83]

Specific areas of the economy can also be encouraged or directed to support the wider industrial effort. The supply and costs of energy are often critical to a competitive industry and official policies in this area may be highly significant. The functioning of the financial system will also be of great importance to business, determining the availability of short and long-term financial support and the terms under which it will be forthcoming. Official policies can have an effect upon the financial system, when and where the political will exists, and may lead to reforms that enhance the support available for the industrial sector.[84]

The range of domestic conditions which are potentially relevant to economic performance and competitiveness, and on which governments may be able to develop effective policies, is far wider than commonly appreciated. The health, education and basic attitudes of the population are germane to economic performance and can be influenced by carefully directed governmental policy. Public health and hygiene campaigns have often been initiated by governments in an attempt to enhance general well-being and vitality. Educational improvements have been at the heart of many countries' pursuit of enhanced economic performance. Great attention was paid to the development of a comprehensive and modern educational system in nineteenth-century Japan. The introduction of a new 'core curriculum' for the secondary educational system by Mrs Thatcher's government in the United Kingdom illustrates a similar concern, as do attempts to secure increased educational standards generally and the fostering an 'enterprise' culture among the young.[85]

There are also numerous external policies and practices open to governments seeking to enhance the international position of their economies. Territorial seizure and imperial control are somewhat unfashionable in the modern world. However, many forms of effective control over other communities may be practised by those states that possess both appropriate resources and the will to exploit them. Sympathetic foreign regimes can be propped up and rewarded with military and economic assistance. Moreover, economic aid can often be manipulated to secure direct benefits for the donors: 'tied' bilateral aid being used to purchase the donor's products; and various forms of conditional aid being used to buy the compliance of the recipient countries.[86] Educational support and provision may, along with various other types of cultural contact, contribute to a form of 'cultural imperialism' which brings many, if often diffuse, benefits to the sources of such influence.[87]

Exports may also be supported by direct subsidies and promotional schemes, or by a variety of helpful domestic policies, including various kinds of subsidy. The blending of economic aid with export credits and guarantees has become a particularly popular form of support of exports to developing countries in a manner that remains relatively, if not entirely, invisible to foreign competitors and international monitoring agencies like the GATT.

A final arena within which governments may mobilize considerable intentional and unintentional assistance for, and provide direction to, industrial developments is that of military research and development (R & D) and subsequent procurement. This area of activity stands at the interface between the external and the internal systems (and demonstrates the artificial nature of their supposed distinction). Military systems are orientated towards external 'threats' and require equipment from the military-orientated sector of industry. However, a significant proportion of the produce of the military supply industry is often sold or donated abroad. In the United Kingdom, France and the United States among the free-enterprise economies, the military industry is highly significant: as a component of industry; as a source of employment; and as a major form of revenue earning exports.[88] Moreover, funding for military-orientated R & D has, at times, been of critical significance to technological progress and wider industrial innovation. The massive developmental funding for micro-electronics and computing, coupled with guaranteed markets for the resulting products, was a major factor in the United States' assumption of the lead in this critical industrial sector in the late 1950s, 1960s and early 1970s.[89]

Finally, governments are able to implement a variety of means of protecting their economies from imports from abroad. *Protectionism* has all too frequently been seen to be the main, if not the only, form of neo-mercantilism practiced by contemporary governments. However, formal tariffs and quotas have been of declining significance during recent years. They are proscribed by the GATT, and have been overtaken by other readily available, and often more subtle, forms of support for domestic industries. Imports have been restricted by extensive non-tariff barriers, ranging from health and safety regulations to voluntary export limitation agreements imposed on foreign would-be exporters. Direct subsidies to sustain the competitiveness of domestic producers and exporters have also been widespread. With the profusion of non-tariff barriers against imports, positive supports for exports, and a range of bilateral trade arrangements with other countries, governments are equipped with many means other than traditional tariffs and quotas when they wish, for whatever reason, to influence the balance and direction of their external trade.[90]

Conclusions

Economic realism, in its many forms, is an approach to political economy that is long-lived, broad in its sources and inspirations, and rich in its analytical insights into the comtemporary global political economy. By eschewing the excessive formalism of liberal, and particularly neo-classical, economics, and by abjuring the determinate dispositions of both liberal and Marxist political economy, it lacks some of their analytical and psychological appeal but retains a greater realism as an approach to the study of a complex, dynamic and turbulent world. The basic concepts and analytical disposition of economic realism do not entail the rejection of all ideas and insights gleaned from the liberal or Marxist approaches, a quality that sometimes renders it difficult to differentiate from these other perspectives. Economic realism provides a filter for the exclusion of the more methodologically or doctrinally extreme elements of alternative approaches while remaining open to the more generally useful contributions. Power and process within a historically conditioned, yet inherently dynamic, context are the central ideas of economic realism and the foundation on which it is able to build flexible, yet orderly and sensitive, analyses of real-world economies and their complex international interconnections.

Economic realism, as outlined here, is also able to accommodate the state and its activities in a flexible and sensitive manner. It is able to avoid the doctrinal repudiation, or analytical relegation, of the state by purer liberals, and some types of Marxist. It is equally able to evade the centralizing implications of state-socialism or the uncritical priority accorded to the state by some international political 'realists.' Morally, and analytically, economic realism accords the state just so much moral force and practical efficacy as conditions and experience appear to warrant; the state is deemed to be neither nothing nor everything!

With regard to the future, economic realism suggests a number of possible courses of development. A constant theme will be that of continuing, and often decisive, action by communities and, when justified, their governments. However, as Robert Gilpin has argued, the loci of power and influence will inevitably move in response to the constant development of the global political economy. The overall shape of the international political economy is, however, less certain. Calleo and Rowland foresee the crystallization of regional mercantilist blocs,[91] while Stephen Krasner envisages the continuation of a fundamental division between an anti-liberal South and the more free-enterprise orientated North.[92]

Economic realism is thus a discriminating and flexible approach to analysis. It permits the construction of realistic recommendations for policy-makers, to be offered with confidence of more widespread acceptability and greater practical success than many of the expectations and prescriptions ushering forth from 'purer' analytical perspectives.

Notes and references

1. For discussions of the nature and reality of mercantilism and its modern echoes, see: D.C. Coleman (ed.), *Revision in Mercantilism* (London: Methuen, 1969); and see also Eric Roll, *A History of Economic Thought* 4th edn (London: Faber and Faber, 1973), pp. 61-85 and 227-31; and Friedrich List, *The National System of Political Economy* (English edition, 1922).
2. See: H.G. Johnson, *The New Mercantilism* (Oxford: Basil Blackwell, 1974), especially 'Mercantilism: Past, Present, Future'; Joan Robinson, 'The New Mercantilism' in Joan Robinson, *Contributions to Modern Economics* (Oxford: Basil Blackwell, 1978), pp. 201-12; and Robert Gilpin, *US Power and the Multinational Corporation: the Political Economy of Foreign Direct Investment* (New York: Basic Books, 1975), esp. pp. 253-8.
3. See, especially, W.J. Samuels, *The Economy as a System of Power, Vols. 1 and 2* (New Brunswick, NJ: Transaction Books, 1979)
4. See, especially, Alfred Eichner, *A Guide to Post-Keynesian Economics* (London: Macmillan, 1979); and Paul Davidson, 'Post Keynsian Economics: Solving the Crisis in Economic Theory' in David Bell and Irving Kristol (eds), *The Crisis in Economic Theory* (New York: Basic Books, 1981), pp. 151-73.
5. See Chris Edwards, *The Fragmented World: Competing Perspectives on Trade, Money and Crisis* (London: Methuen, 1985), esp. Chapter 4; and Ian Steedman *et al.*, *The Value Controversy* (London: Verso, 1981), especially the contributions by Ian Steedman, 'Ricardo, Marx, Sraffa', pp. 11-19, and Eric Olin Wright 'The Value Controversy and Social Research', pp. 36-74; and Ian Steedman, *Marx after Sraffa* (London: New Left

Books, 1977).

6. See Raul Prebisch, *Towards a New Trade Policy for Development* (New York: United Nations, 1964); and D.H. Blake and R.S. Walters, *The Politics of Global Economic Relations*, (Englewood Cliffs, NJ: Prentice-Hall, 1976), esp. pp. 31-6.
7. Hans J. Morgenthau, *Politics Among Nations: The Struggle for Power and Peace* (New York: Alfred Knopf, various editions).
8. For the use of 'realism' as a approach to economic issues, see R.D. McKinlay and R. Little, *Global Problems and World Order*, (London: Frances Pinter, 1986), Chapter 7; and R.J. Barry Jones, *Conflict and Control in the World Economy: Contemporary Economic Realism and Neo-Mercantilism*, (Brighton: Wheatsheaf Books, 1986), esp. Chapter 3.
9. See W.E. Minchinson (ed.), *Mercantilism: System or Expediency* (Lexington, MA: D.C. Heath, 1969), especially the Introduction; and Coleman, *Revision in Mercantilism*.
10. Adam Smith, *The Wealth of Nations* (1766, numerous editions).
11. See Michael Howard, *War in European History* Oxford: Oxford University Press, 1976), esp. Chapter 1.
12. Ibid., Chapter 2.
13. See E.F. Heckscher, *Mercantilism, Vol. 2*, trans. M. Shapiro (London: George Allen & Unwin, 1935).
14. Barry Supple, 'The State and the Industrial Revolution 1700-1914' in Carlo M. Cipolla (ed.), *The Fontana Economic History of Europe: The Industrial Revolution* (London: Fontana/Collins, 1973), p. 317.
15. Phyllis Deane, 'The Industrial Revolution in Great Britain' in Carlo M. Cipolla (ed.), *The Fontana Economic History of Europe: The Emergence of Industrial Societies, Vol. 1*, (London: Fontana/Collins, 1973), p. 208.
16. See Knut Brochardt, 'Germany 1700-1914' in Cipolla *The Fontana Economic History of Europe: The Emergence of Industrial Societies, Vol. 1*, pp. 76-160.
17. Gregory Grossman, 'Russia and the Soviet Union' in Carlo M. Cipolla, *The Fontana Economic History of Europe: The Emergence of Industrial Societies, Vol. 2*, (London: Fontana/Collins, 1973), pp. 486-531.
18. See, for a general discussion of such phenomena, Supple, 'The State and the Industrial Revolution 1700-1914', esp. pp. 319-40 and 344-53.
19. Referenced in C.P. Kindleberger, *Power and Money: The Politics of International Economics and the Economics of International Politics* (London: Macmillan, 1970), pp. 24 and 219.
20. On which see Phyllis Deane, *The Evolution of Economic Ideas* Cambridge: Cambridge University Press, 1978), Chapter 12; William J. Bamber, *A History of Economic Thought* (Harmondsworth: Penguin Books, 1967), Part 4; and A.H. Hansen, *A Guide to Keynes* (New York: McGraw-Hill, 1953).
21. Deane, *The Evolution of Economic Ideas*, Chapter 12.
22. Robinson, *Contributions to Modern Economics*, pp. xi-xix.
23. See Aubrey Silberston, 'Industrial Policies in Britain 1960-80' in Charles Carter (ed.), *Industrial Policy and Innovation* (London: Heinemann, 1981), pp. 39-51.
24. See Wyn Grant's discussion of the debate in the United States on industrial policy in Chapter 4 of this volume.
25. For arguments about the inflationary effects of 'Keynesianism', see Tom Congdon, *Monetarism: An Essay in Definition* (London: Centre for Policy Studies, 1978), esp. pp. 22-32; Milton Friedman (with Rose Friedman), *Free to Choose* (London: Martin Seeker and Warburg, 1980), Chapter 9; Allan H. Meltzer, 'Monetarism and the Crisis in Economics' in Bell and Kristol, *The Crisis in Economic Theory*, pp. 35-45; and J.A. Trevithick, *Inflation: A Guide to the Crisis in Economics* 2nd edn (Harmondsworth: Penguin Books, 1980).
26. See James W. Dean, 'The Dissolution of the Keynesian Consensus' in Bell and Kristol, *The Crisis in Economic Theory*, pp. 19-34.
27. See, for example, J.N. Bhagwati, *The New International Economic Order* (Cambridge, MA: MIT Press, 1977); and E. Laszlo, *et al.*, *The Obstacles to the New International Economic Order* (New York: Pergamon, for UNITAR and CEESTEM, 1980).
28. See, especially, Samuels, *The Economy as a System of Power*.
29. See, as a clear example, Friedman, *Free to Choose*.
30. Eichner, *A Guide to Post-Keynesian Economics*, pp. 11-16.
31. Richard N. Langlois (ed.), *Economics as a Process: Essays in the New Institutional Economics* (Cambridge: Cambridge University Press, 1986), pp. 5-6; and see also John

Foster, *Evolutionary Economics* (London: Allen & Unwin, 1987).
32. Samuels, *The Economy as a System of Power, Vol. 1,* p. iii.
33. Gilpin, *US Power and the Multinational Corporation*, pp. 26-32.
34. Edwards, *The Fragmented World*, Chapter 3 and 4.
35. Ibid., pp. 9-14.
36. See Chapter 2 of this volume. But see also the outline of a model of 'compensatory liberalism', some proponents of which would fall under my economic realist approach, in McKinlay and Little, *Global Problems* esp. pp. 26-41 and 45-8.
37. See Deane, *The Evolution of Economic Ideas, esp.* Chapter 8.
38. See the discussion by Richard R. Nelson, 'The Tension between Process Stories and Equilibrium Models: Analysing the Productivity Growth Slowdown of the 1970s in Langlois, *Economics as a Process*, pp. 135-152.
39. Jones, *Conflict and Control*, pp. 51-2.
40. See, especially, N. Kaldor, 'The Irrelevance of Equilibrium Economics', *Economic Journal*, vol. 82 (December 1972), pp. 1237-55; and J. Hicks, *Causality in Economics* (Oxford: Basil Blackwell, 1979), Chapter 4.
41. See, in particular, Chapters 3 and 7 of this volume.
42. See M.C. Howard and J.E. King, *The Political Economy of Marx*, (Harlow: Longman, 1975) esp. pp. 203-27.
43. See J. Maclean, 'Marxist Epistemology, Explanations of 'Change' and the Study of International Relations' in B. Buzan and R.J. Barry Jones (eds), *Change and the Study of International Relations* (London: Frances Pinter, 1981), pp. 46-67.
44. See, in particular, Ian Steedman *et al., The Value Controversy* (London: Verso, 1981).
45. See Andrew Gamble, 'Critical Political Economy' in R.J. Barry Jones (ed.), *Perspectives on Political Economy: Alternatives to the Economics of Depression* (London: Frances Pinter, 1983), pp. 75-81; and see also Chapter 3 of this volume.
46. Chris Edwards uses it to distinguish Marxist from 'cost of production' analyses of the political economy of North-South economic relations; see Edwards, *The Fragmented World,* esp. pp. 64-82.
47. See Chapter 3 of this volume; also J. Holloway and S. Picciotto (eds), *State and Capital* (London: Edward Arnold, 1978).
48. See Hans J. Morgenthau, *Politics Among Nations: The Struggle for Power and Peace* 4th edn (New York: Alfred Knopf, 1967); E.H. Carr, *The Twenty Years Crisis: An Introduction to the Study of Intermational Relations,* 2nd edn (London: Macmillan, 1946); Robert Gilpin, 'The Richness of the Tradition of Political Realism', *International Organization,* vol 38, no. 2 (Spring 1984), pp. 287-304; and McKinley and Little, *Global Problems,* Chapter 4.
49. See J. Maclean, 'Marxists Epistemology', for a discusssion on such non-observables, not for a rejection of such approaches.
50. See Edwards, *The Fragmented World,* esp. Chapter 3.
51. See, R.J. Barry Jones, *Conflict and Control,* esp. pp. 66-8; and on the significance of uncertainty for economic analysis, see G.L.Shackle, *Uncertainty in Economics and other Reflections* (Cambridge: Cambridge University Press, 1955); and John D. Hey, *Economics in Disenquilibrium* (Oxford: Martin Robertson, 1981).
52. See: Dudley Seers, *The Political Economy of Nationalism,* (Oxford: Oxford University Press, 1983), Chapter 2.
53. On which see Langlois, *Economics as a Process.*
54. See Colin Crouch, 'Corporative Industrial Relations and the Welfare State' in Jones, *Perspectives on Political Economy,* pp. 139-66; Martin Staniland, *What is Political Economy: A Study of Social Theory and Underdevelopment* (New Haven: Yale University Press, 1985), pp. 73-81 and 83-98; and Samuels, *The Economy as a System of Power, vol 1,* part 2; and *vol 2,* Part 4.
55. See Andrew Schonfield *In Defence of the Mixed Economy,* ed. Zusanna Schonfield (Oxford: Oxford University Press, 1984), Part II on Japan; and Takashi Hosomi and Ariyoshi Okumura, 'Japanese Industrial Policy' in J. Pinder (ed.), *National Industrial Strategies and the World Economy* (London: Croom Helm, 1982), pp. 123-57.
56. See the discussion of this problem in Jones, *Conflict and Control in the World Economy,* pp. 116-25.
57. See, in particular, Arghiri Emmanuel, *Unequal Exchange: A Study of the Imperialism of Trade,* trans. Brian Pearce (London: New Left Books 1972).
58. See W.M. Cordon, *Trade Policy and Economic Welfare* (Oxford: Clarendon Press, 1974).

59. See, for example, Peter Kenyon, 'Pricing' in Eichner, *A Guide to Post Keynesian Economics,* pp. 34-45; Gardiner C. Means, 'The Problems and Prospects of Collective Capitalism' in Samuels *The Economy as a System of Power vol. 1,* pp. 123-37; and David Dale Martin, 'Beyond Capitalism; a Role for Markets', in Samuels, *The Economy as a System of Power, vol. 2,* pp. 51-64.
60. Kenyon, 'Pricing'.
61. Emmanuel, *Unequal Exchange.* However, for a critique of the thesis that the South has experienced a long-term decline in its terms of trade, see John P. Powelson, 'The LDCs and their Terms of Trade', *Economic Impact,* vol. 22 (1978), p. 337.
62. Seers, *The Political Economy of Nationalism,* Chapter 6.
63. Ibid., esp. Part B.
64. See, for example, Mancur Olsen, *The Rise and Decline of Nations* (New Haven, CT: Yale University Press, 1982); Frank Blackaby (ed.), *De-industrialisation* (London: Heinemann, 1978); R.E. Caves and L.B. Krause (eds), *Britain's Economic Performance* (Washington, DC: The Brookings Institution, 1980); Ralph Dahrendorf, *On Britain* (London: BBC Publications, 1982); and Charles Carter (ed.), *Industrial Policy and Innovation* (London: Heinemann, 1981).
65. On conservative 'supply-side' economics, see the contributions to vol. 35, no. 3 (1981), vol. 50, no. 2 (1985) and vol. 55, no. 3 (1986) of *Economic Impact*; and on radical 'Supply-side' economics, see *The Alternative Economic Strategy: A Labour Movement Response to the Economic Crisis* (London: CSE Publications, 1980).
66. For an interesting example of such an erroneous view, see C. Fred Bergstern, 'Oil Is Not the Exception' in C. Fred Bergsten, *Toward a New International Economic Order: Selected Papers of C. Fred Bergsten, 1972-1974* (Lexington, MA: Lexington Books, 1975).
67. See Bhagwati, *The New International Economic Order, North-South: A Programme for Survival 'The Brandt Report'* (London: Pan Books, 1980); and S. Krasner, *Structural Conflict: The Third World against Global Liberalism*, (Berkeley: California University Press, 1985).
68. See Laszlo *et al., The Obstacles to the New International Economic Order* and, for a broader perspective, Robert Tucker, *The Inequality of Nations* (New York: Basic Books, 1977).
69. See, especially, Andre Gunder Frank, *On Capitalist Underdevelopment* (Bombay: Oxford University Press, 1975); and Samir Amin, *Accumulation on a World Scale: A Critique of Underdevelopment,* trans. Brian Pearce, (Brighton: Harvester Press, 1974).
70. See, for example, Immanuel Wallerstein, *The Modern World System* (New York: Academic Press, 1974); and Immanuel Wallerstein (ed.), *World Inequality* (Montreal: Black Rose Books, 1973).
71. See, for example, R. Barnet and R. Muller, *Global Reach: The Power of the Multinational Corporations* (New York: Simon and Schuster, 1974); D.P. Calleo and B.J. Rowland, *America and the World Political Economy: Atlantic Dreams and National Realities* (Bloomington: Indiana University Press, 1973), Chapter 7; Robert Gilipin, *US Power and the Multinational Corporation; Samuels, The Economy as a System of Power, Vol. 2,* Part 5 on the international corporate and nation-state systems of power.
72. On which, see Jones, *Conflict and Control*, esp. pp. 104-11 and 125-37.
73. For a discussion of the concept of 'organized capitalism' and its possible dissolution, see Scott Lash and John Urry, *The End of Organized Capitalism* (Oxford: Polity Press, 1987).
74. On the difficulties, see Jones, *Conflict and Control*, pp. 116-31. But on the persistence of internation collaboration, once established, see Robert O. Keohane, *After Hegemony; Cooperation and Discord in the World Political Economy*, (Princeton, NJ: Princeton University Press, 1984).
75. Jones, *Conflict and Control*, esp. pp. 168-78.
76. Marvin J. Wolf, *The Japanese Conspiracy: The Plot to Dominate Industry Worldwide — and How to Deal With It*, (Sevenoaks: New English Library, 1983).
77. Kozo Yamamura and Yasukichi Yasuba (eds), *The Political Economy of Japan, Vol. 1: The Domestic Transformation* (Stanford, CA: Stanford University Press, 1987).
78. Alan Budd, *The Politics of Economic Planning* (London: Fontana, 1970), esp. Chapter 6; and see also B. Lapping, *The Labour Government, 1964-70* (Harmondsworth: Penguin Books, 1970).
79. See M.D. Hancock, 'The Political Management of Economic and Social Change: Contrasting Models of Advanced Industrial society in Sweden and West Germany' in J. Rogers Hollingsworth, *Government and Economic Performance* (Beverly Hills, CA: Sage,

1982); and Jones, *Conflict and Control* pp. 183-4.
80. 'Taxpayer Cash Aid for Laker', *Guardian,* 30 December 1981, p.12.
81. See Jones, *Conflict and Control,* pp. 185-7.
82. Ibid., pp. 187-8. See also many of the contributions in S. Strange and R. Tooze (eds), *The International Political Economy of Surplus Capacity* (London: George Allen & Unwin, 1981).
83. Jones, *Conflict and Control,* pp. 188-93.
84. Ibid., pp. 191-3.
85. Ibid., pp. 193-5 and 197-200.
86. See David Wall, *The Charity of Nations: The Political Economy of Foreign Aid* (New York: Basic Books, 1973); Joan M. Nelson, *Aid, Influence and Foreign Policy* (New York: Macmillan, 1968); Jones, *Conflict and Control* pp. 208-14.
87. Jones, *Conflict and Control*, pp. 214-7.
88. Ibid., pp. 217-22.
89. E. Braun and S. MacDonald, *Revolution in Miniature: The History and Impact of Semiconductor Electronics* (Cambridge: Cambridge University Press, 1978); and Jones, *Conflict and Control* pp. 230-6.
90. Jones, *Conflict and Control*, pp. 253-62.
91. Gilpin, *Gilpin,* US Power and the Multinational Corporation, esp. pp. 253-62.
92. Krasner, *Structural Conflict*.

Notes on Contributors

Chris Brown lectures in politics at the University of Kent. His research interests embrace international political economy, Marxist approaches of international relations and normative theory in international relations. His publications include 'International Political Economy: Some Problems of an Inter-Disciplinary Enterprise', *International Affairs* (1973), and 'Not My Department? Normative Theory and International Relations', *Paradigms: The Kent Journal of International Relations* (1987).

Andrew Gamble is Professor, and Head of the Department, of Politics at the University of Sheffield. Among numerous books and articles he has published are *The Conservative Nation* (1974); *Britain in Decline* (1981); *The Free Economy and Strong State* (1987) and, with P. Walton, *From Alienation to Surplus Value* (1972), and *Capitalism in Crisis: Inflation and the State* (1976).

Wyn Grant is Reader in Politics at the University of Warwick. He has published *The Political Economy of Industrial Policy* (1982), co-authored *Business and Politics in Britain: an introduction* (1987), *The Confederation of British Industry* and co-edited the special edition of *The Journal of Public Policy* on 'Industrial Policies in the OECD Countries' (1982).

R.J. Barry Jones lectures in International Relations and Politics at the University of Reading. He has written on international political economy, transnational corporations and international relations theory. He has published *Conflict and Control in the World Economy: Contemporary Economic Realism and Neo-Mercantilism* (1986), edited *Perspectives on Political Economy* (1983) and co-edited *Change and the Study of International Relations: The Evaded Dimension* (1981) and *Interdependence on Trial: Studies in the Theory and Reality of Contemporary Interdependence* (1984).

David McKay is Senior Lecturer in Government at the University of Essex and Executive Director of the European Consortium for Political Research. He has written widely on American government and politics and on economic and industrial policy. His publications include the co-edited special edition of *The Journal of Public Policy* on 'Industrial Policies in the OECD Countries' (1982).

Roger Tooze is Principal Lecturer in International Relations and Politics at the North Staffordshire Polytechnic. He is the covenor of the International Political Economy Group and his publications in the field of international political economy include *The Failure of International Relations Theory* (1986) and the co-edited *International Political Economy of Surplus Capacity* (1981).

Bibliography

Advisory Council for Applied Research and Development, *The Application of Semiconductor Technology* (London: HMSO, 1978)
Vinod K. Aggarwal, *Liberal Protectionism: The International Politics of Organized Textile Trade* (Berkeley: University of California Press, 1985).
K.J.W. Alexander, *The Political Economy of Change* (Oxford: Basil Blackwell, 1975).
H.R. Alker, 'A Methodology for Design/Research on Interdependence alternatives', *International Organization*, vol. 31, no. 1 (Winter 1977), pp. 29-63.
G.C. Allen, *How Japan Competes: A Verdict on 'Dumping'* (London: Institute of Economic Affairs, 1978).
Samir Amin, *Accumulation on a World Scale*, 2 vols, trans. B. Pearce (Hassocks: Harvester Press, 1974).
Samir Amin, *Neo-Colonialism in West Africa*, trans. F. McDonagh (Harmondsworth: Penguin Books, 1973).
Samir Amin, G. Arrighi, A. Gunder Frank and I. Wallerstein, *Dynamics of Global Crisis* (London: Macmillan, 1982).
D.E. Apter and L.W. Goodman, *The Multinational Corporation and Social Change* (New York: Praeger, 1976)
R.W. Arad, U.B. Arad, R. McCulloch, J. Pinera and A.L. Hollick, *Sharing Global Resources* (New York: McGraw-Hill, 1979).
P. Armstrong, A. Glyn and J. Harrison, *Capitalism since World War II,* (London: Fontana, 1984).
Richard K. Ashley, *The Political Economy of War and Peace* (London: Frances Pinter, 1980).
D. Baldwin, 'Interdependence and Power: A Conceptual Analysis', *International Organization,* vol 34, no. 4 (Autumn, 1980).
D. Baldwin, 'Money and Power', *The Journal of Politics,* vol. 33 (1971), pp. 578-614.
D. Baldwin, 'Power and Social Exchange', *American Political Science Review,* vol. 72 (1978), pp. 1229-1242.
R. Ballance and S. Sinclair, *Collapse and Survival: Industry Strategies in a Changing World* (London: George Allen & Unwin, 1983).
G. Bannock, *The Juggernauts: The Age of the Big Corporation* (London: Weidenfeld and Nicolson, 1971).
P.A. Baran, *The Political Economy of Growth* (New York: Monthly Review Press, 1957).

W.J. Barber, *A History of Economic Thought* (Harmondsworth: Penguin Books, 1967).
C.E. Barfield and W.A. Shambra (eds), *The Politics of Industrial Policy,* (Washington, DC: American Enterprise Institute, 1986).
R.J. Barnet and R.E. Muller, *Global Reach: The Power of the Multinational Corporation* (London: Jonathan Cape, 1975).
Corelli Barnett, *The Collapse of British Power* (London: Eyre Methuen, 1972).
Ian Barron and Ray Curnow, *The Future with Microelectronics* (London: Frances Pinter, 1979).
Brian Barry, *Sociologists, Economists and Democracy* (London: Collier-Macmillan, 1970).
J.N. Behrman, *Conflicting Constraints on the Multinational Enterprise: Potential for Resolution* (New York: Council of the Americas, 1974).
David Bell and Irving Kristol, *The Crisis in Economic Theory* (New York: Basic Books, 1981).
J.N. Behrman, *U.S. International Business and Governments* (New York: McGraw-Hill, 1971).
C. Fred Bergsten, T. Horst and T.H. Moran, *American Multinationals and American Interests* (Washington, DC: The Brookings Institution, 1978).
C. Fred Bergsten, *Toward a New International Economic Order; Selected Papers of C. Fred Bergsten, 1972-1974* (Lexington, MA: Lexington Books/ D.C. Heath, 1975).
C. Fred Bergsten & L.B. Krause (eds), *World Politics and International Economics* (Washington, DC: The Brookings Institution, 1975).
H. Bernstein (ed.), *Underdevelopment and Development: The Third World Today* (Harmondsworth: Penguin Books, 1973).
J.N. Bhagwati (ed.), *Economics and World Order from the 1970s to the 1990s* (New York: Collier-Macmillan, 1972).
J.N. Bhagwati (ed.), *The New International Economic Order: The North-South Debate* (Cambridge, MA: MIT Press, 1977).
Robin Blackburn (ed.), *Ideology in Social Science: Readings in Critical Social Theory* (London: Fontana 1972).
F. Blackaby, (ed.), *De-industrialization* (London: Heinemann, 1978).
D.H. Blake and R.S. Walters. *The Politics of Global Economic Relations* (Englewood Cliffs, NJ: Prentice-Hall, 1976).
H. Block, *Political Arithmetic of the World Economies* (Beverly Hills, CA: Sage, 1974).
Magnus Blomstrom and Bjorn Hettne, *Development Theory in Transition: the Dependency Debates and Beyond: Third World Responses* (London: Zed Press, 1985).
A. Bose, *Marxian and Post-Marxian Political Economy* (Harmondsworth: Penguin Books, 1975).
K.E. Boulding, *Conflict and Defense: A General Theory* (New York: Harper and Row, 1962).
S. Brams, *Game Theory and Politics* (New York: Free Press, 1975).
E.K. Bramsted and K.J. Melhuish (eds), *Western Liberalism: A History in Documents from Locke to Croce* (Harlow: Longman, 1978).
Brandt Report, *North-South: A Programme for Survival* (London: Pan Books, 1980).

Brandt Commission, *Common Crisis North-South: Cooperation for World Recovery* (London: Pan Books, 1983).
E.A. Brett, *International Money and Capitalist Crisis* (London: Heinemann, 1983).
E.A. Brett, *The World Economy Since the War: The politics of Uneven Development* (Basingstoke: Macmillan, 1985).
H. Brookfield, *Interdependent Development* (London: Methuen, 1975).
Christopher Brown, 'Not My Department? Normative Theory and International Relations', *Paradigms: The Kent Journal of International Relations*, vol.1, no. 2 (December 1987), pp. 104-13.
L.R. Brown, *World Without Borders: The Interdependence of Nations* (New York: Foreign Policy Association, 1972)
M. Barratt Brown, *The Economics of Imperialism* (Harmondsworth: Penguin Books, 1975).
M. Barratt Brown, *Models in Political Economy: A Guide to the Arguments*, (Harmondsworth: Penguin Books, 1984).
Robert Brown, *Explanation in Social Science* (London: Routledge and Kegan Paul, 1963).
S. Brown, *New Forces in World Politics* (Washington DC: The Brookings Institution, 1974)
E. Braun and S. MacDonald, *Revolution in Miniature: The History and Impact of Semiconductor Electronics* (Cambridge: Cambridge University Press, 1978).
J.M. Buchanan and G. Tullock, *The Calculus of Consent* (Ann Arbor: University of Michigan Press, 1962).
J.M. Buchanan, *et al.*, *The Economics of Politics* (London: Institute of Economic Affairs, 1978).
Alan Budd, *The Politics of Economic Planning* (London: Fontana, 1970).
H. Bull, 'The Structures that Prevent Collapse into Anarchy', *Times Higher Educational Supplement*, 30 September 1977, p. 13.
J.B. Burbridge, 'The International Dimension' in Alfred S. Eichner, *A Guide to Post-Keynsian Economics* (London: Macmillan, 1979), pp. 139-50.
Barry Buzan, *People, States, and Fear: The National Security Problem in International Relations* (Brighton: Wheatsheaf, 1983).
Barry Buzan and R.J. Barry Jones (eds), *Change and the Study of International Relations: The Evaded Dimension* (London: Frances Pinter, 1981).
M. Caldwell, *The Wealth of Some Nations* (London: Zed Books, 1977).
D.P. Calleo and B.J. Rowland *America and the World Political Economy: Atlantic Dreams and National Realities* (Bloomington: Indiana University Press, 1973).
J.A. Camilleri, *Civilization in Crisis: Human Prospects in a Changing World* (Cambridge: Cambridge University Press, 1976).
Fernando Henrique Cardoso and Enzo Faletto, *Dependency and Development in Latin America* (Berkeley: University of California Press, 1979).
Charles Carter (ed.), *Industrial Policy and Innovation* (London: Heinemann, 1981).
C.F. Carter and J.L. Ford, *Uncertainty and Expectations in Economics: Essays in Honour of G.L.S. Shackle* (Oxford: Basic Blackwell, 1972).

Robert Cassen, *et al., Does Aid Work?* (Oxford: Oxford University Press, 1986).
F. Castles, *Politics and Social Insight* (London: Routledge and Kegan Paul, 1971).
R.E. Caves and L.B. Krause (eds), *Britain's Economic Performance*, (Washington DC: The Brookings Institution, 1980).
R.E. Caves and H.G. Johnson (eds), *Readings in International Economics* (London: George Allen & Unwin, 1968).
A. Cawson (ed.), *Organized Interests and the State* (London: Sage, 1985).
Carlo M. Cipolla (ed.), *The Fontana Economic History of Europe, Vol. 3, The Industrial Revolution* and *Vol. 4, The Emergence of Industrial Societies*, (London: Fontana, 1973).
D.C. Coleman (ed.), *Revision in Mercantilism* (London: Methuen, 1969).
Conference of Socialist Economists, *The Alternative Economic Strategy: A Labour Movement Response to the Economic Crisis* (London: CSE Books, 1980).
Conference of Socialist Economists, *Microelectronics: Capitalist Technology and the Working Class* (London: CSE Books, 1980).
Tim Congdon, *Monetarism: An Essay in Definition* (London: Centre for Policy Studies, 1978).
P.L. Cook and A.J. Surrey, *Energy Policy: Strategies for Uncertainty* (Oxford: Martin Robertson, 1977).
R.N. Cooper, *The Economics of Interdependence: Economic Policy in the Atlantic Community* (New York, McGraw-Hill, 1968).
W.M. Corden, *Trade Policy and Economic Welfare* (Oxford: Clarendon Press, 1974).
Counter Information Services, *The New Technology* (London: Counter Information Services).
Andrew Cox, 'Corporatism as Reductionism: the Analytical Limits of the Corporatist Thesis', *Government and Opposition*, vol. 16 (1981), pp. 78-95.
Robert W. Cox, 'Ideologies and the New International Economic Order: Reflections on Some Recent Literature', *International Organization*, vol. 32, no. 2 (Spring 1979), pp. 257-302.
R.W. Cox and H.K. Jacobson (eds), *The Anatomy of Influence: Decision-Making in International Organizations* (New Haven, CT: Yale University Press, 1974).
Tom Crowe and John Hywel Jones, *The Computer Society* (London: Fabian Society, 1978).
G. Dalton, Economic *Systems and Society: Capitalism, Communism and the Third World* (Harmondsworth: Penguin Books, 1974).
R.A. Dahl and C.E. Lindblom, *Politics, Economics and Welfare* (New York: Harper Row, 1953).
Ralph Dahrendorf, *On Britain* (London: BBC Publications, 1982).
Phyllis Deane, *The Evolution of Economic Ideas* (Cambridge: Cambridge University Press, 1978).
G. Denton, 'European Monetary Co-operation: the Bremen Proposals', *World Today*, vol. 34 (1978), pp. 435-46.
W.D. Diebold, 'Adapting Economies to Structural Change: the International Aspect', *International Affairs* vol. 54 (1978), pp. 573-88.
Peter Donaldson, *Worlds Apart: The Development Gap and What it Means*,

2nd edn (Harmondsworth: Penguin Books, 1986).
C.F. Doran, 'Oil Politics and the Rise of Co-dependence' in D.W. Orr and M.S. Soroos, *The Global Predicament* (Chapel Hill: University of North Carolina Press, 1979).
D. Dosser, D. Gowland and K. Hartley (eds), *The Collaboration of Nations: A Study of European Economic Policy* (Oxford: Martin Robertson, 1982).
Anthony Downs, *An Economic Theory of Democracy* (New York: Harper & Row, 1957).
J.H. Dunning, 'The Future of the Multinational Enterprise', *Lloyds Bank Review*, no. 113 (July 1974), pp. 15-32.
J.H. Dunning (ed.), *The Multinational Corporation* (London: Allen & Unwin, 1972).
J.H. Dunning, *International Production and the Multinational Enterprise* (London: George Allen & Unwin, 1981).
M. East, *et al.*, *Why Nations Act* (Beverly Hills, CA: Sage, 1978).
John Eaton, *Political Economy: A Marxist Textbook* (London: Lawrence and Wishart, 1963).
Chris Edwards, *The Fragmented World: Competing Perspectives on Trade, Money and Crisis* (London: Methuen, 1985).
Alfred S. Eichner (ed.), *A Guide to Post-Keynesian Economics* (London: Macmillan, 1979).
Alfred S. Eichner, *The Megacorp and Oligopoly: Micro Foundations of Macro Dynamics* (White Plains, NY: M.E. Sharpe, 1976).
Peter Ekeh, *Social Exchange Theory: The Two Traditions* (London: Heinemann, 1974).
Electronics Economic Development Committee, *Policy for the UK Electronics Industry* (London: National Economic Development Office, 1982).
P.T. Ellsworth, *The International Economy*, 3rd edn (New York: Collier Macmillan, 1964).
Diane Elson (ed.), *Value* (London: CSE Books, 1969).
Arghiri Emmanuel, *Unequal Exchange, A Study of the Imperialism of Trade*, trans. Brian Pearce (London: New Left Books, 1972).
Christopher Evans, *The Mighty Micro: The Impact of the Computer Revolution* (London: Gollancz, 1979).
P. Evans, *Dependent Development* (Princeton, NJ: Princeton University Press, 1979).
N.S. Fatemi, G.W. Williams and T. de Saint-Phalle, *Multinational Corporations: Problems and Prospects* (South Brunswick, NJ: A.S. Barnes, 1975).
Otto Feinstein (ed.), *Two Worlds of Change: Readings in Economic Development* (New York: Anchor Books, 1964).
R. Fels (ed.), *The Second Crisis of Economic Theory* (Morristown, NJ: General Learning Press, 1972).
Ben Fine and Laurence Harris, *Rereading Capital* (London: Macmillan, 1979).
Tom Forester (ed.), *The Microelectronics Revolution* (Oxford: Basic Blackwell, 1980).
John Foster, *Evolutionary Macroeconomics* (London: Allen & Unwin, 1987).
Andre Gunder Frank, *Capitalism and Underdevelopment in Latin America*, (Harmondsworth: Penguin Books, 1971).
Andre Gunder Frank, *Crisis: In the Third World* (London: Heinemann, 1981).

Andre Gunder Frank, *Crisis: In the World Economy* (London: Heinemann, 1980).
Andre Gunder Frank, *Dependent Accumulation and Under-Development* (London: Macmillan, 1978).
Andre Gunder Frank, *On Capitalist Underdevelopment* (Bombay: Oxford University Press, 1975).
Robert Freedman (ed.), *Marx on Economics* (Harmondsworth: Penguin Books, 1962).
C. Freeman and M. Jahoda, *World Futures: The Great Debate* (Oxford: Martin Robertson, 1978).
Bruno S. Frey, 'The Public Choice View of International Political Economy', *International Organization*, vol. 38, no. 1 (Winter 1984).
Milton Friedman, *Free to Choose: A Personal Statement* (London: Martin Secker and Warburg, 1980).
N. Frolich and J.A. Oppenheimer, 'I get By With a Little Help from My Friends', *World Politics*, Vol. 20 (1970), pp. 104-20.
N. Frolich, J.A. Oppenheimer and O.R. Young, *Political Leadership and Collective Goods* (Princeton, NJ: Princeton University Press, 1971).
N. Frolich and J.A. Oppenheimer, *Modern Political Economy* (Englewood Cliffs, NJ: Prentice-Hall, 1978).
David Fromkin, *The Independence of Nations* (New York: Praeger, 1981).
J.K. Galbraith, *American Capitalism: The Concept of Counterveiling Power* (London: Hamish Hamilton, 1957).
J.K. Galbraith, *The Liberal Hour* (London: Hamish Hamilton, 1960).
J.K. Galbraith, *The new Industrial State* 2nd edn (London: André Deutsch, 1972).
J.K. Galbraith, *Economics and the Public Purpose* (London: André Deutsch, 1974).
J.K. Galbraith, *The Age of Uncertainty* (London: André Deutsch, 1977).
Johan Galtung, 'A Structural Theory of Imperialism', *Journal of Peace Research*, vol. 13, no. 2 (1971), pp. 81-94.
Andrew Gamble, *Britain in Decline: Economic Policy, Political Strategy and the British State* (London: Macmillan, 1981).
Andrew Gamble, *The Free Economy and Strong State* (London: Macmillan, 1987).
J.C. Garnett, *Commonsense and the Theory of International Relations* (London: Macmillan, 1984).
Susan George, *How the Other Half Dies: The Real Reasons for World Hunger* (Harmondsworth: Penguin Books, 1976).
Robert Gilpin, *The Political Economy of International Relations* (Princeton, NJ: Princeton University Press, 1987).
Robert Gilpin, *US Power and the Multinational Corporation: The Political Economy of Foreign Direct Investment* (New York: Basic Books, 1975; London: Macmillan, 1976).
Robert Gilpin, 'The Richness of the Tradition of Political Realism', *International Organization,* vol. 38, no. 2 (Spring 1984), pp. 287-304.
M. Godet and O. Ruyssen, *The Old World and the New Technologies,* (Luxembourg: Office for Official Publications of the European Communities, 1981).
Wynne Godley and Francis Cripps, *Macroeconomics* (London: Fontana,

1983).
Kjell Goldman and Gunnar Sjostedt, *Power, Capabilities, Interdependence* (London: Sage, 1979).
L. Gomes, *International Economic Problems* (London: Macmillan, 1978).
G. Goodwin and J. Mayall, 'The Political Dimension of the UNCTAD Integrated Community Scheme', *Millenium: Journal of International Studies,* vol. 6, no. 2 (Autumn 1977), pp. 146-61.
F. Gordon-Ashworth, *International Commodity Control: A Contemporary History and Appraisal* (London: Croom Helm, 1984).
Wyn Grant, 'Large Firms and Public Policy in Britain', *Journal of Public Policy,* vol. 4 (1984), pp. 1-17.
Wyn Grant and David McKay (eds), 'Industrial Policies in OECD Countries', special edition of *Journal of Public Policy,* vol. 3 (February 1982).
Wyn Grant and Jane Sargent, Business and Politics in Britain: An Introduction (London: Macmillan, 1987).
F. Green and P. Nore, *Economics: An Anti-Text,* (London: Macmillan, 1977).
H.G. Grubel, 'The Case against the New International Economic Order', *Review of World Economics,* vol. 113 (1977), pp. 284-307.
H.G. Grubel, *The International Monetary System,* 3rd edn (Harmondsworth: Penguin Books, 1977).
S. Haggard and Beth A. Simmons, 'Theories of International Regimes', *International Organisation,* vol. 41, no. 3 (Summer 1987), pp. 491-517).
Peter Hall, *Governing the Economy* (Oxford: Polity Press, 1986).
A.H. Hansen, *A Guide to Keynes* (New York: McGraw-Hill, 1953).
Vilho Harle (ed.), *The Political Economy of Food* (Westmead, Hants: Saxon House, 1978).
N. Harris, *Of Bread and Guns: The World Economy in Crisis* (Harmondsworth: Penguin Books, 1983).
K. Hartley, *Problems of Economic Policy* (London: George Allen & Unwin, 1977).
D. Harvey, *The Limits to Capital* (Oxford: Basil Blackwell, 1982).
F.A. Hayek, *The Road to Serfdom* (London: Routledge and Kegan Paul, 1944).
F.A. Hayek, *The Constitution of Liberty* (London: Routledge and Kegan Paul, 1960).
Teresa Hayter, *Aid as Imperialism* (Harmondsworth: Penguin, 1971).
Teresa Hayter, *The Creation of World Poverty* (London: Pluto Press, 1981).
Anthony Heath, *Rational Choice and Social Exchange: A Critique of Exchange Theory,* (Cambridge: Cambridge University Press, 1976).
E.F. Heckscher, *Mercantilism,* 2 vols, trans. M. Shapiro (London: George Allen & Unwin, 1935).
R.L. Heilbroner, *Between Capitalism and Socialism: Essays in Political Economics* (New York: Vintage Books, 1970).
C.R. Hensman, *Rich Against Poor: The Reality of Aid* (Harmondsworth: Allen Lane, 1971).
P. Hertner and G. Jones, *Multinationals: Theory and History* (Aldershot: Gower, 1986).
J.D. Hey, *Economics in Disequilibrium* (Oxford: Martin Robertson, 1981).
John Hicks, *Causality in Economics* (Oxford: Basil Blackwell, 1979).
Brian Hindley and Eri Nicolaides, *Taking the New Protectionism Seriously*

(London: Trade Policy Research Centre, 1983).
Fred Hirsch, 'Is there a New International Economic Order?', *International Organization,* vol. 30, no. 3 (Summer 1976), pp. 521-31.
Fred Hirsch, *Social Limits to Growth* (London: Routledge and Kegan Paul, 1977).
Fred Hirsch, M. Doyle and E.L. Morse, *Alternatives to Monetary Disorder* (New York: McGraw-Hill, 1977).
Fred Hirsch and J.H. Goldthorpe, (eds), *The Political Economy of Inflation* (Oxford: Martin Robertson, 1978).
A.O. Hirschman, *National Power and the Structure of Foreign Trade* (Berkeley: University of California Press, 1945; expanded edn, 1980).
E.J. Hobsbawm, *Industry and Empire: Pelican Economic History of Britain vol. 3* (London: Weidenfeld and Nicolson, 1968; and Harmondsworth: Penguin, 1969).
M. Hodges, *Multinational Corporations and National Government: A Case Study of the United Kingdom's Experience 1964-1970* (Farnborough: Saxon House, 1974).
S. Holland, *The Socialist Challenge* (London: Quartet, 1975).
S. Holland (ed.), *Beyond Capitalist Planning* (Oxford: Basil Blackwell, 1978).
S. Holland, *The Global Economy: from Meso to Macro Economics* (London: Weidenfeld and Nicolson, 1987).
J. Rogers Hollingsworth (ed.), *Government and Economic Performance,* special edition of *The Annals,* (Beverly Hill, CA: Sage, 1982).
J. Holloway and S. Picciotto, (eds), *State and Capital: A Marxist Debate* (London: Edward Arnold, 1978).
M.C. Howard and J.E. King, *The Political Economy of Marx* (Harlow: Longman, 1975).
E.K. Hunt, *Property and Prophets: The Evolution of Economic Institutions and Ideologists* (New York: Harper and Row, 1981).
T.W. Hutchinson, *Knowledge and Ignorance in Economics* (Oxford: Basil Blackwell, 1977).
W.H. Hutt, *Politically Impossible* (London: IEA, 1971).
W.F. Ilchman and N.T. Uphoff, *The Political Economy of Change* (Berkeley: University of California Press, 1971).
Alex Inkeles, 'The Emerging Social Structure of the World', *World Politics,* vol. 27 (1975), pp. 467-95.
A.P. Jacquemin and H.W. de Jong (eds), *Markets, Corporate Behaviour and the State* (The Hague: Martinus Nijhoff, 1976).
C. Jenkins and B. Sherman, *The Collapse of Work* (London: Eyre Methuen, 1979).
Robin Jenkins, *Exploitation: The World Power Structure and the Inequality of Nations* (London: MacGibbon and Kee, 1970).
Bob Jessop, *The Capitalist State* (Oxford: Martin Robertson, 1982).
R.A. Johns, 'Transnational Business, National Friction Structures and International Exchange', *Review of International Studies*, vol. 10, no. 2 (April 1984), pp. 125-42.
C. Johnson (ed.), *The Industrial Policy Debate* (San Francisco: ICS Press, 1984).
H.G. Johnson (ed.), *The New Mercantilism: Some Problems in International Trade, Money and Investment* (Oxford: Basil Blackwell, 1974).

H.G. Johnson (ed.), *Planning and Productivity in Sweden* (London: Croom Helm, 1976).
R.J. Barry Jones, 'International Political Economy: Problems and Issues', *Review of International Studies*, vol. 7, no. 4 (1981), pp. 245-60.
R.J. Barry Jones, 'International Political Economy: Perspectives and Prospects' *Review of International Studies,* vol. 8, no. 1 (1982), pp. 39-52.
R.J. Barry Jones, (ed.), *Perspectives on Political Economy: Alternatives to the Economics of Depression* (London: Frances Pinter, 1983).
R.J. Barry Jones, *Conflict and Control in the World Economy: Contemporary Economic Realism and Neo-Mercantilism* (Brighton: Wheatsheaf, 1986).
R.J. Barry Jones and P. Willetts (eds), *Interdependence on Trial: Studies in the Theory and Reality of Contemporary Interdependence* (London: Frances Pinter, 1984).
Antonio Jorge, *Competition, Cooperation, Efficiency, and Social Organization: Introduction to a Political Economy* (Cranbury, NJ: Associated University Presses, 1978).
N. Kaldor, 'The Irrelevance of Equilibrium of Economics', *Economic Journal* vol. 82, no. 328 (December 1972) pp. 1237-55.
P.J. Katzenstein, *Between Power and Plenty: Foreign Economic Policies of Advanced Industrial States* (Madison: Wisconsin University Press, 1978).
P.J. Katzenstein, 'International interdependence: Some long-term trends and recent changes', *International organization*, vol. 29, no. 4, pp. 1021-34.
G. Kay, *Development and Underdevelopment* (London: Macmillan, 1975).
Estes Kefauver, *In a Few Hands: Monopoly Power in America* (Harmondsworth: Penguin Books, 1966).
C.W. Kegley and P. McGowan, *The Political Economy of Foreign Policy Behavior* (Beverly Hills, CA: Sage, 1981).
W. Kennet, L. Whittey and S. Holland, *Sovereignty and Multinational Corporations* (London: Fabian Society, 1971).
A.G. Kenwood and A.L. Lougheed, *The Growth of the International Economy, 1820-1980* (London: George Allen & Unwin, 1983).
R.O. Keohane, *After Hegemony: Cooperation and Discord in the World Political Economy* (Princeton, NJ: Princeton University Press, 1984).
R.O. Keohane and J.S. Nye, *Power and Interdependence: World Politics in Transition* (Boston: Little, Brown, 1977).
R.O. Keohane and J.S. Nye (eds), *Transnational Relations and World Politics* (Cambridge, MA: Harvard University Press, 1972).
Michael Kidron, *Western Capitalism Since the War* revised edn (Harmondsworth: Penguin, 1970).
V.G. Kiernan, *Marxism and Imperialism* (London: Edward Arnold, 1974).
R. Kimber, 'Collective Action and the Fallacy of the Liberal Fallacy', *World Politics* vol. 33 (1981), pp. 178-96.
C.P. Kindleberger, *Power and Money: The Politics of International Economics and the Economics of International Politics* (New York: Basic Books, 1970).
C.P. Kindleberger, *International Economics*, 5th edn (Homewood IL: 1973)
John Knapp, 'Economics or Political Economy', *Lloyds Bank Review*, (January 1973), pp. 19-43.

K.W. Knapp, *The Social Costs of Business Enterprise*, extended edn (Nottingham: Spokesman Books, 1978).
Klaus Knorr, *Power and Wealth: The Political Economy of International Power* (London: Macmillan, 1973).
Stephen D. Krasner, 'State Power and the Structure of International Trade', *World Politics*, vol. 28 (1976), pp. 317-47.
Stephen D. Krasner, *International Regimes* (Ithaca, NY: Cornell University Press, 1983).
Stephen D. Krasner, *Structural Conflict: The Third World Against Global Liberalism* (Berkeley: University of California Press, 1985).
K. Kumar, *Prophecy and Progress* (Harmondsworth: Penguin Books, 1978).
Sanjaya Lall, *et al.*, *The New Multinationals: the Spread of Third World enterprises* (New York: John Wiley, 1984).
R.N. Langlois (ed.), *Economics as a Process: Essays in the New Institutional Economics* (Cambridge: Cambridge University Press, 1986).
Peter Large, *The Micro Revolution* (London: Fontana, 1980).
Scott Lash and John Urry, *The End of Organized Capitalism* (Oxford: Polity Press, 1987).
E. Laszlo, *et at.*, *The Obstacles to the New International Economic Order*, New York: Pergamon for UNITAR and CEESTEM, 1980).
E. Laszlo and J. Kurtsman (eds), *The Structure of the World Economy and Prospects for a New International Economic order* (New York and London: 1980).
M. Laver, *The Politics of Private Desires* (Harmondsworth: Penguin, 1981).
G. Lean, *Rich World, Poor World* (London: George Allen & Unwin, 1978).
W.I. Lenin, *Imperialism: The Highest State of Capitalism* (1916), various editions, available in Vol. 22 of Collected Works, (Moscow: Progress Publishers).
S. Lens, *The Military-Industrial Complex* (London: Stanmore Press, 1971).
J.C. Leontiades, *Multinational Corporate Strategy* (Aldershot: Gower, 1985).
W. Arthur Lewis, *Evolution of the International Economic Order* (Princeton, NJ: Princeton University Press, 1978).
L. Lindber, *et al.*, (eds)., *Stress and Contradiction in Modern Capitalism* (Lexington, MA: D.C. Heath, 1975).
George Lichtheim, *Imperialism* (London: Allen Lane, 1971).
Merle Lipton, *Capitalism and Apartheid: South Africa, 1910-84.* (Aldershot: Gower, 1985).
Friedrich List, *The National System of Political Economy* (1841), trans, S.S. Lloyd (London: Longmans, Green, 1904).
W.N. Loucks, *Comparative Economic Systems* 6th edn (New York: Harper and Row, 1961).
Evan Luard, *Economic Relationships Among States* (London: Macmillan, 1984).
Evan Luard, *The Management of the World Economy* (London: Macmillan, 1983).
Andrew Mack, 'Theories of Imperialism: The European Perspective', *Journal of Conflict Resolution,* vol. 18, no. 3 (September 1974), pp. 514-35.
C.B. Macpherson, *The Political Theory of Possessive Individualism* (Oxford: Clarendon Press, 1962).
Karl Marx, *Capital, vols 1 and 2,* (London: Everyman/Dent, 1930 (originally,

1867 and 1885 respectively)).
Karl Marx, *Grundrisse,* trans. M. Nicolaus (Harmondsworth: Penguin, 1973).
Gordon H. McCormack and R.E. Bissell (eds), *Strategic Dimensions of Economic Behaviour* (New York: Praeger, 1984).
R.D. McKinlay and R. Little, *Global Problems and World Order* (London: Frances Pinter, 1986).
Gerald M. Meier, *Leading Issues in Economic Development* 3rd edn (New York: Oxford University Press, 1976).
F.V. Meyer, *International Trade Policy* (London: Croom Helm, 1978).
Michael Michaely, *Concentration in International Trade* (Amsterdam: North-Holland Publishing Co., 1962).
Ralph Milliband, *The State in Capitalist Society: The Analysis of the Western System of Power* (London: Weidenfeld and Nicolson, 1969).
W.E. Minchinson (ed.), *Mercantilism: System or Expediency* (Lexington, MA: D.C. Heath, 1969).
E.J. Mishan, *The Costs of Economic Growth* (London: Staples Press, 1967).
G. Modelski (ed.), *Multinational Corporations and World Order* (Beverly Hills, CA: Sage, 1972).
M. Moran, 'The Politics of International Business', *British Journal of International Studies,* vol. 8, no. 2 (April 1978) pp. 217-36.
Hans J. Morgenthau, *Politics Among Nations: The Struggle for Power and Peace* (New York: Alfred Knopf, numerous editions).
E.L. Morse, *Modernization and the Transformation of International Relations* (New York: Free Press, 1976).
D.C. Mueller, *Public Choice* (Cambridge: Cambridge University Press, 1979).
R.E. Mueller and R.J. Barnet, *Global Reach: The Power of the Multinational Corporation* (New York: Simon and Schuster, 1974).
R. Murray, *Multinational Companies and Nation States* (London: Spokesman Books, 1975).
Gunnar Myrdal, *The Political Element in the Development of Economic Theory,* trans. Paul Streeten (London: Routledge and Kegan Paul, 1953).
J.H. Nagel, *The Descriptive Analysis of Power* (New Haven, CT: Yale University Press, 1975).
Joan M. Nelson, *Aid, Influence, and Foreign Policy* (New York: Macmillan, 1968).
Theo Nichols (ed.), *Capital and Labour: A Marxist Primer* (London: Fontana, 1980).
M. Nicholson, *Conflict Analysis* (London: English Universities Press, 1970).
Kwame Nkrumah, *Neo-Colonialism: The Last Stage of Imperialism* (London: Heinemann, 1965).
S. Nora and A. Minc, *The Computerization of Society: A Report to the President of France* (Cambridge, MA: MIT Press, 1981).
P. Norbury and G. Bownas (eds), *Business in Japan: A Guide to Japanese Business Practice and Procedure,* 2nd edn (London: Macmillan, 1980).
C. Norman, *Microelectronics at Work: Productivity and Jobs in the World Economy,* Worldwatch Paper 39 (Washington, DC: Worldwatch Institute, 1980).
Fred Northedge, 'Transnationalism: The American Illusion', *Millennium: Journal of International Studies,* vol. 5 (1970).

R. Cruise O'Brien (ed.), *Information, Economics and Power: The North-South Dimension* (London: Hodder and Stoughton, 1983).
R. Cruise O'Brien and G.K. Helleiner, 'The Political Economy of Information in a Changing International Economic Order', *International Organization,* vol 34, no. 4 (Autumn 1980), pp. 445-70.
James O'Connor, *Accumulation Crisis* (Oxford: Basil Blackwell, 1984).
James O'Connor, *The Fiscal Crisis of the State* (New York: St Martin's Press, 1978).
Peter R. Odell, *Oil and World Power: Background to the Oil Crisis,* 3rd edn (Harmondsworth: Penguin, 1974).
Peter R. Odell and Luis Vallenilla, *The Pressures of Oil: A Strategy for Economic Revival* (London: Harper and Row, 1978).
C. Offe, *Disorganized Capitalism* (Cambridge: Polity Press, 1985).
Mancur Olson, *The Logic of Collective Action: Public Goods and the Theory of Groups* (Cambridge; Cambridge University Press, 1965).
Mancur Olson, *The Rise and Decline of Nations: Economic Growth, Stagflation and Social Rigidities* (New Haven, CT: Yale University Press, 1982).
R.K. Olson, *U.S. Foreign Policy and the New International Economic Order: Negotiating Global Problems, 1974-1981* (Boulder, CO: Westview Press, 1981).
R.L. O'Meara, 'Regimes and Their Implications for International Theory', *Millennium,* vol. 13, no. 3 (Winter 1984), pp. 245-64.
John O'Neill, (eds.), *Modes of Individualism and Collectivism* (London: Heinemann, 1973).
R. Owen and B. Sutcliffe, (eds), *Studies in the Theory of Imperialism* (London: Longman, 1972).
Michael Parkin and George Zis (eds), *Inflation in Open Economies,* (Manchester: Manchester University Press, 1976).
T. Pateman (ed.), *Counter Course: A Handbook for Course Criticism* (Harmondsworth: Penguin, 1972).
Cheryl Payer (ed.), *Community Trade of the Third World* (London: Macmillan, 1975).
Cheryl Payer, *The Debt Trap; The IMF and the Third World* (Harmondsworth: Penguin, 1974).
Lester B. Pearson, *et al., Partners in Development: Report of the Commission on International Development* (New York: Praeger, 1969).
M. Peston, *Whatever Happened to Macro-economics?* (Manchester: Manchester University Press, 1980).
E.H. Phelps-Brown, 'The Underdevelopment of Economics,' *Economic Journal,* vol. 82 (1972), pp. 1-10.
A.J. Pierre (ed.), *Unemployment and Growth in the Western Economies* (New York: Council on Foreign Regulations. 1984).
Kees van der Pijl, *The Making of an Atlantic Ruling Class* (London: Verso, 1984).
J. Pinder (ed.), *National Industrial Strategies and the World Economy.,* (London: Croom Helm, 1981).
M.J. Piore and C.F. Sabel, *The Second Industrial Divide* (New York: Basic Books, 1984).
D. Pirages, *Global Ecopolitics: The New Context for International Relations,*

(Belmont, CA: Duxbury, 1978).
Karl Polanyi, *The Great Transformation: The Political and Economic Origins of Our Time* (Boston: Beacon Press, 1957).
Sidney Pollard, *The idea of Progress: History and Society* (London: C.A. Watts, 1968).
Sidney Pollard, *The Integration of the European Economy since 1815*, (London: George Allen and Unwin, 1981).
Sidney Pollard, *The Wasting of the British Economy* (London: Croom Helm, 1984).
Nicos Poulantzas, *State, Power, Socialism* (London: New Left Books, 1978).
J.P. Powelson, 'The LDCs and the Terms of Trade', *Economic Impact*, vol. 22 (1978), pp. 33-7.
Raul Prebisch, *Towards a New Trade Policy for Development* (New York: UN Publications, 1964).
R.D. Putnam and N. Bayne, *Hanging Together: The Seven Power Summits* (Cambridge, MA: Harvard University Press, 1984).
J. Rada, *The Impact of Micro-electronics* (Geneva: International Labour Office, 1980).
H. Radice (ed.), *International Firms and Modern Imperialism* (Harmondsworth: Penguin, 1975).
A. Rapoport, *Conflict in a Man-Made Environment* (Harmondsworth: Penguin, 1974).
J.L. Ray and T. Webster, 'Dependency and Economic Growth in Latin America', *International Studies Quarterly*, vol. 22, no. 3 (September 1978), pp. 409-34.
P.A. Reynolds and R.D. McKinley, 'The Concept of Interdependence: Its Uses and Misuses', in Kjell Goldmann and Gunnar Sjostedt, *Power, Capabilities, Interdependence* (London: Sage, 1979).
J.H. Richards, *International Economic Institutions* (London: Holt, Rinehart and Winston, 1970).
A.R. Riddell (ed.), *Adjustment or Protectionism: The Challenge to Britain of Third World Industrialisation* (London: Catholic Institute for International Relations, 1980).
Roger Riddell, *Foreign Aid Reconsidered* (Baltimore: Johns Hopkins University Press, 1987).
Joan Robinson, *Economic Philosophy* (London: A.C. Watts, 1962).
Joan Robinson, *Contributions to Modern Economics* (Oxford: Basil Blackwell, 1978).
Joan Robinson and John Eatwell, *An Introduction to Modern Economics*, revised edn (London: McGraw-Hill, 1973).
John Robinson, *Multinationals and Political Control* (Aldershot: Gower, 1983).
Eric Roll, *A History of Economic Thought* (London: Faber and Faber, 1973).
R. Rosecrance, 'International Theory Revisited', *International Organization*, vol. 35 (1981), pp. 691-713.
R. Rosecrance and A. Stein, 'Interdependence: Myth or Reality?', *World Politics*, vol. 26, no. 1 (October 1973), pp. 1-27.
R. Rosecrance, *et al.*, 'Whither Interdependence?', *International Organization*, vol. 31, no. 3 (Summer 1977), pp. 425-71.
J.N. Rosenau, *Linkage Politics* (New York: Free Press, 1969).

J.N. Rosenau, *The Study of Global Interdependence* (London: Frances Pinter, 1980).
W.W. Rostow, *The Stages of Economic Growth* (Cambridge: Cambridge University Press, 1960).
Bruce M. Russett, *Economic Theories of International Politics* (Chicago: Markham, 1968).
D.A. Rustow and J.F. Mugno, *OPEC: Success and Prospects* (Oxford: Martin Robertson, 1976).
A. Sampson, *The Sovereign State: The Secret History of ITT* (London: Hodder and Stoughton, 1973).
A. Sampson, *The Seven Sisters: The Great Oil Companies and the World They Made* (London: Hodder and Stoughton, 1975).
A. Sampson, *The Arms Bazaar* (London: Hodder and Stoughton, 1977).
A. Sampson, *The Money Lenders: Bankers in a Dangerous World* (London: Hodder and Stoughton, 1981).
W.J. Samuels (ed.), *The Economy as a System of Power*, 2 vols (New Brunswick, NJ: Transaction Books, 1979).
W.J. Samuels (ed.), *The Methodology of Economic Thought: Critical Papers from the Journal of Economic Thought*, (New Brunswick, NJ: Transaction Books, 1980).
K.P. Sauvant and F.G. Lavipour, *Controlling Multinational Enterprises: Problems, Strategies, Counterstrategies* (London: Wilton House Publications, 1976).
T.C. Schelling, *The Strategy of Conflict* (Oxford: Oxford University Press, 1963).
H.O. Schmitt, 'Integration and Conflict in the World Economy', *Journal of Common Market Studies*, vol. 7 (1969), pp. 1-18.
J.A. Schumpeter, *Capitalism, Socialism and Democracy*, 5th edn (London: George Allen & Unwin, 1976).
E. Sciberras, *Multinational Electronics Companies and National Economic Policies* (Greenwich, CT: JAI Press, 1977).
Dudley Seers, *The Political Economy of Nationalism* (Oxford: Oxford University Press, 1983).
Dudley Seers and Leonard Joy, *Development in a Divided World* (Harmondsworth: Penguin, 1971).
Jean-Jacques Servan-Schreiber, *The American Challenge,* trans. R. Steel (London: Hamish Hamilton, 1968).
G.L.S. Shackle, *Uncertainty in Economics and other Reflections* (Cambridge: Cambridge University Press, 1955).
G. Shepherd, F. Duchene and C. Saunders, *Europe's Industries: Public and Private Strategies for Change* (London: Frances Pinter, 1983).
Martin Shaw, *Marxism and Social Science: The Roots of Social Knowledge* (London: Pluto Press, 1975).
A. Shonfield, *Modern Capitalism: The Changing Balance of Public Power* (Oxford: Oxford University Press, 1965).
A. Shonfield, *International Economic Relations: Washington Papers No. 42*, (Beverly Hills, CA: Sage, 1976).
A. Shonfield, *In Defence of the Mixed Economy*, ed. Z. Shonfield, (Oxford: Oxford University Press, 1984).
A.M. Sievers, *Revolution, Evolution and the Economic Order* (Englewood

Cliffs, NJ: Prentice-Hall, 1962).
H.A. Simon, *Administrative Behavior: A Study of Decision-Making Processes in Administrative Organizations,* 2nd edn (New York: Free Press, 1957).
D. Simpson, *The Political Economy of Growth* (Oxford: Basil Blackwell, 1983).
Hans Singer, John Wood and Tony Jennings, *Food Aid: The Challenge and the Opportunity* (Oxford: Oxford University Press, 1987).
Hans Singer and Javed Ansari, *Rich and Poor Countries,* 2nd edn (London: George Allen & Unwin, 1978).
A. Sivanandan, *Imperialism in the Silicon Age: Race and Class Pamphlet No. 8* (London: Institute of Race Relations, 1980).
E.B. Skolnikoff, *The International Imperatives of Technology: Technological Development and the International Political System* (Berkeley: Institute of International Studies, University of California, 1972).
Adam Smith, *An Inquiry into the Nature and Causes of the Wealth of Nations* (1776), numerous editions.
A. Smith, *The Geopolitics of Information* (London: Faber, 1980).
M.H. Smith, *Western Europe and the United States: the Uncertain Alliance* (London, Allen & Unwin, 1984).
Tony Smith, 'The Underdevelopment of Development Literature: The Case of Dependency Theory', *World Politics,* vol. 31 (1979), pp. 247-88.
Douglas C. Smyth, 'The Global Economy and the Third World: Coalition or Cleavage?', *World Politics,* vol. 29, no. 4 (July 1977), pp. 584-609.
J.E. Spero, *The Politics of International Economy Relations,* 2nd edn (London: George Allen & Unwin, 1982).
Martin Staniland, *What is Political Economy? A Study in Social Theory and Underdevelopment* (New Haven, CT: Yale University Press, 1985).
Robert B. Stauffer (ed.), *Transnational Relations and the State* (Sydney: University of Sydney Transnational Relations Research Project, 1985).
Ian Steedman, *et al., The Value Controversy* (London: Verso, 1981).
Michael Stewart, *Controlling the Economic Future: Policy Dilemmas in a Shrinking World* (Brighton: Wheatsheaf Books, 1983).
Susan Strange, 'International Economics and International Relations: A Case of Mutual Neglect', *International Affairs,* vol. 46 (1970), pp. 304-15.
Susan Strange, *Sterling and British Policy: A Political Study of an International Currency in Decline* (London: Oxford University Press, 1971).
Susan Strange, 'Who Runs World Shipping?', *International Affairs,* vol. 52, no. 3, (July 1976), pp. 346-67.
Susan Strange (ed.), *Paths to International Political Economy* (London: George Allen & Unwin, 1984).
Susan Strange, 'Protectionism and World Politics', *International Organization,* vol. 39, no. 2 (Spring 1985), pp. 233-59.
Susan Strange, *Casino Capitalism* (Oxford: Basil Blackwell, 1986).
Susan Strange and Roger Tooze (eds.), *The International Political Economy of Surplus Capacity: Competition for Market Shares in the World Recession* (London: George Allen & Unwin, 1981).
Paul Streeton, 'The Political Economy of the Environment: Problems of Method', in C.F. Carter and J.L. Ford, *Uncertainty and Expectations in Economics: Essays in Honour of G.L.S. Shackle* (Oxford: Basil Blackwell, 1972), pp. 276-90.

Dennis Swan, *The Economics of the Common Market,* 4th edn (Harmondsworth: Penguin, 1978).
Dennis Swan, *Competition and Industrial Policy in the European Community* (London: Methuen, 1983).
Mary Ann Tetreault, 'Measuring Interdependence', *International Organization,* vol. 34, no. 3 (Summer 1980), pp. 429-516.
Mary Ann Tetreault and Charles F. Abel (eds), *Dependence Theory and the Return of High Politics* (Greenwood Press, 1986).
G. Thayer, *The War Business: The International Trade in Armaments* (London: Weidenfeld and Nicolson, 1969).
J.E. Tilton, *International Diffusion of Technology: The Case of Semiconductors* (Washington, DC: The Brookings Institution, 1971).
Jan Tinbergen (ed.), *Reshaping the International Order: A Report to the Club of Rome* (London: Hutchinson, 1977).
L. Tivey, *The Politics of the Firm* (Oxford: Martin Robertson, 1978).
R. Tooze, 'Economics, International Political Economy and Change in the International System' in Barry Buzan and R.J. Barry Jones (eds), *Change and the Study of International Relations: The Evaded Dimension* (London: Frances Pinter, 1981).
R. Tooze, *The Failure of International Relations Theory* (London: Frances Pinter, 1986).
Trades Union Congress, *Employment and Technology: A TUC Interim Report* (London: TUC, 1979).
M. Trebilcock, *The Political Economy of Economic Adjustment* (Toronto: University of Toronto Press, 1986).
J.A. Trevithick, *Inflation: A Guide to the Crisis in Economics* 2nd edn (Harmondsworth: Penguin, 1980).
R.W. Tucker, *The Inequality of Nations* (New York: Basic Books, 1977).
C. Tugendhat, *The Multinationals* (London: Eyre and Spottiswoode, 1971).
L. Turner, *Politics and the Multinational Company* (London: Fabian Society, 1969).
L. Turner, 'The Oil Majors in World Politics', *International Affairs,* vol. 52, no. 3 (July 1976), pp. 368-80.
L. Tyson and J. Zysman (eds), *American Industry in International Competition* (Ithaca NY: Cornell University Press, 1983).
J. Vasquez, *The Power of Power Politics* (London: Frances Pinter, 1983).
R. Vernon, *Sovereignty at Bay: the Multinational Spread of US Enterprises* (London: Longman, 1971).
A. Vincent, 'The Hegelian State and International Politics', *Review of International Studies,* vol. 9 (1983).
Jacob Viner, 'Power versus Plenty as Objectives of Foreign Policy in the 17th and 18th Centuries', *World Politics,* vol. 1 (1946), pp. 1-29.
David Wall, *The Charity of Nations: The Political Economy of Foreign Aid* (New York: Basic Books, 1973).
R. Dan Walleri, 'The Political Economy Literature on North-South Relations', *International Studies Quarterly,* vol. 22 (1978), pp. 587-624.
Immanuel Wallerstein (ed.), *World Inequality* (Montreal: Black Rose, 1973).
K. Waltz, *Theory of International Politics* (Cambridge, MA, Addison-Wesley, 1979).

Benjamin Ward, *The Ideal Worlds of Economics: Liberal, Radical and Conservative Economic World Views* (New York: Basic Books, 1979).
Benjamin Ward, *What's Wrong With Economics?* (New York: Basic Books, 1972).
Dwayne Ward, *Toward a Critical Political Economics: A Critique of Liberal and Radical Economic Thought* (Santa Monica, CA: Goodyear Publishing Co. Ltd, 1977).
Bill Warren, *Imperialism: Pioneer of Capitalism* (London: Verso, 1980).
G.D.N. Warswick, 'Is Progress in Economic Science Possible?', *Economic Journal,* vol. 82, no. 325 (March 1972), pp. 73-86.
M.J. Weiner, *English Culture and the Decline of the Industrial Spirit, 1850-1980* (Cambridge: Cambridge University Press, 1981).
Rudi Weisweiller, *Foreign Exchange* (London: George Allen & Unwin, 1972).
John White, 'The New International Economic Order: What Is It?', *International Affairs,* vol. 54, no. 4 (October 1978), pp. 626-34.
Paul Whiteley, *The Political Control of the Macroeconomy: The Political Economy of Public Policy Making* (London: Sage, 1986).
O.E. Williamson, *Markets and Hierarchies: Analysis and Antitrust Implications: A Study in the Economics of Internal Organization* (New York: Free Press, 1975).
M.J. Wolf, *The Japanese Conspiracy* (New York: Empire Books, 1983; and London: New English Library, 1984).
A. Woodcock and M. Davis, *Catastrophe Theory* (New York: Dutton, 1978).
Jack Woodis, *Introduction to Neo-Colonialism* (London: Lawrence and Wishart, 1967).
Martin Wright, *Power Politics* (Leicester: Leicester University Press, 1979).
D. Wrong, *Power: Its Forms, Bases and Uses* (Oxford: Basil Blackwell, 1979).
Kozo Yamamura and Yasukichi Yasuba (eds), *The Political Economy of Japan, vol. 1: The Domestic Transformation* (Stanford, CA: Stanford University Press, 1987).
D. Yergin and M. Hillenbrand, *Global Insecurity: A Strategy for Energy and Economic Renewal* (New York: Houghton Mifflin, 1982).
Oran Young, 'Interdependencies in World Politics', *International Journal,* vol. 24 (1969).

Name Index

Subject Index